AF540639

# TRIBAL EDUCATION IN INDIA

*By*

Dr. A.V. Yadappanavar

*Associate Professor*

*Centre for Women Development*

*NIRD*

*Hyderabad*

*(A.P.)*

2003

DISCOVERY PUBLISHING HOUSE

NEW DELHI-110002

First Published-2003
**Reprinted 2012**
ISBN 81-7141-672-1



*Published by*
**DISCOVERY PUBLISHING HOUSE**
4831/24, Ansari Road, Prahlad Street,
Darya Ganj, New Delhi-110002 (India)
Phone: 3279245 • Fax: 91-11-3253475
E-mail:dphtemp@indiatimes.com

***Printed at:***
**Dynamic Printers, Delhi**

# Preface

The problem of tribal education has remained crucial for the educational planners and policy makers. Several studies were conducted in this direction and innovative approaches were also adopted. However, the impact of the progress was not much on the overall development of the tribal communities. This has resulted in a widening distance between tribes and non-tribes giving rise to various forms of inequalities. Moreover, the tribes in India are heterogenous with varied cultures and economy which indents for a local need based effort by the government both at state and central levels.

There are various developmental activities which are planned and implemented for the tribals, education is one among such activities. It is perceived that by educating these disadvantaged groups it will enable them to have wider avenues of occupations and also facilitate in the overall socio-economic development as well as mobility in these communities.

This books is based on a field-based research in the tribal concentrated Paderu block of Vizag District in Andhra Pradesh. An attempt has been made to understand the ways the schools function and stands organized in the tribal villages. The analysis of various schools and the extent to which they are serving the purpose of these tribal communities are presented in the study, will be of great use to the policy makers and planners.

I am grateful to former Director General, NIRD Mr. T.L. Shankar and Mr. P. Vanamali, Dy. Director General for their guidance and encouragement for undertaking this study.

Prof. M.L. Santhanam and Dr. S. Srinivasan have helped me with their incisive comments on the draft report, and I gratefully acknowledge their services.

At the faculty level secretarial assistance rendered Mr. B. Adi Ratnam, Ms. G. Shobha and Mr. D. Anantha Reddy are also being acknowledged.

My sincere thanks are also due to Shri Wasan for making all efforts to print this research study in the form of Book.

**Arvind Yadappanavar**

# Acknowledgement

I owe my profound gratefulness and gratitude to my professor Purushottam Panday, Mahatma Gandhi Kashi Vidyapeeth, who very patiently kept on encouraging and inspiring me through his scholarly guidance and suggestions from time to time. I am also thankful to Dr. Subhas Chaturvedi, Reader in Economics, Kashi Vidyapeeth for his timely help and guidance.

I would also like to place on record my deep sense of gratitude to Shri. T.L. Shankar, Former Director General, National Institute of Rural Development, who has been a source of inspiration and guidance given in completion of my study. I express my sincere thanks to our Director General, Shri R.C. Choudhury, Shri P. Vanamali, Dy. Director General and Shri D. Satya Murthy, Registrar who have encouraged me to undertake this field based study.

I am grateful to Dr. M.L. Santhanam, Dy. Director i/c for Centre for Behavioural Organisation Development and Shri A.R. Bandyopadhyay (consultant to NIRD), Dr. Om Prakash, Dy. Director, Centre for Micro Planning and Dr. S. Srinivasan, Asst. Director, Centre for Human Resources Development who have gone through the report meticulously.

At field level many persons have contributed for the successful completion of the fieldwork. Among them special mention has to be made about Shri Pareda, Project Officer, ITDA, Paderu mandal for sparing the service of BDO and District Tribal Welfare Officer. I express my thanks in facilitating fieldwork and my stay comfortable at respective places.

Above all, the district officials, the mandal officials, the teachers, students, parents need special appreciation for their keen interest in answering several questions posed to them.

The author is thankful to Mr. B. Adi Ratnam, Mrs. G. Shobha, Mr. Ananatha Reddy and Mrs. Anitha for their excellent secretarial assistance and computerizing the entire report, but for their help and cooperation, this study would not have been completed in time.

**A.V. Yadappanvar**

Hyderabad

# CONTENTS

# 1

# Introduction

## PREAMBLE

It is time and again emphasised that education is the key to the progress of the nation. According to the Constitution of India, states are directed to make provision for securing the right of children to education within the limits of its economic capacity, and to provide free and compulsory education to all children up to the age of 14 by 1960. Further, it has stated that the State shall promote with special care the educational and economic interest of the weaker sections of the community such as Scheduled Caste and Scheduled Tribes (Report of the Expert Group 1994). As long as illiteracy continues be the prevalent in rural and tribal areas, attempts to bring about social and economic changes will not yield the desired results. The Education Commission appointed by Government of India during 1964-66 recommended that high priority to be given to the "liquidation of illiteracy". In spite of completing 50 years of independence, still the literacy rate as per 1991 census, is at 52.2 per cent level for All India (NIRD, 1995) and at 29.54 per cent level for Andhra Pradesh. The Rural Literacy rates as per 1991 Census is as follows:

**Table—1.1 Population and Rural Literacy**

| | *Male* | *Female* | *Total* |
|---|---|---|---|
| All India | 57.9 | 23.9 | 44.7 |
| Andhra Pradesh | 47.3 | 30.6 | 35.7 |

## Education and Literacy—Concepts

The changed socio-economic conditions, particularly after independence, have witnessed opportunities for tribals to receive education and employment, and have provided them with new avenues to express and assert their equality. This along with the newly granted politico-legal privileges is liable to affect their feelings, thoughts and life style.

For Learner (1962) education is, therefore, undoubtedly one of the keys that unlocks the doors to modernisation, providing most important channels of transition from traditional to modern sectors. Literacy, therefore, is both the index and agent to modernisation.

Placing all-out stress on the need of education for the people in the underdeveloped areas of the world in particular, Mead (1953) avers, "education is needed in all these areas to cope with and repair the destruction already introduced and beyond this to make it possible for the people if they choose the place in the community of nations, and to take advantage of progress of science and technology in improving the standards of living". Education, also, constitutes an essential ingredient for the economic modernisation of the society, as in illiterate society is neither to be in the fore-front of technological creativity nor for that matter to know how to use new technologies even if they exist for taking (Gill, 1965). Moreover, in developing societies education is construed to be a kind of crucial investment, as it generates much needed skills and knowledge for economic growth ". . . literacy is a value in itself. In addition there is an economic reason—developmental reason—for primary education for it enables children to acquire literacy and to retain it in adulthood besides cultivating in them the capacity to acquire skills and develop right attitude to work on production" (Rao, 1966).

Evidences are many to the fact that the manifold programmes of socio-economic developments undertaken in the tribal areas in India are not making much headway chiefly because of the ignorance and illiteracy of the tribals. Even to take advantage of the various development schemes a certain degree of education is necessary (Sachchidananda, 1967). The problem of education is thus obviously circular (Anderson, 1970). To speak in pragmatical terms the socio-economic development and educational expansion should be viewed as interdependent processes, both should therefore, go hand in hand. This approach also takes into account the inter sub system interaction and exchange as stressed in Parsonian mode of analysis (Parsons, 1940).

The relevance of general education in terms of literacy is recognized in every type of society irrespective of its socio-economic basis. The problem, however, arises as to the type of special vocational and other skills that need to be developed in a given community. Evidently, the level and type of such skills depend on the developmental stage of the society concerned. The tribal communities which remained ignorant for a long time require, not only the general literacy but also other skills which equip them to face boldly and experience the exogenous force of modernisation. (Grigson 1943). From his first hand experience of problems of tribals argues that it is necessary to introduce among the tribals such kind of education which would restore confidence in them. To put it exactly in his own words, "we have to restore and foster the aboriginal's self-respect by protecting him from loss of land, bond service, debt and oppression, to shield him from malaria yaws and other sickness, to teach him agriculture and economic organisation suited to his habit and mentality and to educate him not merely to retain and value his own tribal culture, but also to take and hold his due place in the economic, political and culturai life of modern India".

It is evident from the above discussion that although education is an essential ingredient of socio-economic development, it is never an independent variable. Educability is dependent upon personal and situational factors. To be very brief, the social determinants of educability are inequality and school provision, social class and cultural ingredients such as the language, the social distance between the teachers and the pupil, the level of educational aspiration, the definition of roles in the nature of peer groups in childhood and adolescence (Halsey, 1970). Education can provide very good opportunities for the socially disadvantaged groups provided they have the necessary facilities and life chances to get education (Tilak, 1987). Inequalities in educational facilities and life chances lead to inequalities in educability and thus minimize the chances of social mobility.

The role of education in traditional societies was largely confined to cultural accomplishment. In the context of development of modern science and technology which are being used as tools of qualitative change in human lives, education has come to be acknowledged as a tool of human development and empowerment. In the context of transformation of a traditional society into a modern one the centre of authority shifts from the known-informal systems to formal systems which are supposedly based on the principles of equity and justice. The weaker sections belonging to SC and ST who have been at the lowest rung of the ladder of development have a genuine difficulty in understanding and assimilating the rationale and modus operandi of this transformation, functioning of the formal modern institutions and class character of the people who may be occupying a commanding position in the new system. They get seriously handicapped on account of this ignorance. Literacy and education provide a key to such understanding: they also help in demystifying and demythologising and aura of false consciousness which clouds our mind and tends to perpetuate the unjust and inequitable system. In this sense they become important tools of liberation of the weaker sections of the society while simultaneously working for their identification with the State and national mainstream.

India has declared herself as the sovereign democratic Republic and takes an enviable credit of being the largest democracy in the world. Like any democratic country, she aims at providing equal educational opportunities to all the citizens. In this context the Education commission (1964-66), rightly remarks", one of the important objectives of education is to equalize opportunity, enabling the backward or underprivileged classes and individuals to use education as a level for the improvement of their condition. Every society that values social justice and is anxious to improve the lost of the common man and cultivate all available talent, must insure progressive equality of opportunity to all sections of the population. This is the only guarantee for the building up of an egalitarian and human society in which exploitation of the weak will be minimized".

Indian Constitution also prohibits discrimination and promotes social welfare by taking care of the educational and economic interests of all:

*(a)* Article 29 maintains that no citizen can be denied admission into any educational institution maintained by the state or receiving aid out of state funds.

*(b)* Article 46 enjoins upon the state to promote with special care the educational and economic interests of the weaker sections of the people, and in particular, of the scheduled castes and the scheduled tribes and to protect them from social injustice and all forms of exploitation.

In addition to these, the universal Declaration of Human Rights, adopted by the General Assembly to the United Nations on the 10th December, 1948, proclaims not only the principle of non-discrimination but also the right to education, the purpose of which are given below:

*(a)* Everyone has the right to education. Education shall be free, at least in the elementary and the fundamental stages. Elementary education shall be compulsory.

*(b)* Education shall be directed to the full-development of the human personality and to the strengthening of respect for human rights and fundamental freedom.

*(c)* Parents have a prior right to choose the kind of education that shall be given to their children.

Education for the tribal people has today become a matter of great concern. Ever since India gained independence a considerable amount of money has been spent so that the tribal people, who are undeveloped and neglected, could get a fair deal. It has been generally recognised that India being welfare state cannot afford to have a particular section of its population behind in the field of education. This would be against the principles of democratic development of the country. There is hardly any necessity, therefore, to emphasize the need and importance of education for the tribal people in India. Concerted efforts are made, from time to time, to better the tribal situations in India. Both the central and state governments are, therefore extending facilities in various shapes for the promotion of tribal education. Generally, the facilities have been extended by providing school buildings, teachers, free studentship, free textbooks, and, at selected places, free boarding and lodging facilities and mid-day meals. In this context it is worthwhile to make a mention of the remarks of education Commission (1964-66) which states, "It is necessary to pay special attention to the education of children from the backward classes which include the scheduled castes, the scheduled tribes, denotified communities and a few nomadic and semi-nomadic groups."

## The Historical Background of Tribal Education

The historical situation of education could possibly provide the background of the present educational developmental of the Scheduled Tribes and other weaker sections. The system in general seems to have had an adverse effect on the tribals and the trend seems to continue even today. Going back to the British period we observe that the colonisers never wanted India to become self-reliant. The educational structures during the British period were meant to play a crucial role in maintaining the colonial rule and not to favour indigenous education. The Government did not take any interest in making provision for educating the masses. As A.R. Desai (1967: 102-103) observes, "the Government did not consider the supply of education entirely its own responsibility, nor did it consider it as an essential necessity to every Indian to be provided free of cost and compulsory".

The Britishers wanted their colony (India) to lose its identity and become part of their colonising power. Also a handful of so-called 'Indian Elite' did not want to bring about any developmental change in India through a dynamic educational system. Keeping these mind Britishers as well as the so-called 'Indian Elite' did not attempt to set up institutions of technical educational and vocational courses on a large scale in tribal areas.

Before the British, the major function of education was character-building and learning religious scriptures. Of the four varnas only the upper three had the right to study the religious scriptures and the Shudras were deprived of any opportunity for education. Though some claim that in Ancient India women had an equal right to education, in practice they were outside the mainstream of the educational system. In other words, the weaker sections were excluded from education, though they were essential for the mainstream economic activity. What is said about the Shudras is equally true about the tribals. In the words of N. Minz (1982) "the feudal economic structure before and during the British, exploited the tribals and suppressed and oppressed them very much".

Since there was no intention of developing the masses, no effort was made to educate the people, particularly the tribals and other living in the remote areas. No facilities such as hostels were available to the weaker sections. Whatever facilities that were available, were monopolised by the powerful who could pay for them. As English became the medium of instruction, the majority of the population including tribals were excluded from education. The situation was much worse among tribal women and all along the colonial era, their literacy remained very low (Patel 1984).

What little effort was made in the education of the poor was by charitable organisations. In the 19th century missionaries began welfare activities among the poor. In the beginning they were working among the 'untouchables' but in the latter part of the century they attempted to spread education also among a few tribal groups who were residing in the hills and forest areas isolated from the mainstream. Hence one can see traces of education among the aborigines. The quality of education that was spread among the tribals varied from place to place. Efforts of the missionaries in this field were scattered. More concentrated efforts were required to spread education among the tribals if this pioneering work was to be effective. Where there was such an effort, the result was much better than in other areas. For example, the East India Company did not show any concern for the education of the aboriginal population or hill tribes. Nurullah and Naik (1951) have shown that Assam and Bengal had taken up the issue of education for the tribals. But the missionaries were mainly instrumental in achieving this. Only later the governments of these states also encouraged them. Hence one notices high literacy among the north-eastern tribals.

After 1882-83 provision was made for special schools free schooling and award of scholarships to tribal students. But the progress of tribal education till the beginning of the 20th century was not at all impressive as can be seen in Table—1.2.

In absolute numbers Bengal and Assam had the highest number of tribal students in 1901-1902. But literacy rate was the highest in Bombay so was to disparity between male and female literates. In other words, even when some effort was made in the education of tribal males, the gap between male and females literacy continued.

**Table—1.2 Educational Development of Tribals (1901-1902)**

| *Province* | *No. of students* | *No. of Literates per 1000* | |
|---|---|---|---|
| | | *Males* | *Female* |
| Madras | 4,534 | 47 | 1 |
| Bombay | 7,663 | 105 | 2 |
| Bengal | 30,203 | 89 | 4 |
| Central Province | 2,980 | 40 | 2 |
| Assam | 16,094 | 89 | 13 |
| Bihar | 296 | 18 | 2 |

**Source :** Nurullah and Naik (1951)

Around 1920, it was realised that tribals should be educated systematically and that the education of the backward classes are not be isolated from their social, political, religious and economic situation (Government of Bombay 1958).

The year 1921 is a landmark in the history of elementary education as Indian ministers took the responsibility of spread of elementary education. Also education among the tribals was slow developing and during the period 1921-47 in Gujarat these types educational institutions were working for educating the tribals 1985) they are *(a)* Day Schools, run by the department of instruction and later by the local board; *(b)* Boarding schools by local boards and *(c)* Ashram type schools run by Gandhian organisations. Similar schools were opened also in a few other areas of tribal concentration but with limited success.

## The Post—Independence Situation

Briefly, until independence tribal education was in a very bad shape. They were educationally, socially and economically exploited right from the ancient times till independence. These exploitation was reflected also in their exclusion from education situation does not seem to have changed much even after independence. The Constitution of 1950 provides certain protection of safeguards to the Scheduled Tribes along with the Scheduled Castes and other Backward Classes. Its objective is to bring them up nationally and economically to a level where they can be on par with others.

Inspite of this, during the last three and a half decades has not been any significant in the educational system of the country except to have a uniform duration (10 + 2 + 3) i.e. 15 years for the first degree. During this period there has been tremendous increase in the number of educational institutions and in the enrolments, but correspondingly there have not been job opportunities. A feeling of disenchantment has been growing in everyone's mind.

According to Fourth all India Education Survey only 83.00 per cent of tribal people were covered by primary levels within 1 km of the tribal habitat. Out of the remaining 17 per cent, 13.9 per cent did not have a school within 1.5 km and 8.3 per cent did not have a school within 2 km in Andhra Pradesh. The percentage of uncovered population is as follows, 36.37 per cent unserved within habitation, 22.20 per cent unserved within 1 km, 11.30 per cent unserved within 2 km. There is a sharp drop from primary stage 101.79 per cent to middle stage 35.65 per cent. Nearly two third of scheduled Tribe boys and girls dropped out ascending from primary to middle stages based on the available figures figure of retention of 5 per cent in the high school classes is available. Thus the overall picture is dim. To arrest the wastage and stagnation State and Central Government have taken some steps and have given some incentives to the parents as well as to the children to encourage them to come to school and continue in it. But somehow the results are not very encouraging.

Incentives and facilities given by the Central Government to the Scheduled Tribe children and for the development of their education are in terms of establishment of schools, colleges, freeships, Scholarships, uniforms, text books, mid-day meals etc. In the first year of the First Five Year Plan (1951-52) a sum of Rs. 300,000 was sanctioned for the award of scholarships to Scheduled Tribe students (Commissioner for SCs and STs 1951). According to this report during 1952-53, 1,094 ST students were awarded scholarships. It was observed that 95 per cent of the Scheduled Tribe applicants were able to get scholarships during that year. In the same year the number of enrolments of Scheduled Tribe students in professional institutions like medical, engineering, agriculture, etc. was much higher than the number in 1951-52. For the first time during the year 1953-54, the IIT Kharagpur encouraged Scheduled Caste and Scheduled Tribes students to join the Institute by relaxing admission criteria. Reservation of seats for the Scheduled Castes and Scheduled Tribes was introduced during the First Five Year Plan in Assam, Bihar, Madras, Punjab, Uttar Pradesh, Rajasthan, Hyderabad and Mysore in some medical, agricultural, engineering, polytechnic colleges and also in schools and colleges for general education. The Union Ministry of Education recommended in 1954 two important points for easy access of the Scheduled Castes and Tribes to technical as well as general educational institutions. 20 per cent of the seats were reserved for them and where admissions are restricted to candidates who obtain a certain minimum percentage of marks there may be a 5 per cent reduction for them provided that the lower percentage prescribed does not fall below the minimum required to pass the qualifying examination (Commissioner for SCs and STs 1955).

During the Second Five Year Plan Rs. 58 lakhs were spent on the education of the Scheduled Tribes. Stipends were given to a few students who were residing in hostels but the amount was not sufficient. During the Third Five Year Plan under the scheme 'Scholarships for Post-matric Studies', the number of scholarships awarded was 61,000. State Governments were requested by the

Central Government to provide safeguards and concessions for the education of the Scheduled Castes and Tribes. Only a few states complied. During the Fourth Plan period Rs. 22 crores were spent on the Scheduled Tribes for their education. During this period it was realised that even after three five year plans, schools in tribal areas were poorly equipped and did not have a sufficient number of trained teachers. Hence in the Fourth Plan emphasis was laid on training of teachers, hostel facilities for students, introduction of science teaching in schools in the tribal areas, improvement in the teaching of mathematics and provision of vocational courses for tribal schools with the hope that Scheduled Tribe schools leavers would be enabled to fit into the agricultural and other programmes of tribal development. During the Fifth Five Year Plan it was observed that only if the financial condition of the Scheduled Tribes and Castes was improved their educational level would be raised. But measures tribal culture, language and their social organisation. If it can be grasped, it would facilitate tribal education. To this should be added the culture of the tribals themselves.

Reviewing of the Sixth Plan performance, the lack of progress in some areas may be noted. For the tribal sub-plan states have not been able to prepare even by the end of sixth plan project for all ITDPS or for tribal pockets or for the development of primitive tribes. Coordination between the different tribal programmes which are taken up at the project level has been lacking.

The Sixth Plan outlay for socio-economic programmes for Schedule Caste and Schedule Tribes and Backward Class was Rs. 3,521 crores (under the state allocation under tribal sub-plan*), and the expenditure was Rs. 3,409 crores. Under special central scheme Rs. 485 crores was kept as an outlay and the same has been spent. (*estimate).

Emphasis was placed more on family oriented programmes than on infrastructure development unlike in the previous plans.

Seventh Five Year Plan indicates that independent academic and research organisations will be deployed for evaluation studies on the important various development projects meant for the socio-economic uplift of tribals.

The Madhya Pradesh Government have a Kanya Shiksha Parishad at Chhindwara where education and training is imparted to tribal women in a unified manner such centres can be considered for establishment by other states, for assisting women under Income Generating Activities (IGA).

Keeping the state and national priorities in view the process of plan formulation generally and also the planning of specific projects need to attach importance to the ethos, needs and aspirations of specific tribal group.

In order to increase the school enrolment ST children provision will be made for 100 per cent coverage, along with the supply of free textbooks and stationary, provision of free uniforms and provision of attendance scholarships particularly for girls (including possibly some compensation to their parents for their opportunity cost) other incentives like midday meals hostel facilities special coaching in school/colleges in classes IX, X, XI and XII for such children as are weak in some subjects particularly English, Science and Mathematics will also be provided in the seventh plans. Introduction of merit scholarship at the post-matric stage at the rate of one and half times the rate of normal scholarships and removal of the present restriction limiting scholarships to two children of the same parent are also envisaged. Book banks for all professional courses, liberalisation of pre-metric scholarship for children of those engaged in unclean occupation and inclusion of day scholars in the scheme for pre-metric scholarships and other educational schemes suitable modifications of the schemes for educational development keeping in view of the needs of S.T and the introduction of preparatory training residual teaching and special coaching for professional courses at the district level will be undertaken.

Research and training will be expanded to fund research/ surveys on ST programmes not only by the Tribal Research and Training Institute in the State but also by voluntary bodies, academic institutions and research workers.

Participation of voluntary organisations will be solicited not only for implementing the socio-economic programmes and specific schemes for STs, but also to organise motivate and assist STs to come forward to avail themselves of developmental programmes.

For all these programmes an allocation of Rs. 1239.21 crores has been provided in the State Plans and Rs. 281.22 crores in the central sectors.

Stipends and Scholarships were award to 115 lakhs children belonging to SCs/STs/and other backward classes and another 113 lakhs children belonging to these categories were covered by other educational incentives like free supply of uniforms, stationary books etc., post metric scholarships were awarded to about 9 lakhs ST/SC students and 3000 hostels and 9000 Ashram Schools were established.

An encouraging feature of the special component plans drawn up by the States for the socio-economic development of the scheduled classes in that the quality of schemes and their implementation has shown improvements over the previous plans. However, much still needs to be done towards organisations improvements, coordination among various implementation agencies and programmes and scheme aimed at the same target groups need to be strengthened.

During the Eighth Plan (1992-97) for the educational developmental of ST, existing programmes for prematric and post matric education of ST will be continued. Residential schools including ashram schools will be expanded. As envisaged in the national policy on education 1986, priority will be accorded to the opening of primary schools in tribal areas. The social cultural milieu of the ST will be taken into consideration in developing the curricula and devising the instructional material in tribal languages at the initial stages with arrangements for switching over to the regional language.

Anganwadis, non-formal and adult centres will be established in tribal areas on a priority basis.

Further the curriculum at all stages of education will be so designed as to create an awareness of the rich cultural identify of the tribal people as also of their enormous creative talent.

Emphasis was laid in the Seventh Plan on the educational developmental of SC and ST pre-matric stipends and scholarships were given by the state governments to 190 lakhs SC/ST/Other

BC students. Other educational incentives included free supply of uniform, stationary and text books to about 100 lakhs students. Post metric scholarships were given to about 15 lakhs SC and ST students in 1991-92 as against 9.75 lakhs scholarships in 1985-86 and only 1.56 lakhs scholarships in 1968-69.

These scholarships were given for study of post-matriculation/post-secondary courses of study in arts, and science, commerce as well as professional and technical degree/ diploma and certificate courses on the basis of a graded means test.

For SC and ST students studying in medical and engineering college, a scheme of books was started in 1978-79 which benefitted about 21,000 students in 1990-91. Hostels facilities for SCs and STs were considerably expanded.

## Outlay on Education

At the inception of planning, in 1950-51 education claimed 1.2 per cent of the gross national product (GNP). The Education Commission (1966) expected that the expenditure on education would rise from 3 per cent to 6 per cent. But, presently, India spends only 3.2 per cent of its NP on education. The February 1994 conference on education of Chief Ministers, presided over by the Prime Minister, called for allocation of financial resources equivalent to above 6 per cent of the NP. The Prime Minister has expressed the hope at least on two occasions that the outlay would increase to 6 per cent before the country enters the next century. Linking expenditure to education on the NP means that the allocation to education will increase as the economy grows. Should the commitment be honoured from the Ninth Five Year Plan onwards, it should enable an even higher percentage of funds in the Tribal Sub-Plan (TSP), considering that special central assistance is available for it. The total outlay on tribal developmental during Fifth Plan period during which the Tribal sub-plan strategy was introduced seems to have been a little over a thousand crore of rupees. During the Sixth Plan period, the expenditure reported was Rs. 3,400 crores, while that projected for the Seventh Plan period was Rs. 6,500 crores. Thus, according to the report of the Planning Commission's Working Group for Tribal Development during the Eighth Plan period, financial investment during the Fifth, Sixth and Seventh Plan periods amounted to about eleven thousand crores of rupees. Further, the Working Group projected a figure of over Rs. 16,000 crores for the Eighth Plan period. TSP deals with very high levels of investment.

The same Working Group estimated a flow of nearly Rs. 400 crores to education sector from a total states plan outlay for education of Rs. 2,700 crores for the period 1985-86 to 1988-89, representing a percentage of about 15. If the same percentage of flow from the Sixth to Eighth Plan is assumed, an outlay of Rs. 4,000 crores on education seems a feasible proposition. If additionalities in the shape of special Central assistance etc. are reconed, the order of investment in tribal education would be higher.

It is generally conceded that rural areas in general and tribal areas in particular, have failed to attract resources, personnel and infrastructure facilities. In this context, both physical and financial planning acquire added importance.

The results of the 1991 census imply that out of 100 scheduled tribe persons in the country, 70 were illiterate. Further, the 1991 ST literacy percentage of 29.60 conceals the widening gap over years between the levels of literacy of scheduled tribes and non-SC-non-ST population as well as the dismal picture of female ST literacy percentage. It also masks inter-state, urban-rural, male-female, inter-tribe and inter-district disparities.

It is further noteworthy from the following figure of differentials in literacy rates of scheduled tribes, scheduled caste and non-ST-non-SC sections that the gap in literacy percentage of non-SC and non-ST sections and STs has gone on increasing during the inter-decennial census period 1961-91 from 19.33 to 33.05.

During the three decades, the average annual growth-rate for the former has been 1.17 and for the latter 0.70. It is evident that the regression will continue and will not close at this rate.

**Table—1.3 Comparison of Literacy among Tribals and others**

| *Census year* | *Scheduled Castes* | *Scheduled Tribes* | *Non SC Non ST popula-tion* | *Literacy gap between non SC-non ST and* | |
|---|---|---|---|---|---|
| | | | | *SCs* | *STs* |
| 1961 | 10.27 | 8.53 | 27.86 | 17.59 | 19.33 |
| 1971 | 14.67 | 11.30 | 33.80 | 19.13 | 22.50 |
| 1981 | 21.38 | 16.35 | 41.30 | 19.84 | 24.87 |
| 1991 | 37.41 | 29.60 | 62.25 | 25.24 | 33.05 |

**Source :** Educational Statistics of Scheduled Castes and Scheduled Tribes, Ministry of Human Resource Development, 1993.

The state-wise ST literacy rates show wide variations among the 22 states and 4 Union Territories. While the 1991 all-India percentage of ST literacy is indicated as 29.60 (compared with the total all-India figure of 52.51), the variation among states is from 17.16 in Andhra Pradesh to 82.73 in Mizoram. Seven States and Union Territories have literacy percentage less than the all-India figure of 29.60. Thus, two-thirds of the total ST population has been at a literacy level less than the all-India ST average and less than half of the literacy levels of the total population.

The ST female literacy rates varied from 4.42 per cent in Rajasthan to 78.70 per cent in Mizoram. The average all-India literacy rate was 18.19 per cent. The 5 states which together account for 5.69 per cent of the females ST population in the country continued to remain below the national average of ST female literacy during the decade 1981-1991:

**Table—1.4 Literacy among ST Female—1981-1991**

| *States* | *Per cent age* |
|---|---|
| Rajasthan | 4.42 per cent |
| Andhra Pradesh | 8.68 per cent |
| Orissa | 10.21 per cent |
| Madhya Pradesh | 10.73 per cent |
| Bihar | 14.75 per cent |

The gender difference in attainment of literacy levels calls for notice. It is apparent that the bulk of ST female population subsists at a literacy level below 20 per cent. Only 5 States and Union Territories i.e. Lakshadweep, Mizoram, Kerala, Nagaland and Sikkim have been able to make more than 50 per cent of their ST females literates.

There are inter-tribe variations. Even in one State the divergence is very wide. For example, in Kerala, the Kochu Velan and Kattunayakan exhibited respectively literacy rates of 75 per cent and 1.96 per cent as per the 1981 census. Several tribes showed such divergences, cutting out the scope for a generalised education approach for scheduled tribes considered as one homogenous mass. One striking result of the uniform approach is that education has been benefitting largely the articulate and dominant tribes situated around urban power centres.

The progress in enrolment percentages in the age-group 5-11 relative to Class I—IV has been from 10.45 per cent in 1955 to 101.79 per cent in 1988-89. For the age-group 11-14 relative to Classes VI—VIII the percentage rose from 1.24 in 1955-56 to 35.65 in 1988-89. Particularly in the primary level the enrolment drive seems to have yielded results. However, enrolment in the first primary class can present a misleading picture: It merely shows figures of enlistment into the schools for the first time. Studies have shown that some parents averred that they did not admit their children into the schools, yet the names of children appeared as enrolled. Further, among children really admitted, there are early drop-outs. The effective enrolment is, hence, lower.

Indeed, a high degree of wastage is a dilemma of education for tribals. There is a sharp drop from primary stage 101.79 per cent to middle stage 35.65 per cent. Nearly two-third ST boys and girls dropped out ascending from primary to middle stages, retention is 5 per cent in the high school classes. Thus, the overall picture is dim.

**Factors which Contribute to Educational Deprivation of the Scheduled Tribes**

The Fifth All India Educational survey has given a graphic account of the various infrastructural bottlenecks which contribute to the educational deprivation of the Scheduled Tribes in India.

This is not very much different from the findings of the fourth All India Educational Survey according to which only 83 per cent of the tribal people were covered by primary schools within 1 kilometre of the tribal habitat. Out of the remaining 17 per cent, 13.9 per cent did not have a school within 1.5 kilometre and 8.3 per cent did not have a school within 2 kilometres. The position has deteriorated in the Fifth All India Educational Survey as would be evident from the following:

A. Habitations predominantly inhabited by ST and served by Primary Schools

(Average of population ranging between 100 to 5000 and above)

| | |
|---|---|
| Within habitation | 45.43 per cent |
| Upto 0.5 km. | 57.71 per cent |
| Upto 1 km. | 74.46 per cent |
| Upto 1.5 km. | 79.33 per cent |
| Upto 2 kms. | 87.60 per cent |

It is not as if the entire population within the habitation is served by primary school as would be evident from the following.

B. Percentage of population in habitations predominantly inhabited by ST served primary schools.

C. There is a sizable percentage of habitation predominantly populated by Scheduled Tribes which continue to be unserved by primary schools as would be evident from the following.

| | |
|---|---|
| Upto 1 km. | 25.54 per cent |
| Upto 1.5 km. | 20.67 per cent |
| Upto 2 kms. | 12.50 per cent |

D. The percentage of rural population in habitations predominantly populated by ST which continue to be unserved.

| Kilometres | per cent age |
|---|---|
| Upto 1 km. | 11.65 per cent |
| Upto 1.5 km. | 9.50 per cent |
| Upto 2 kms. | 5.00 per cent |

E. The scenario is not uniform and varies from State of State, District to District and even within the district. Infrastructure development is partly a legacy of history and partly a question of uneven dispersal of resources amongst different regions of the country, the reasons of which are not easily explainable. The consequence of inequitable distribution of resources is, however, clearly visible in as much as well endowed regions as a result of the seemingly unreasonable patronage get more endowed and less endowed regions go down, further on the ladder of development. Punjab has the highest percentage (99.59 per cent) of the population served within 1 km. while Arunachal Pradesh has the lowest per cent of population served. That is 73.3 per cent Among the major states having tribal population, Andhra Pradesh, Arunachal Pradesh, Assam, Himachal Pradesh, Madhya Pradesh, Maharashtra, Manipur, Maghalaya, Orissa, Rajasthan, Sikkim and Tripura have sizable habitation and population which do not have primary schooling facilities within 1 km. and 2 kms. and remain unserved till date.

**Table—1.5 Percentage of Uncovered Population—Statewise**

| *States* | *Unserved per cent within habitation* | *Per cent served within 1 km.* | *Per cent served within 2 km.* |
|---|---|---|---|
| **1** | **2** | **3** | **4** |
| Andhra Pradesh | 36.37 | 22.20 | 11.30 |
| Arúnachal Pradesh | 35.65 | 29.12 | 53.03 |
| Assam | 35.18 | 11.14 | 1.28 |
| Bihar | 41.13 | 12.51 | 3.10 |
| Himachal Pradesh | 41.69 | 10.16 | 7.75 |
| Madhya Pradesh | 33.99 | 12.58 | 5.30 |
| Maharashtra | 44.82 | 8.77 | 4.09 |
| Manipur | 6.02 | 4.32 | 3.54 |
| Meghalaya | 20.10 | 4.21 | – |

*(Table Contd.)*

| 1 | 2 | 3 | 4 |
|---|---|---|---|
| Orissa | 33.65 | 16.42 | 9.12 |
| Rajasthan | 25.00 | 12.93 | 9.06 |
| Sikkim | 35.69 | 18.43 | – |
| Tripura | 59.27 | 24.58 | 11.14 |
| Uttar Pradesh | 29.57 | 12.61 | 3.80 |
| West Bengal | 25.00 | 5.28 | – |
| Andaman and Nicobar Islands | 31.92 | 17.57 | – |

F. The above description does not present complete picture of educational deprivation. The same distance in the plains and areas with developed communication is not a serious hurdle but in the tribal areas with hills and forests and with following streams, even 1 km. may be a long distance and absence of schools within the habitation may be a double disadvantage. Access to education would not only depend on the location of the schools within easy reach out but also the nature of the terrain, the willingness of the teachers to come from the plain areas to stay in the tribal areas and to hold on to their interest in teaching. Willingness of parents to send their children over long distances to the school, the hiatus in matters of food, dress, architecture and the overall school and hostel environment and home which may be responsible for pull out or push out of children from the school which is different from the dropout phenomenon etc. The position is regard to enrolment and retention at primary, middle and secondary levels is equally deceptive i.e. it does not reflect the actual situation. The figures obtained from the All India Educational Survey may undoubtedly generate hope on the surface but they have more to hide than to reveal.

H. In the three States of Bihar, Madhya Pradesh and Orissa which account for more than 44 per cent population, the level of enrolment at primary stage has been 88.37 per cent, 74.33 per cent and 78.38 per cent respectively. The enrolment of girls in these states, however, falls to 59.9 per cent, 49.83 per cent and 49.41 per cent respectively. The real indicators of educational achievement, however, come out in much sharper focus of the high level on dropouts and low level of retention. The enrolment in the cases of children belonging to the ST community declines sharply from 88.37 per cent to 23.19 per cent in Bihar, from 74.33 per cent to 21.41 per cent in Madhya Pradesh and from 78.38 per cent to 21.60 per cent in Orissa.

I. Rajasthan has the invidious distinction of having the enrolment of girls at only 5.03 per cent which is the lowest in the country. Harsh geography and topography, prevalence of feudal tradition characterised by Parda system, incidence of early child marriage and prevalence of a culture of discrimination against the fair sex have all contributed to this unfortunate situation. Even in advanced State like Maharashtra where Tata Institute of Social Sciences, Bombay had conducted a study, the rates of wastage and stagnation among SC and ST students are reported to be much higher than those among non-SC and ST students are reported to be much higher than those among non-SC and ST students at primary and middle level of schooling.

J. Insufficient retention in formal school system leads of inadequate participation in the class room activities and acquisition far below the desired levels of learning leading to relapse to the old world of illiteracy and accretion to the ranks of illiterates. Existence of high percentage of single teacher schools, absence of women teachers belonging to the Scheduled Tribe community, absence of physical facilities like production and distribution of teaching-learning materials which will be attractive, relevant and enjoyable and of good quality, scarcity of teaching aids (blackboard, roll up board, globe, charts, posters etc.) at reasonable price, closure of schools in tribal areas for certain period of time, posting of teachers from the plain areas to tribal areas by way of punishment are all factors which lead to the state of educational deprivation of the members of the Scheduled Tribe community.

## The Equity Perspective

Equity in dissemination of education among different strata of society is a live issue. The following figures illustrate growing disparity during 1961-91 in literacy percentage between tribal population and the total general population:

**Table—1.6 Comparison of Tribal Literacy with General Population**

| | *1961* | *1871* | *1981* | *1991* |
|---|---|---|---|---|
| ST | 8.53 | 11.30 | 16.35 | 23.62 |
| General | 24.00 | 29.45 | 36.23 | 52.21 |

The trend shows that, progressively, in the matter of literacy percentage, the tribals continue to fall backwards, notwithstanding the new policy on education of the Government of India and action taken in accordance herewith. The access to schools, hostels, etc. has improved, but not commensurate with the requirement. Rêsidential schools have been found to be more appropriate to the tribal milieu but they need reformation; further they are expensive and cannot be expected to cover the tribal areas intensively. Owing to paucity of funds, teaching-learning aids are in short supply. Official figures of enrolment of children in the primary, middle and higher classes are generally flattering, but they ignore the large-scale drop-outs. Parental indifference towards children's education arises out of a mix of rational economic factors, incomprehensible pedagogy and absence of tradition. The situation is aggravated by an air of superciliousness of generality of non-tribal teachers. A new philosophic approach is called for. Then there are issues like inter-tribe, inter-district, urban-rural, male-female educational disparities and a few others. The canvas of tribal education is very large.

## The Present Situation

Public statements are made that education of the tribals must be viewed as enriching national education and that nation-building is incomplete without their joining the mainstream. Consequently, the Central and State Governments have been stressing considerably the spread of education among the Scheduled Castes and Scheduled tribes. But the efforts have not been as foreseen. They have not got the benefits of education and the cause of this anomaly have to be identified.

There are more than 573 tribal communities in India. They differ from each other in their dialect, social organisation, political system etc. But except in the north-east where they are the dominant group, in the rest of India literacy among them is low. This can be seen when we compare the present literacy percentage of the tribals with the total population of our country. Enrolment among the Scheduled Tribe students is significantly lower than that among the upper castes. It is much worse among tribal girls. According to the 1991 census, literacy among tribal was 29.60 per cent as against total literacy of 52.21 per cent. Literacy among tribal women was extremely low at 10.19 per cent. According to the 1991 census there were 67.8 million tribals in the country, forming 8.08 per cent of the total population of 846 million, of which 40.65 per cent were males and 18.9 per cent were females. In 1991, tribals formed 8 per cent of the total population. In other words, unlike the rest of the country which had fewer women than men, among tribals, the male-female ratio was favourable to women. But literacy among their women was much lower than that among their male literacy. Literacy has made considerable progress in the rest of the population over the last decade. But its growth has not been very high among the scheduled Tribes and castes. It is lower in the rural areas than among towns.

**Table—1.7 Literacy Rates: Male–Female, Caste–Class and Rural–Urban Difference in India**

| | *1991* | *1981* | | | | |
|---|---|---|---|---|---|---|
| | *Male* | *Female* | *Total* | *Male* | *Female* | *Total* |
| Urban | 81.09 | 42.14 | 73.09 | 65.83 | 47.82 | 57.40 |
| Rural | 57.87 | 30.62 | 44.69 | 40.79 | 17.96 | 29.65 |
| Total | 64.13 | 39.29 | 52.21 | 46.89 | 24.82 | 36.23 |
| Scheduled Castes | | | | | | |
| Urban | 66.60 | 42.29 | 55.61 | 36.60 | 47.54 | 24.34 |
| Rural | 45.95 | 19.46 | 33.25 | 27.91 | 8.45 | 13.43 |
| Total | 49.91 | 23.76 | 37.41 | 31.12 | 10.93 | 21.38 |
| Scheduled Tribes | | | | | | |
| Urban | 66.56 | 45.66 | 56.60 | 47.60 | 27.32 | 37.93 |
| Rural | 38.45 | 16.02 | 27.38 | 22.94 | 6.81 | 14.92 |
| **Total** | **40.65** | **18.19** | **29.60** | **24.52** | **8.04** | **16.35** |

Tribes are the most disinherited group in the country, Even the scheduled castes are ahead of them. Literacy among the tribals in north-east is relatively high but it is extremely low among the other most tribal areas of the rest of India.

Hence, one can see an extremely low percentage at the national level. In other words, in several groups of tribals in Central India literacy is lower than the national average for tribals. Studies in India show that in most tribal areas of Orissa, literacy is as low as 10.21 per cent.

Tribal concentration is the highest in the north-eastern states and is high in Union Territory of Lakshadweep, Dadar, Nagar Hawali, Arunachal Pradesh, Meghalaya, Tripura, and states of Madhya Pradesh, Sikkim, Orissa, Gujarat, Assam and Rajasthan.

In 1991 the percentage of tribal population to total population was the highest in the states of Mizoram (84.75) and Meghalaya (85.53) in the north-east. The other states having a relatively high tribal population are Madhya Pradesh (23.27), Orissa (22.21), Gujarat (14.92), Rajasthan (12.44), Maharashtra (9.27) and Bihar (7.66)* (Census of India 1991 series—1, paper 2 Final Population Tables, New Delhi, 1993. Among the Union Territories, Lakshdweep had the higher percentage in 1991 i.e. 93.15 per cent. However, except for the north-east where tribals are a dominant group, their enrolment in schools in the rest of India is not proportionate to their numbers in the state.

**Table—1.8 Percentage of Scheduled Tribe Population to Total Population in 1991**

| *State/Union Territories* | *Percentage* |
|---|---|
| 1 | 2 |
| Andhra Pradesh | 6.31 |
| Arunachal Pradesh | 63.66 |
| Assam | 12.82 |
| Bihar | 7.66 |
| Goa | 0.03 |
| Gujarat | 14.92 |

*(Table Contd.)*

| 1 | 2 |
|---|---|
| Himachal Pradesh | 4.22 |
| Karnataka | 4.26 |
| Kerala | 1.10 |
| Madhya Pradesh | 23.27 |
| Maharashtra | 9.27 |
| Manipur | 34.41 |
| Meghalaya | 85.53 |
| Mizoram | 94.75 |
| Nagaland | 87.70 |
| Orissa | 22.21 |
| Rajasthan | 12.44 |
| Sikkim | 22.36 |
| Tamil Nadu | 1.03 |
| Tripura | 30.95 |
| Uttar Pradesh | 0.21 |
| West Bengal | 5.59 |
| Andaman and Nicobar Islands | 9.54 |
| Dadra and Nagar Haveli | 78.99 |
| Daman and Diu | 11.54 |
| Lakshadweep | 93.15 |

**Source:* Census of India 1991, Series 1, Paper 2, 1992, Final Population Totals, New Delhi, 1993

Literacy rate among tribals is 24.00 per cent than the general population 52.00 per cent also than the SCs 30.00 per cent, female literacy among tribals is 15.00 per cent compared to 39 per cent in the general population and 19 per cent among the Scheduled Castes. The rural tribal literacy (13.00 per cent) in much lower than literacy in the Rural General Female Population. The Table presented below gives rest of the details of literacy of general population in comparison to tribals.

**Table—1.9 Literacy among Scheduled Tribe and General Population**

| | *1981* | *1991* |
|---|---|---|
| Tribal Male | 24.52 | 32.50 |
| Tribal Female | 8.04 | 14.50 |
| General Male | 46.89 | 64.13 |
| General Female | 24.82 | 39.29 |
| Rural Tribal Female | 6.81 | 12.74 |
| Rural General Male | 17.96 | 30.62 |
| Tribal | 16.35 | 23.63 |

*Source:* Primary Census Abstract for General Population and Scheduled Tribes, 1981, 1991.

**Table—1.10 Percentage of Tribal Literacy (1981-91)**

| | *Total* | *Male* | *Female* |
|---|---|---|---|
| Andhra Pradesh | 17.16 | 25.25 | 8.68 |
| Mizoram | 82.71 | 86.66 | 78.70 |
| Rajasthan | 19.44 | 33.29 | 4.42 |
| Orissa | 22.31 | 34.44 | 10.21 |
| Madhya Pradesh | 21.54 | 32.16 | 10.73 |
| Bihar | 26.78 | 38.40 | 14.75 |
| Kerala | 57.22 | 63.38 | 51.07 |
| Nagaland | 60.59 | 66.27 | 54.51 |
| Sikkim | 59.01 | 66.80 | 50.37 |
| Lakshadweep | 80.58 | 89.50 | 71.72 |

*Source:* Computed on the basis of Census of India 1991, Union Primary Census Abstract Scheduled Tribes, 1993.

**Table—1.11 National Scenario of ST Enrolment**

| *ST Enrolment* | | | *1990-91* | *1992-93* |
|---|---|---|---|---|
| Class | I—IV | Girls | 76.6 | 88.64 |
| | | Total | 103.3 | 109.19 |
| Class | I—VIII | Girls | 27.5 | 32.4 |
| | | Total | 39.7 | 45.64 |

*Source:* Revised National Policy on Education 1992.

As regards gross enrolment ratio the Scheduled Tribes have claimed total 108.19 per cent in the Classes I—V in the year 1992-93. This figure was 103.3 per cent during the year 1990-91. The enrolment figures is comparatively poorer 78.6 per cent to 88.64 per cent in respect of Scheduled Tribes for a period of 1990-1991 to 1992-93. The enrolment of Scheduled Tribe students for Classes V—VIII has shown an enhancement from 39.7 per cent in 1990-91 to 45.64 in 1992-93. ST girls enrolment has increased from 27.5 per cent in 1990-91 to 32.04 per cent. But on the whole ST population is yet to be improved upto expectation. The above table gives an idea about this position.

One can notice that Nagaland and other north-eastern states, where tribals are a majority, have the highest gross enrolment of tribals. Their percentage comes down as soon as one comes to states like Orissa, Bihar, Madhya Pradesh where tribals are a minority living in its backward areas, Here they are a suppressed group and are denied access to education. The low level of literacy is only a sign of the exploitative status of the tribals in most states where they are a small minority living in remote areas. Middlemen, contractors and money lenders have exploited them and turned them into their bonded labourers. Studies have indicated that around 90 per cent of them live below the poverty line and that 90 per cent of the bonded labourers in the country belong to the Scheduled Castes and Scheduled Tribe categories (Marla 1981). Studies have shown that these dominant groups have a vested interest in the contribution of this exploitative state of the tribals. The riches of these groups depend on the poverty of the tribals and the Scheduled Castes. Hence they ensure that these weaker sections are deprived of facilities like schools which can be instrumental in making them aware of their state of exploitation (Jetley 1977).

Given their poverty and state of bondage, they cannot afford to send their children to school since they are required to supplement the meagre income of their parents. If they enter class 1, often they are forced to drop out of school even before they complete elementary education. Hence dropout rate is very high among tribals. This is true particularly among women, as may be seen in their very low literacy rate shown in Table—1.10. The governments, both at the Centre and in the States, have enunciated policies to encourage education among tribals. Official statistics show that many schools have been built in the tribal areas. But studies show that often these schools exist only on paper. The vested interest of the dominant sections mentioned above control the official machinery and ensure that plans made for the tribals are not implemented.

Several other factors could be mentioned as possible causes for the slow progress of the Scheduled Tribes in this field. It is already mentioned poverty, lack of social and political awareness, vested interests, faulty planning, improper implementation, and the highly bureaucratic administrative structures. To this one may add the appointment of teachers who are ignorant of tribal culture, religion and tradition. The vicious circle is closed by tribal traditions and culture which, by and large, do not encourage educational progress. If we are to find a solution to this state of affairs, we need to go deeper into this situation and find out the real causes. With J.P. Naik (1971) we too need to ask the following questions:

1. Why is the co-efficient of equality of the Scheduled Tribes still low? Why is this co-efficient especially low in some states?
2. Why are the rates of wastage and stagnation at the school stage higher in the case of the Scheduled Tribes than in any community as a whole? What measures can be taken to reduce them?
3. Who are the Scheduled Tribe Students are the transferred from primary stage to secondary stage and then to the university stage?

4. What difficulties are experienced by Scheduled Tribe students in getting admission to good secondary schools, good college and universities and technical schools in the country? How can these difficulties be overcome? What other difficulties do they face? What type of guidance do they receive to overcome these difficulties.
5. How is the programme of scholarships to Scheduled Tribe students at the university stage operating in practice? What are the practical difficulties experienced by them in this regard and how can they be overcome?
6. How are the Ashram schools and hostels for Scheduled Tribe students at the secondary and university stages being managed at present? How can their management be improved? What measures can be adopted to secure increased accommodation for Scheduled Tribe students in the general hostels.

If these issues are dealt with properly and the right measures taken, then the educational problems of the Scheduled Tribes can be solved to a considerable extent and with that the co-efficient of equality can be maintained at the required level. In the process of doing that, cumulative inequality which is so clear in the case of the tribals, can be controlled.

Andhra Pradesh is one of the nine educationally backward states in the country and has the dubious distinction of being the only state in the south to have a lower literacy rate than the national average. Using a composite index of five indicators, P.R. Panchmukhi ranks the State third lowest in the country in educational development. To some extent this backwardness can be ascribed to historical reasons, and systematic efforts to improve the standard of education were started only after 1956.

In 1956-57, enrolment in primary school was 57.94 per cent in the 6 to 11 age group, and this had reached 89.1 per cent by 1984-85, whereas enrolment upper primary school in the 11 to 14 age group is not even 50 per cent now. This shows that the constitutional objective of universalisation of elementary education (6 to 14 age group) has not been achieved yet in the State. The rate of growth of enrolment in the post-secondary level (intermediate, post-graduate and professional and degree level) has been much higher than at the school level, and expenditure on higher education has also grown faster than expenditure on elementary education. All this suggests that the growth of education has been very uneven in Andhra Pradesh.

Learning in India has been a prerogative of a new groups in society. Even after the advent of a secular and democratic government, groups which are closer to the power structure have derived greater benefit from the government programmes of education while regions and groups which are at a distance and in a disadvantaged position are further marginalised. In 1981, for instance, the literacy rate of the urban male population was around 70 per cent, while the rates of literacy among disadvantaged groups like S.C. and S.T. and women were very low, as low as 2.78 per cent for rural ST women.

A minimum of 4 years of schooling is essential for any individual to satisfy the census definition of literacy. However, the drop-out rates in primary education, (particularly in the 5th standard,) indicated that the socially disadvantaged groups and the districts inhabited by these groups are educationally backward, with very high drop-out rates. Among the 23 districts in the States, Srikakulam and Vizianagaram in Coastal Andhra had a drop-out rate of 70 per cent, while Anantapur in Rayalaseema had a drop-out rate of 64 per cent. These districts are generally categorised as the most backward districts in the state.

It is a well-known fact that there is a relationship between the level of educational development and the socio-economic structure. As long as the economy derives a major proportion of its domestic product from the traditional primary sector (which requires very little modern skills) the demand for education would be small. Apart from other socio-economic factors, the demands of industry for skills and upgradation of technology contribute in a major way to the expansion of education in a country.

The National Policy on Education, 1986 (NPE) provides the broad outlines under which educational policy should be laid down in the states. The NPE stresses consolidation and retention rates in school education, open learning systems in higher education and mass literacy by 1995 as priority areas. The government of Andhra Pradesh also seems to have been influenced in its educational policy by the World Bank recommendations for opening up the educational system to the private sector for improving its efficiency. But this neo-classical approach to human capital development is inappropriate in the conditions prevailing in underdeveloped countries like India.

## Policy Suggestion for the Eighth Plan

1. Adult literacy programmes should be strengthened since the State has an illiterate population of 1 crore women and 70 lakh men in the 20 to 59 age group.
2. In the identified backward districts like Nizamabad, Ranga reddy, Medak, Anantapur, Srikakulam and Vizianagaram, a crash programme of universalisation of primary education must be taken up, with incentives like mid-day meals to induce parents to keep their children in school.
3. As funds for Operation Block are made available by the Centre and from various developmental programmes, the scheme should be implemented rigorously, especially in the backward regions.
4. A comprehensive programme of child-care, nutrition and preparation for schooling must be introduced for the rural pre-primary age children, especially those belonging to socially disadvantaged groups.
5. More innovative mechanisms of augmenting resources for higher education need to be evolved, rather than encouraging commercialisation which will worsen socio-economic imbalances in the long run.

Andhra Pradesh initially did increase allocations to social services, but has not been able to raise the allocations for education. There are two sets of arguments which are often levelled against allocation of additional resources to education, health and other social services. The first set of arguments suggests that the differences in the performance relating to the literacy, enrolments, infant mortality etc. are more due to the diversity in cultural and institutional factors rather than in the allocation of resources.

A recent study by the World Bank explicitly argues a case for "private provision of public services" like education, health etc. Given the present state of development and the state of the poor, this is a dangerous tendency which leads to the creation of class-differentiated institutions like schools for the rich and schools for the poor.

The argument that education and health facilities are becoming a heavy burden on the state is a lie. Andhra Pradesh, with a per capita domestic product equivalent to that of Kerala, spends only half of what Kerala has been spending on education per capita. Andhra Pradesh's allocation for education has been around twenty per cent of the state budgeted expenditure and it could be increased to thirty per cent. Further Andhra Pradesh can mobilise more resources from the past investments by raising the water rates in command areas to at least a universally recommended level of fifteen per cent of the value of the output from irrigated agriculture. There is also a very strong case against any further allocation for irrigation or command area development or drainage systems from public funds, because this expenditure can be met from farmers' contributions as was done earlier in India, and is being done elsewhere in the world. This would also reduce the disproportionate rural surpluses searching out high profit and low productive investments and conspicuous consumption.

It is therefore imperative that Andhra Pradesh should bring about a second tilt in budgetary allocation, a tilt in favour of education, especially school education. The first tilt in favour of social services expenditure is a desirable one, but may not be adequate to effect improvements in the quality of life of the poor without proper educational facilities. The Eighth Five Year Plan of Andhra Pradesh should aim towards raising the per capita allocation to education to the level obtained in Kerala, at least in two phases. The first phase should take into consideration the vast regional differences in primary education in the state, as shown in Table—1.12. Higher allocations should go to those districts where the enrolment in primary schools is less than 50 per cent of the population in the corresponding age group. The second phase should be increasing the number and improving the quality of primary and secondary education. Hopefully, this may change the direction of the dialectics of development in Andhra Pradesh.

**Table—1.12 District-wise Distribution of Pupils in Primary Schools**

| *Sl. No.* | *District* | *Population of (1984-85) 5-9 Age group* | *No. of Scholars in Elementary Schools* | *Percentage of Scholars in Elementary School Population in 5-9 Age group* |
|---|---|---|---|---|
| **1** | **2** | **3** | **4** | **5** |
| 1. | Srikakulam | 292614 | 198000 | 67.67 |
| 2. | Vizianagaram | 265703 | 166000 | 62.48 |
| 3. | Visakhapatnam | 393296 | 229000 | 59.75 |
| 4. | East Godavari | 542554 | 328000 | 60.46 |
| 5. | West Godavari | 424959 | 292000 | 68.71 |
| 6. | Krishna | 436624 | 281000 | 64.36 |
| 7. | Guntur | 484306 | 297000 | 61.32 |
| 8. | Prakasam | 343410 | 241000 | 70.18 |
| 9. | Nellore | 292184 | 164000 | 56.13 |
| | Coastal Andhra | 3465649 | 2226000 | 64.23 |
| 10. | Chittoor | 404416 | 276000 | 69.25 |
| 11. | Cuddapah | 301707 | 266000 | 88.17 |
| 12. | Ananthapur | 421940 | 249000 | 59.01 |
| 13. | Kurnool | 403145 | 228000 | 56.56 |
| | Rayalaseema | 1531207 | 1019000 | 66.55 |
| 14. | Mahabubnagar | 401125 | 134000 | 32.67 |
| 15. | Rangareddi | 261071 | 97000 | 37.15 |

*(Table Contd.)*

| 1 | 2 | 3 | 4 | 5 |
|---|---|---|---|---|
| 16. | Hyderabad | 3323345 | 183000 | 55.06 |
| 17. | Medak | 294105 | 126000 | 42.84 |
| 18. | Nizamabad | 261819 | 57000 | 21.44 |
| 19. | Adilabad | 277925 | 76000 | 27.25 |
| 20. | Karimnagar | 374818 | 117000 | 31.22 |
| 21. | Warangal | 373940 | 118000 | 31.56 |
| 22. | Khammam | 295468 | 90000 | 30.46 |
| 23. | Nalgonda | 355320 | 147000 | 41.37 |
| | Telangana | 3240936 | 1143000 | 35.26 |
| **Andhra Pradesh** | | **8237790** | **4388000** | **53.26** |

* 1981 Population has been adjusted to 1984-85 on the basis of population growth rate for the period.

** These figures differ from the enrolment rates.

*Source:* *(i)* Census of India 1981, Series 2, Andhra Pradesh, Part IV—A Social and Cultural Tables, 1986 for 1981 district-wise Population of age group 5-9.

*(ii)* For 'Scholars in the Primary Schools', Commissioner of School education as given in Andhra Pradesh Economic Association, Fifth Annual Conference Papers, Volume—II.

Since no significant achievement can be made without the co-operation of the parents, teachers have to be in regular touch with the parents, especially of irregular children. In this aspect, some of the anti-poverty programmes can also be used to make the parents aware of their responsibility in sending their wards regularly to school.

At present different schemes like distribution of text books note books, bags etc. are in implementation. Scholarships are also given to children belonging to Scheduled Tribes. These schemes have not resulted in maximum benefit because they are not linked to educational performance. For instance, instead of giving a scholarship once in a year in a lump sum, it is better to make it quarterly, and distribute the amount only after proper assessment in terms of attendance and learning.

The equation estimated to explain the variation in literacy rate showed that the literacy rate is lower in areas with high proportion of Scheduled Tribes and agricultural labourers. Hence more attention should be paid to the mandals with higher proportion of these categories. Given the socio-economic conditions of the mandals, the expected literacy rate is computed from the estimated equation and mandals are classified on the basis of the difference between the actual and the expected literacy rate (Table—11). Out of the 57 mandals in the district, 14 mandals have a performance lower than expected, and most of them (10 mandals) belonging to the low literacy category. One mandal in high literacy category also has a less than expected performance.

This does not call for a very big investment. But even if it entails some cost, it is very much worth the while, as without a secure base for the tribals to stand on, one cannot plan for tribal development. It may be good to heed to advice of B.D. Sharma, an experienced administrator with long involvement in tribai development, in this regard. He said: "It is logical to take effective protective measures through suitable administrative and legal action before launching a developmental programme. The economic issues get a second priority in the new development strategy next to protective measures and building up of the inner strength of community.

The second item which must be imphasised in the Eighth Plan is literacy. If the tribals are to benefit from other development schemes, they must first receive the gift of education. Without the requisite level of awareness amongst them, there is bound to be a high degree of wastage and seepage in developmental work.

As already stated, the tribals of Andhra Pradesh have the lowest level of literacy among all the states of our country. Within the Scheduled Tribes of the State again, there are considerable regional variations in the literacy levels, as seen in Table—1.12. It is to be noted that the literacy levels among the tribes of Telangana districts are uniformly low.

Strangely there is no correlation between the number of existing schools in the Scheduled Areas of a district and the level of literacy. At the beginning of the Fifth Plan, as a part of the exercise of formulating the first Tribal Sub-Plan (TSP), the Tribal Welfare Department compiled information on the number of existing institutions in 1974-75 in the Scheduled Areas of different districts. Combining the ordinary primary schools and Ashram schools together and looking at their total against the population of the ITDAs, it was found that for every one lakh population there were 80 such institutions in Adilabad, 310 in Warangal, 380 in Khammam, 320 in West Godavari, 320 in West Godavari, 320 in East Godavari, 160 in Visakhapatnam and 140 in Srikakulam. Whatever other things these figures might mean, there is one clear indication, i.e., not only the number of schools but the quality of the institutions should be augmented in districts that have a very low literacy level.

In trying to figure out the existing situation in the field of education, one runs into some difficulties in the absence of published 1981 Census data on individual tribes and in the absence of village census books. A further difficulty arises from the fact that there are two district domains in which the Tribal Welfare Department operates. Some of the schemes of this department are addressed to all the tribes in the State, while some are location specific. This department is also the apex body for the ITDAs. In preparing reports and compiling, figures, sometimes the scope of coverage is not clearly indicated. Hence there is a possible confusion at times between the data pertaining to the ITDAs and the data for the entire State, which is particularly evident in regard to school enrolment figures.

The Tribal Sub Plan for the Seventh Plan period gives a resume of the aims and achievements of the Sixth Plan. The primary school enrolment at the beginning of the Sixth Plan was 2,39,000 and rose to 3,85,000 by the end of the Sixth Plan. The area and the population to which the data refer is matter of doubt. If we take it to pertain only to the ITDAs (to which the TSP applies), the total population including tribals and non-tribals in 21.88 lakhs in the area. The children in the 6-11 age group can be only about 2.64 lakhs. Even if we take the enrolment figures as pertaining to all the tribal population in the state, the children of tne primary school age group can only be about 3.84 lakhs in the total tribal population of 31.76 lakhs. This means that the enrolment targets were over fulfilled by the end of the Sixth Plan itself. The Sixth Plan achievements in enrolment at upper primary school level are given separately. Here the enrolment increased from 15,000 to 75,000 during the Sixth Plan.

If there were 2,39,000 children in primary schools and 15,000 children in upper primary schools at the beginning of the Sixth Plan, their impact should have been felt in the returns of the 1981 Census. Even if we take only those 2,54,000 childrten enrolled in the primary schools at the beginning of 1980, they constitute 8 per cent of the total tribal population of 31.76 lakhs. If we add the literates among the older age groups the literacy level among the tribes of Andhra Pradesh must have been much above the 7.8 per cent that was recorded in the 1981 Census.

Further anomalies turn up when we look at other data. The Fifth Plan.TSP gives detailed base-line data which show that, in 1974-75, there were only 60,077 children enrolled in the schools within the Scheduled Areas of the State. Then the question arises as to whether the efforts undertaken during the Fifth Plan alone could push up school enrolment from 60,000 at the beginning of the Plan period to 2,39,000 at the end of the Plan period, which would have needed five or six thousand additional teachers and corresponding institutional infrastructure. There is no evidence that such a gigantic investment was made during the Fifth Plan. Then again, from the beginning to the end of the Sixth Plan period, the school enrolment rose from 2,39,000 pupils to 3,85,000 children which should be reckoned as a stupendous achievement. But, on the other hand, we find in the Seventh Plan TSP document a rueful entry regarding the results of the Sixth Plan which reads: "After a detailed review of the educational programme, it was found that the gap in the literacy level has further widened because of lack of sufficient investments".

Let us trace of educational progress achieved in the Scheduled Areas of the State beginning with the Fifth Plan period, which also coincided with the launching of the first Tribal Sub Plan. While the estimated number of children of school-going age was given as 1,96,000 the actual enrolment in the schools was only 60,000 in 1974-75. The number of primary schools in Scheduled Areas at the time was 1,513 and the number of upper primary schools was only 20. Ashram schools numbered 210. Leaving the negligible numbers that could be enrolled in the upper primary schools, we could take that the enrolment at the primary school level was just 60,000 at the beginning of the Fifth Plan. The total number of teachers in the schools was 1,821. The fifth Plan TSP calculated the number of additional teachers required to impart instruction if all the children of the school-going age were to be enrolled, and put the figures at 5,888. It showed a shortfall of 4,067 teachers and an equal number of classrooms. The fifth Plan TSP estimated that an outlay of Rs. 7.61 crore would be needed to fill this gap and to achieve enrolment of at least 95 per cent of the children of school-going age.

The realism of the Fifth Plan TSP is not reflected in the subsequent plan documents. In fact, it seems to have become infra dig even to mention the name of primary schools in the Sixth and Seventh Plan documents. They only spoke of Ashram schools to some extent and, more enthusiastically, of the new-angled variety, the residential schools. The project-wise data submitted to the Parliamentary Committee in the year 1985 showed that in the 8 ITDAs, there were 1,742 primary schools and 366 Ashram schools. This meant that during the one decade between 1974-75 and 1984-85 the number of primary schools in the Scheduled Areas rose from 1,513 to 1,742 and the number of Ashram schools from 210 to 366, if these figures are to be relied upon, there was an addition of 299 primary schools and 156 Ashram schools during this one decade. It is then evident that only a small fraction of the Fifth Plan projections of about 4,000 additional teachers and corresponding infrastructure could be fulfilled. The meagre additional of a few hundred schools could be fulfilled. The meagre addition of a few hundred schools could not have raised the enrolment from 60,000 at the beginning of the Fifth Plan TSPs projections regarding 4,000 additional teachers aimed only to achieve a total enrolment of 1,76,000 pupils.

The parliamentary Committee was informed that there was a proposal to open 2,090 more primary schools during the Seventh

Plan period, of which 1,000 were to be opened in 1986-87 and the remaining in the subsequent year. Following in the same vein, a recent paper by the Director of Tribal Cultural Research Institute has stated that 3,317 single teacher schools have already been opened during the Seventh Plan-period. But if we look at the Seventh Plan TSP document it only aimed at taking the primary school enrolment from 3,85,000 to 3,96,000. To increase enrolment by just 10,000 one does not need 3,317 single teacher schools. There is something grossly amiss in the reported schemes and in the data regarding tribal education in Andhra Pradesh. The level of statistical information seems to be on par with the level of literacy among the tribes of Andhra Pradesh.

The Seventh Plan TSP indicates that the share of outlay from the Director of Schools was of the order of Rs. 8.1 crores. Out of this, Rs. 5.6 crores were earmarked for 10 residential schools alone. Where then was the money for 3,317 additional primary schools? We may look at the budget estimates of recent years and examine whether these schemes were backed up by requisite financial outlays. The Tribal Welfare Department's Plan budget account for 1986-87 under the head of 'Schools' was Rs. 29,38,600, and the TSP's account under the head of Elementary Education was Rs. 68,58,900. The two together make up approximately Rs. 98.0 lakhs. If we assume that the salary of a teacher plus contingencies would amount to Rs. 20,000 per year, this alone would come to Rs. 2 crores per year for 1,000 teachers, apart from the building cost. How could this feat be achieved within Rs. 98.0 lakhs? In the following year, the outlay had indeed been steeped up. The revised estimate for 1987-88 for school education (Tribal Welfare Department Plan and TSP taken together) was Rs. 3 crores. But that would not be sufficient to support the appointment and maintenance of another batch of 2,317 teachers in addition to 1,000 teachers appointed in the previous year. The total Plan budget estimates for school education in the tribal sector for the year 1988-89 added up to only Rs. 2.74 crores. This might have been just enough for the maintenance of 1,300 teachers for one year. Hence, it is a matter of surprise as to how 3,317 schools were suddenly conjured up in the Scheduled Areas during the Seventh Plan period. What about the cost of constructing such a large number of school buildings?

If really such a large number of schools were started, perhaps they are being run without proper accommodation and the teachers perhaps and paid a few hundred rupees per months.

It would ultimately, be better for the credibility and success of development programmes to have fewer but well-run institutions than to have several units. Before a teacher is appointed, necessary care should be taken in his selection. While single teacher schools are a necessary to serve some remote villages, the majority of the schools must be manned by 2 or 3 teachers. In the case of single teacher schools, the teachers should be, as far as possible, numbers of the local tribal community. Women teachers should be recruited wherever possible and posting of a teacher couple will be ideal for Ashram schools. The Government of India has a scheme to subsidise the salary of women teachers working in tribal schools, and advantage should be taken of it. Schools without blackboards have been heard of. But in our anxiety to boost enrolment figures, we seen to be contriving to have schools even without walls and roofs. A durable school building should be constructed before any unit is entered in official statistics. And every school building should have residential quarters for teachers.

The Seventh Plan TSP notes the effective enrolment of pupils in primary schools is only 60 per cent because of heavy drop-out rates at the initial stage itself. The retention rate was said to be between 70 and 80 per cent among the boys and between 40 and 50 per cent among the girls. (The enrolment is reported to be 82 per cent among the girls as against 100 per cent among the boys). Another report reveals that more than 60 per cent of tribal children drop out of the school before they reach the end of the lower primary stage, and even lapse into illiteracy. Hence not only enrolment but regular attendance and retention in school, at least up to the end of the primary stage, are important if schooling is to leave its indelible imprint on tribal children.

A number of incentives are offered at present to school-going tribal children, like text books, note books, school dress, pre-metric scholarships etc. One decisive addition that should be made to the existing incentives is the mid-day meal of primary school children. The Eighth Plan should provide for the progressive introduction of this scheme so as to cover all the children in the primary schools in the Scheduled Areas, who would number about two lakhs, excluding in inmates of Ashram schools. (It should be noted that literacy levels are lower in the Scheduled areas than among the tribes living in the plains). An annual provision of Rs. 200 per child may be made for the mid-day meal programme.

In the field of primary education, the Eighth Plan should aim at consolidation and not haphazard expansion. The construction of four thousand pucca primary school buildings along with cottages for teachers should be targeted for the Eighth Plan period. This is to cover the 3317 primary schools said to have been started during the Seventh Plan. About Rs. 50,000 should be allotted for each unit for this purpose. Every school should be provided with standard instructional material. After first providing for the consolidation of the existing institutions, new units should be taken up, and these should be mostly in the form of Ashram schools.

An Ashram school with three teachers and about 100 should be ideal for tribal areas. Unfortunately, the initial enthusiasm for this types of institutions has waned, for no obvious reason. During the Sixth Plan, 436 new Ashram schools were proposed but only 175 were completed and 119 were reported to be in progress. Today there are only 366 Ashram schools in the Scheduled Areas of the State. The seventh Plan proposed 315 Ashram schools, but there is no evidence of any progress in that regard. Emphasis suddenly shifted to what are called residential schools, each claiming a huge outlay of Rs. 50 lakhs, but each catering only to about 300 students. There are 24 such institutions at present. These institutions may be all right to serve the needs of education at upper primary level and above. But, at the primary level, they would soon reach a saturation point in the tribal areas or only serve the elite of the society, whether tribal or non-tribal, uniform improvement of all schools should be the aim, particularly at the primary level. During the Eighth Plan, 500 new Ashram schools should be established by converting, it necessary, (and not abolishing) existing primary schools wherever that suits the needs of the situation.

The expansion of education at the upper primary and school levels should proceed at a pace so as to ensure that a 50 per cent of those enrolled in primary schools get into the next and 25 per cent of them can find a place in the high schools should be Teachers Training colleges in each major ITDA in-service training and refresher courses must be offered to teachers in tribal school on a regular basis.

The administration should outgrow its thinking consolidation and improvement of existing institutions are development activity worthy of inclusion in Plan schemes. Eighth Plan TSP in Andhra Pradesh should aim at consolidation of the existing educational infrastructure by allocating about courses for the construction of 4,000 school buildings and the quarters, about Rs. 15 crores for the mid-day meal programme and about Rs. 10 crores for establishing 500 new Ashrams are already stated, the strategy for tribal development. The Eighth Plan should not be based on financial outlays on in the same proportions as in the State Plan, but they provide major thrusts in the most crucial areas.

The mid-term appraisal of Eighth Plan revealed that serious attention to the literacy problems of the weaker sections of society, specially STs was emphasised by the Eighth Plan. Efforts have therefore, been directed to the districts/regions which are educationally backward and have high concentration of STs population with low female literacy.

During the 9th Plan period the enrolment of girls, of Scheduled Tribes has shown an increases at the primary stage and the drop out rates have shown a declining trend. However, there is still a long way to go to achieve UEE. The National Literacy Mission (NLM) with a mandate to make 100 million people literate in the age group of 15-35 by the year 1997 has achieved (1996) a target of 56.1 million.

In the Ninth Plan, apart from carrying out the directions given by NPE (1992), and keeping in view of declaration of education as an aspect of fundamental human right to life, making the nation fully literate by the year 2005 will be a committed goal. Around 6 per cent of the GDP will be earmarked for the education sector by the year 2000 and 50 per cent of that will be spent on primary education. Further, substantial funds will be earmarked for imparting technical and vocational skills and training, in order to turn out more employable and self-employed youths. NLM will achieve the coverage of 100 million adults by the year 1998-89 with special attention and effort for the spread of literacy among women and in the States with high incidence of illiteracy. The Mid-day Meal Scheme will be implemented in all the States to ensure regular attendance and retention in primary and middle schools. In every initiative to promote the spread of education, the girl child will be a special focus of attention.

The unfinished task of UEE will be completed with special focus on the backward States/districts, the girl child and other disadvantaged population groups, emphasising decentralised and disaggregated planning with the participation of Non-government Organisations (NGOs), the corporate sector and various other groups. Linkages will be developed between adult education and formal and non-formal education including open learning. Quality in UEE will be achieved through better pedagogical and management practices. Performance of teachers will be improved through better content and facilities for training programmes and community participation in supervision. Strategies will be developed for mobilising financial support through community effort.

## Conclusion

Most of the time planners appear to have ignored aspects such as the culture and exploitation of the Scheduled Tribes while providing incentives and persuading them to come for formal education. During the First Five Year Plan itself our government realised this but nothing was done in concrete terms except exempting these students from the payment of tuition fees, relaxing the admission criteria, providing overseas scholarships etc. This has in no way helped the Scheduled Tribes to develop a genuine interest in formal education since it made no efforts to change the exploitative structures that have kept them poor. Besides this, their cultural aspects are also not attended to. No special measures were taken by the Ministry of Education, Planning Commission, the Department of Social Welfare or other Government agencies to develop tribal education keeping in view their tradition, culture, religion, geographical location and language. Whatever small initiatives are taken, get shattered because of lack of proper implementation. There is a big gulf between planning and implementation and for this most of the time government officials at the implementation level are responsible.

From all facts and figures discussed above, one could arrive at a rational conclusion that there should be many changes brought about in the existing educational system with special reference to the weaker sections, particularly the Scheduled Tribes. The Challenge of Education has pointed out many difficulties and constraints that are responsible for ineffectiveness of the present educational system and it has also suggested some situations (Ministry of Education 1985). But none of them seems to deal with the basic causes which make education inaccessible to the tribals. Studies have mentioned six points which should be taken into consideration while finding out some solutions to tribal education *viz.* tribal social structures, their economic organisation, their accessibility to education, their language, their psychology and taken for this were inadequate. In spite of these efforts, not much has happened in tribal education. According to the 6th Five Year Plan document (1980-85), 59 per cent Scheduled Tribe children (49 per cent boys and 70 per cent girls) are yet to receive elementary education. The approach paper to the seventh five year plan lays stress on general and technical education and states that the education of girls and children belonging to the Scheduled Castes and Tribes would be especially promoted. It emphasises the promotion of a non-formal educational approach.

This plan claims to pay special attention to the problems of Scheduled Tribe women. As already mentioned earlier, the literacy among the Scheduled Tribe women is nowhere near that of their counterparts in the general population. This can be seen not merely in literacy but also at every stage of education, in schools, in colleges and in universities.

**Continuing Repression**

The real cause for this continuing low literacy and educational level and for their lack of access to facilities such as education should be found in the continuing existence and even strengthening of the vested interests of the rural areas. These areas are controlled by landlords and moneylenders, many of whom are also the local politicians. They have been exploiting the tribals, forcing them into indebtedness, alienating them from their land and often turning them into bonded labourers.

Besides, the forest departments revenue inspectors, tehsildars and often the B.D.O. and other government officials too exploit the tribals. In connivance with these government officials, local rich non-tribals exploit the tribals to such an extent that they fail to acquire any interest in education and if at all they do, they lose it in no time. The existence of these vested interests and the consequent improverishment of the tribal population have been substantiated by several studies. Tara Patel (1984), and Shah and Patel (1985) have shown it in Gujarat, Pamecha (1985) in Rajasthan, Fernades, Menon and Viegas (1984) in Orissa and others elsewhere.

For this situation to continue, it is important to keep them away from proper education. Hence even after independence these vested interests have ensured the exclusion of tribals from education. In many cases schools and colleges are deliberately not set up in areas predominantly inhabited by Scheduled Tribes. When they exist, the school teacher in a tribal area is rarely a tribal. The non-tribal teacher does not understand and sometimes does not try to grasp proper choice of teachers in schools meant for them (Pattanayak 1981). But little has been done in this direction and the new document does not deal with these aspects.

The long experience of tribal education leads us to realise that its implementation process has to be changed or replaced by a new educational system. After so many years of the Government's attempts, the tribals remain even today an educationally backward community. This is true particularly about their women. It is a matter of serious concern since today they constitute 7.76 per cent of the total population of our country. As such they simply cannot be neglected any more.

# 2

# Review of Literature

## Introduction

The progress of education among the tribals has been very slow. Number of factors seems to be acting as barriers for the educational progress among them. Fairly large number of research studies have highlighted these factors and the government has been initiating the number of measures to overcome the problems involved. A closer analysis of the variables brought out by the research overview reveals that difficulties and disparities in educational progress among the tribals stem from three sets of structural constraints i.e. the ecological, the socio-economic and internal elements of the school system.

Review of the status of educational development among the tribals and the various factors which have inhibited educational progress among them clearly highlight the fact that socio-economic development and education should not be divorced, but viewed as inter-dependent process.

The review indicate the gaps to be filled and also the methodology is used by various authors. The present study was designed based on the extensive review made in the chapter an attempt is made to present the studies in India on the various aspects of tribal education *viz.*, absenteeism, wastage and stagnation.

Ambasht (1970) made a study of Christian Missionaries helping for tribal education in Ranchi, Bihar. His study indicated that distance of school, economic reasons, toughness of syllabus, different medium of instruction are the various reasons for wastage among tribal students of Ranchi.

Desai et al (1976) in his study of Gujarat State indicated that Ashram Sales are costly in terms of low enrolment.

Toppo (1979) in her study in Ranchi in Bihar stated that Christian missionaries are helping for tribal education. Tribal showed more drop-outs and stagnation than non-tribal children. The various reasons for the drop-outs indicated are—lack of encouragement by parents, illiteracy of parents, lack of follow up by teachers, absenteeism of students during harvest seasons and festivals, different medium of instruction.

Shah and Patil (1985) in their study of Gujarat reveal that literacy rate of harijans is higher than that of Girijans. Literacy among urban tribals is higher than among the rural tribals.

Rao (1987) in his study of Andhra Pradesh showed that adult education programme is not successful, so it is essential to concentrate on children's education, little supervision on the functions of teachers, lack of parental interest in school functioning, lack of knowledge of tribal culture among teachers are the main reasons for poor functioning of adult education programme.

Reddy (1990) in his study of Andhra Pradesh revealed that, Andhra Pradesh tribal literacy rate is less than other South Indian States. Female literacy is still worse. Tribal literacy is lower than that of Harijans and other communities, so separate schools for girls is being proposed.

Lachaiah (1990) is his study of Banjaras of Karimnagar district of Andhra Pradesh revealed that parents are interested to educate their children.

Bara and Bhangra and Minz (1991) in their study of Ranchi district of Bihar reported that Christian Schools are helping for girls enrolment.

Srivastava (1986) made a socio-psychological study of stagnates among tribal and non-tribal students of class VIII, with reference to their mode of stagnation, academic achievement, personality traits socio-economic status and groups and 250 stagnates from non-tribal role of living in the same area. The findings implied that the programmes for the development of students from different tribes should be in accordance with their needs and their mother tongue should invariably be used as the medium of instruction at the primary stage.

Srivastava and Joshi conclude that inadequate schools and poverty in the tribal region, insufficient learning material, language, parents compulsion were the causes responsible for the non-enrolment as well as dropping out of ST students from the school. Thus, drop-out is one of the major reasons for slow progress of education among tribes. The poor economic condition, household activities, inadequate schools and traditional prejudices are the main causes responsible for it.

The first contribution of the study of educational problems of Scheduled Tribes in India was made as early as 1944 by Professor Furer-Haimendorf. He presented the outlines of educational schemes by conducting an empirical study among the Gonds of Adilabad district of Nizam's dominion of Hyderabad. Problems of language and script and teachers were highlighted. This was the first time it was pointed out that an education programme for tribals has to be in consonance with their habitat, economy and culture. The dawn of independence and establishment of tribal research institutes in various states having a sizeable tribal population boosted research efforts in the tribal welfare of which education was an important component. Eminent Anthropologists like Chattopadhyay, M.N. Basu, and Biswas made valuable suggestions regarding tribal education. Various research reports and dissertations have focused on the issues related to education of tribals.

Balarkishna (1986) highlighted the effects of socio-cultural deprivation on tribal adolescents. He found that the Christian tribal students possess more intelligence, better reasoning ability and higher achievement motivation than non-Christian tribal students. Moreover, the Christian tribal groups were found to have higher aspiration and goals than the non-Christian tribal group.

Chand (1985) compared various Naga tribal students in relation of their self-perception, socio-economic status and allied aspects. It was found that the boys belonging to Angami and Sema tribes were significantly different from the girls of same tribe in self perception. The girls belonging to the three different tribes were found similar on self-perception. The vocational choice of girls belonging to those three tribes were not found to differ significantly from one another. Likewise the educational aspirations of the boys were also found to be similar.

Chowdhury (1985) focused on the education and social change among the Scheduled Tribes of North Bengal. Some of his findings are as follows. The indigenous Scheduled Tribes were generally more advanced compared to migrant Scheduled Tribes, both plantation workers and village settlers in the field of literacy and gainful occupation. Migrant Scheduled Tribes at the village were alarmingly backward in education in relation to migrant Scheduled Tribes in the tea estate and indigenous Scheduled Tribes in the village.

Dutt (1983) studied the socio-psychological aspects of the tribal high school male students of Himachal Pradesh with high achievement motivation. He found that the tribal students with high achievement motivation were better than the students with low achievement motivation, with regard to intelligence and extraversion, there was no effect of achievement motivation of tribal students on their anxiety, emotional adjustment social adjustment educational adjustment, neuroticism and perceived parental support, parental control and parental punishment. The study highlighted that for betterment of tribal students personalities, guidance and counselling programmes should be encouraged. Also non-formal education, co-curricular activities and adult education programmes should be encouraged in tribal areas.

Gupta (1965) surveyed Adivasi students in Ranchi district. He concluded that the overall situation posed by the Adivasi students was far from satisfactory. Their problems of adjustment to different spheres of life—social, financial, personal and academic—dependent on various factors such as social class, accommodation, personality traits, distance from the native place, financial incentives and level of education.

Koul (1983) attempted at case studies of Scheduled Tribe failure students at middle and matriculation level in Himachal Pradesh. He found that tribal failure students compared to passed tribal students have the following characteristics—lower verbal and non-verbal creative thinking, higher average age, lower socio-economic status, lower degree of adjustment in emotional and social spheres, more anxiety, poor study habits, more insecurity, lower self-conception, etc.

Kumar (1978) made systematic enquiry into higher education among Scheduled Tribes. He conducted his study among 300 tribal students (100 I.A./I.Sc, 100 B.A./B.Sc., 50 M.A./M.Sc. and 50 students of professional colleges were included). He inferred that inspite of the many facilities provided to tribal students in higher education, they have not yet come up to the level of non-tribal students. In professional education tribals dropped out and stagnated most in low courses. Majority of the tribal students belonged to literate families with comparatively high economic and social status in their community. There was comparatively less indiscipline among the tribal students.

Nagaiah (1986) investigated home environment and parenting style among the disadvantaged tribal student population in Madhya Pradesh. It was found that home environment in the two tribal groups, *i.e.* Gonds and Bhils was not found to differ significantly from that of the urban group. However, the parenting style of Bhils and Gonds was markedly different from that of urban parents.

Panda (1989) focused on personality adjustment, mental health and acculturation among Saora tribal students. He found that the Oriya boys and girls possessed better personality adjustment than the least acculturedSaora boys and girls.

With the aim of understanding the usefulness of education in tribal life and also finding out the nature of impediments and hurdles to the overall educational programmes of the tribal people of Orissa, Panda (1980) conducted an empirical study. Some of his findings were:

*(i)* The caste composition of teachers showed that the largest proportion of teachers belonged to Brahmin caste with Khandayat teachers next in number.

*(ii)* Medical facilities provided to tribal school children was very-poor.

*(iii)* A majority of teachers felt that the syllabus was not suitable to the daily usage of tribal children.

*(iv)* Teachers participation in workshops/seminars was very poor.

*(v)* Many students felt that they were unable to pursue their studies well because they had insufficient reading and writing materials.

*(vi)* The relationship between teachers and students was cordial.

Rout (1985) made an indepth study on tribal education in Orissa. He found that out of 13 districts (undivided) of Orissa, Koraput, Sundergarh, Mayurbhanj, Phulbani and Keonjhar have been seriously neglected. Low scholastic achievement and low achievement motivation were marked amongst tribal children. Parental indifference, cultural differences and socio-economic status were identified as major factors for the aforesaid problems. A downward trend in enrolment was marked with increase in educational level. Only 7 per cent of the teachers were from the tribal community. The major causes of dropouts were socio-economic, psychological and educational. In general the qualifications and standard of teachers were not upto the mark.

Binata (1984) identified the problems of education of Santals as follows:

1. Apathy of community members to education
2. Enrolment
3. Retention
4. Stagnation/retardation
5. Relevance of content of education
6. Employment scope

7. Alienation and
8. Communication

He concluded that the real problem lies in the lack of adequate coordination of resources. For this it was necessary that:

(a) the system of education be locally adoptable,
(b) content and strategies be based on local culture, and
(c) appropriately trained teachers be provided.

Singh (1979) reported that Santal students were significantly higher in anxiety but lower in intelligence, achievement motivation and academic achievement than non-Santals. In addition it was also found that extroversion was negatively but not significantly related to academic achievements of Santals, whereas it was positively and significantly related in the case of non-Santals.

Srivastava (1986) investigated into the mode of stagnation, academic achievement, personality traits, socio-economic status and intelligence of the tribal and non-tribal students. He found that Bhotia and Jaunsari tribals were more intelligent than non-tribal students. Bhotia and Jaunsari students exhibited a positive attitude towards most of the personality factors, whereas Tharu, Boxa and Raji tribals showed a negative attitude towards the personality traits. The stagnates of Bhotia, Tharu, Jaunsari and Boxa tribes did not show any significant differences from non-tribals. The stagnates from Raji tribe had comparatively poor socio-economic background. Bhotia and Jaunsari showed better academic performances than non-tribal students. Academic performances of Tharu and Jaunsari and Raji students were inferior to non-tribals.

Madan (1951) conducted a study on the education of tribals in India. To hi in for the total progress of the country it was necessary to educate the tribals. He suggested that: *(i)* economic improvement should be given first priority because no educational experiment could be successfully conducted on the people who were suffering from economic backwardness; *(ii)* all the existing modes of education must be studied and utilized; *(iii)* basic type of education should be given preference; *(iv)* vocational education must find the proper place in their educational set up; *(v)* there should be some provision for adult education also, and *(vi)* three main points namely, local teachers, local method of instruction and local dialects were essential in order to make literacy digestible to the tribals.

Raj (1951) conducted a study to work out the immediate steps that should be taken to educate the huge mass of tribals or 'adivasis' in the country. He suggested that the total programme of tribal education should be carried out in the following stages: *(i)* rousing intellectual curiosity in the advisasis for their own culture; *(ii)* writing books on the stories of their origin, culture and history in their own languages; *(iii)* making them conversant about their attitude, nature, customs, village clothes, houses, neighbours etc. with the help of plays, songs and pictures, *(iv)* writing and publishing easy books containing their own stories and the stories of other people also; *(v)* introducing them with the book-lets and showing them in slides on other people, other occupations, other environments, etc., *(vi)* motivating them to read the books of their own history, and publishing the books on their own and others' myths and the realities of life and *(vii)* introducing them with the books of physiology and other natural sciences. One more important point that was mentioned by the author is that all the teachers engaged in tribal education should be given a special training before they were actually put to work.

A study on the education in tribal culture was conducted by Mutatkar (1973). In the study he discussed various problems which would occur while educating the tribals in their own culture. He suggested some recommendations to solve the problems in tribal education. According to him, *(i)* a creche or 'Balwadi' should be attached to the primary schools; *(ii)* some classes should be held in the open air where the tribals could graze their cattle also; *(iii)* spacious and well-lighted classrooms should be made; *(iv)* several visual aids like picture, model and museum should be employed for training the tribals; *(v)* teachers should become the friends and playmates of the children; and *(vi)* co-curricular activities like dancing, crafts, etc. should also be introduced in their educational system.

The author furthered emphasized that the curriculum for tribal education should be essentially based on: *(i)* physical education;

*(ii)* health and hygiene; *(iii)* nature study; *(iv)* language; and *(v)* arithmetic. These subjects should be taught in natural surroundings in an informal conversational manner. To make the tribal societies more homogeneous, the education provided to them must cover all the spheres of life.

Sachchidananda (1973) conducted a study on socio-economic aspect of tribal education. In his study he reiterated that there was a major link between education and economy. According to him, education could increase the human efficiency which ultimately turned into production. After independence the urgent need for bettering the living condition of the tribal people was realized by the government and large sum of money was allocated for the development programme of the tribals. Firstly, there was a big controversy among the social workers regarding the relative importance of educational and economic development. It was urged by them that once they were educated, they would themselves improve their economic condition. But after different surveys, it was accepted by all the sections of the people that for the educational development of tribals, it was necessary to improve their economic condition. It was found that tribal parents did not send their children to schools because they helped them increasing their family income.

The author suggested some solutions to overcome this hurdle. The solutions were: reducing the school hours; special attention to be paid on their festivals, sowing and harvesting seasons, etc. Educational authorities should be prepared to make arrangements lest education would interfere with the economic pursuits of their households. The author concluded the report by commenting that economic development was a never ending process, therefore, both economic and educational development should go hand-in-hand.

Khurana (1978) conducted a study on tribal education. According to him, after Africa, India had the largest concentration of tribals. Though the Indian Constitution (under Article 46) had given the special responsibility to the state and central governments for the development of these weaker sections, yet the progress was not upto the mark. There was a wide gap between the education of tribal children and that of their non-tribal counterparts. The number of enrolment was less and there was a huge wastage and stagnation among the tribals.

The author suggested that the problem of tribal education should be tackled in the two stages. Firstly, the tribal children needed to brought to the school; and secondly, they were to be retained in the school until they completed at least the elementary level of education, say upto class V. To carry out these programmes; *(i)* village-wise survey should be conducted to find out the number of children not attending the school; *(ii)* a survey map of the existing institutions in the tribal areas should be prepared to tell the tribal children the exact location of the school nearest to their locality; *(iii)* Ashram type schools should be opened; *(iv)* the areas which had a literacy rate below 5 to 10 per cent should be identified at block levels and special attention should be given to them; *(v)* a programme for providing husband-wife teams for these schools should be made wherever possible; *(vi)* to ensure proper functioning of schools, an administrative or inspecting authority should be appointed; *(vii)* provision should be made for residential quarters for the teachers, and *(viii)* every effort should be made for the economic development of these tribals.

### Socio Economic Correlates

In his report "The Education and Adivasis in Thana District", Koppikar (1956) enlists a number of difficulties of parents in sending their children to schools, like *(i)* they require their older children and especially girls to look after the younger ones in the creche when they are out of work; *(ii)* they wish that their children should supplement the family income by doing domestic work, grazing the cattle etc. *(iii)* they need their help during the field operations, transplantation, and harvesting or in the jungle in the dry season for collecting dry leaves and fuel, and *(iv)* they believe that their children need training in manual work. While they desire that their children should go to school, they also wish they should learn the family occupation and be trained for the hard life while they are young.

Das Gupta (1963) in his study of Tribal Education and Santals, found out that the most uncongenial home environment affected the education of Santals. They remained absent in school because they were to spend long hours on domestic or outdoor work that brought some economic relief to the family. Economic causes, than any other, were found to be coming in their way of education.

Sachchidananda (1967) was of the opinion that the principal reasons, for the failure of tribal students, are a poor socio-economic development, and a weak foundation, and the inability to afford the necessities of education, hence the drop out.

**Psychological Correlates**

The study of tribal education and Santals of Das Gupta (1963) reveals the following difficulties faced by their parents in sending the children to schools: *(i)* lack of cooperation and real contact between parents and schools; *(ii)* apathetic or indifferent attitude of the parents towards education of their children. Further he gives a list of several reasons for their indifferent attitude, which covers: *(i)* the present system of education is not adjusted to their immediate needs and interests; *(ii)* they are suspicious of the sincerity of the non-tribal people who generally organise and run the educational institutions intended for them; *(iii)* the present system of education takes no notice of their indigenous system of training or the skill and interest which they already possess, and *(iv)* there is an acute dearth of tribal teachers who can handle properly the children.

For Deutsch (1965) cumulative deficit phenomenon was responsible for making one drop-out. Such deficits in Class-I become more marked than in the higher classes. There is a great deal of experimental evidence to show that developmental process before the age of 5 and 6 are extremely important for proper cognitive growth (Bloom et al. (1965).

Moreover, the inferiority and low esteem of the tribal children do elicit very derogatory responses in their teachers towards there children. Such reactions of the teachers in a teaching-learning situation cause irreparable damage in the tribal children who already harbour strong psychological traits in the strange class-room situation which belongs to a sub-culture.

Lack of ambition and unfavourable attitude towards education were, according to Sachchidananda (1967), were the main reasons for the failure of tribal children.

Mehta (1967) finds that the deprived children lag behind in language development in learning of various concepts and symbols. Recent researches (Bloom et al., 1965) show that in children growing up under adverse conditions, the I.Q. may be depressed by 10 to 15 points. For Rath (1976) the subtle psychological and cultural problems of the tribals will stand in the way of their integration. By the time the tribal child comes to primary school at the age of 5 to 6, his cognitive growth is already depressed (Rath, 1974b). The uneducated parent cannot possibly satisfy his natural curiosities about environment. Whatever language is used at home is quite different from the standard language used in the primary schools. The text-books used in the schools are written by people belonging to culturally advantaged class, so the concepts and images symbolized in the standard use of words are quite foreign to the tribal children. So when a tribal child comes to class—I, and reads the first reader written in the standard language he starts with zero linguistic information and conceptualization, whereas a child belonging to the advantaged class has quite a few familiar concepts and linguistic associations in common. This deficiency acquired in class-I will accumulate progressively as the child goes through other classes and his accumulated deficiency is ultimately responsible for stagnation, dropout and weaker motivation for higher education.

Rath (1976) expresses his feelings by stating that in the atmosphere of sub-culture the tribal children may develop low self-esteem and inferiority in comparison with others. This itself may be the single major cause of early drop out. He (1973) also ascribe weak motivational factors for learning in case of these children which lead to drop out.

Das Gupta (1963) in his study of tribal education and Santals, found that the problem of the medium instruction was felt to a great extent since none of the tribal language has a script of its own and these students are expected to be taught through the medium of their mother-tongue, it would be a difficult task to find a solution. Furthermore, the curriculum for the tribal education need to be different from that of socially advanced groups. The economic conditions of the Santal is bad, and therefore, their curriculum should have a vocational bias suitable for their occupation and need. While studying some of the basic problems of tribal education, Srivastava (1967) concludes that the mother tongue and the medium of instruction are major problems. For him, none of the tribal language has a script since the tribal literature is not well developed, tribal children cannot be taught through their mother-tongue for more than three years, and tribal children have little knowledge of the regional languages; and instructions cannot be imparted through the regional languages. He further highlighted the following difficulties encountered by the tribal children: *(i)* inadequacy of schools; *(ii)* one teacher schools; *(iii)* distances from home; *(iv)* lack of enthusiasm in parents for opening schools in their villages. Another potent factor he has studied is about the low percentage of trained teachers. The low qualification of a teacher naturally effects the standard of education. But at the same time. The emoluments given to teachers, by and large, are low and incentives for the hard life are absent.

Sachchidananda (1967) says that the principal reasons for the failure of tribal students are, the lack of study atmosphere at home, an irregular attendance, education in an alien tongue, the heavy curricula, and the irregular payment of government scholarships.

The study conducted by Ambasht (1970) on tribal children of Ranchi district forged a common complaint that the schools remained closed because of the absence of a teachers and they often went home for personal work and were engaged in their own cultivation. The tribal children did not like non-tribal teachers, because they belong to a different community and they did not know the tribal language; instead they have shown a liking for tribal Christian teachers because they have found them clean, loving, helpful, sympathetic, and speaking their language. And the tribal teacher also enjoyed more respect and status than the non-tribal teachers. Further he found that the schools of tribal children at Ranchi were badly constructed with tiled roofs; the government schools had normally one room and no furniture. Some residential schools exclusively meant for tribals isolated them more and thus the aim of education was not achieved.

While studying the educational condition of the tribal people of six villages of the states of Bihar and M.P., Srivastava et al.

(1971a) reported that one of the chief reasons for the slow progress of education among the tribes is attributed to the problems of wastage and stagnation. The causes of drop out are: *(i)* failure in examination; *(ii)* economic hardship of the families; *(iii)* bad treatment by teachers; *(iv)* death in the family; *(v)* illness, and *(vi)* negative attitude towards education.

Rath (1974) tends to feel that the text-books are biased towards culturally advantaged children. The disadvantaged and deprived children who lag behind in language development, generally do not follow such text-books. Such curriculum and text-books tend to accentuate the feelings of alienation in poverty stricken children. Many become alien to school and the school alien to them, coupled with irrelevant curriculum and biased text-books; the non-mother-tongue medium of instruction makes it doubly difficult for deprived children to understand the class-room lessons. For tribal and other categories of economically and culturally backward children, a different medium of instruction can be a strong reason for lack of interest in the school. They are forced to lag behind. This reinforces their alienation and the feeling of incompetence. Further, the traditional system of examination is totally outside the realm of experience of the millions of children from poorer homes. The system perpetuates the vested interest in educational stagnation.

Sujatha (1987) undertook a study in Nellore district of Andhra Pradesh to find out the underlying causes of absenteeism, stagnation and wastes among Yanadi tribe. She also studied the effect of socio-economic condition of parents on enrolment of the children; and sex difference was also studied. She found that absenteeism was more among Yanadi girls both in mixed villages and tribal colonies; absenteeism was more among Yanadi girls (58.5 per cent) than the boys (40.5 per cent) in mixed villages, whereas the difference between girls (27.5 per cent) and boys (25.5 per cent) in tribal colonies was negligible; and absenteeism among Yenadi boys and girls put together was lower in tribal colonies (26 per cent) than in the mixed villages (49.5 per cent).

Further she found that the incidence of wastage among the Yenadi children at the primary stage ranged between 75 to 92 per cent. Generally the education of Yenadi children in the schools situated in the mixed villages is not found encouraging. The incidence of wastage is on the top at the first standard itself among both boys and girls in both categories of schools. Incidence of wastage steadily decreases from second grade onwards and again shows an upward trend in fifth grade among boys and fourth and fifth grades among girls.

Only for the first time the educational problems of the Saoras of Orissa were identified by Srivastava et al. (1971b). They found that the important causes of educational backwardness of the Saoras and their comparatively inferior educational performance had been because they were taught through Oriya and not through their mother-tongue. Also the primary schools functioning in the Saora area did not fulfil their real purpose due to various factors. Most of the primary schools functioning in the Saora area did not possess school buildings of their own and classes were conducted in residential houses. The inspecting staff had also to face many problems in inspecting the schools mainly due to inaccessibility of the Saora villages. They found one of the greatest hurdles in the development of education in the Saora area was the problem of wastage and stagnation. The problem was mainly economic in nature.

# 3

# Approach to Tribal Development

To understand the dynamics of educational development among scheduled tribes, it is quite essential to examine how education has been viewed in their total development process. The approach to development of tribes in India can be broadly studied under four phases. The first phase covers pre-independence period. During this period the British adopted a policy of isolation and maintained status-quo of the tribes; and the second phase from 1947 to 1952 was more of transition period for development of both the general population and as well as tribals' since the administration system has undergone structural changes during this period. Between 1952-1974 the formulation of five year plans and systematic approach for planned development was adopted along with community development approach followed by formulation of five year plans and systematic approach for planned development was adopted along with community development approach followed by formulation of multipurpose Tribal Development Blocks. A breakthrough in developmental approach was conceived from the Fifth Five Year Plan onwards with the formulation of Tribal Sub-Plans. This continued during sixth and seventh five year plans.

## Approach Before Independence: First Phase

The approaches during pre-independence period to effect tribal welfare or development was of a different type. It was mainly ameliorative in nature. The tribal areas were the last to come under the British Power because of their difficult terrain and inaccessibility. By all accounts it is clear that the character of the tribal policy of British Government was isolcationist. The British Government inclined, on the whole to follow the policy of laissez faire, partly because of the task of administration was difficult and unrewarding. However, their policy helped zamindars, landlords and moneylenders and traders to exploit the tribals by way of depriving their right on land and forest and reducing them to labourers. The main purpose of the British policy was to secure peace and not necessarily to help the people to advance on the road to progress either by integration with the plains Hindus or otherwise. Consistently with keeping the peace, gradual survey settlement was carried out, and by slow stages regular land revenue was levied, whenever and whenever possible (Ghurye 1963). There was no deliberate attempt either to strengthen the economic base or to educate the tribals.

Simultaneous with their general policy of isolation characterised by non-intervention or limited intervention under dire political need was their often covert and sometimes direct encouragement to an undeniable fact that the Christian missionaries had done something for the well-being of the tribes, the scope of which was wide, and that was an activity of spirited social service and reforms as a result of which many of the tribal areas had acquired schools, hospitals, etc. The missionaries, therefore, must be considered as the pioneers who initiated the process of organised socio-economic transformation in the hitherto stagnant tribal life. However, Christian missionaries canvassed service to the suffering humanity as their duty, they coupled it with the right of conversion to Christianity. This resulted in large-scale conversion of many tribal groups, especially of the states in Eastern India. With the passage of time it became more and more apparent to people here that the primary goal of the missionaries was conversation and opening of schools, hospitals and other welfare agencies were only bait in the trap of conversion", (Srinivas 1962). A careful analysis of the missionary activities thus leads to the conclusion that under the cover of humanitarianism, the political motives of the colonial partially excluded and adopting the policy of isolation, the British Government was subjected to criticism of the Nationalists who "viewed their measures as part of a diabolic conspiracy to create a new separatist minority", (Dube 1968). Thus the effects of the British to educate tribes were not significant, as alien rulers they had limited objectives of education which were mostly meant to run their administration rather than imparting knowledge and skills.

During the period of freedom movements, in the context of tribal education the impact of two social movements needs to be noted, the first was the national movement led by Mahatma Gandhi, which inspire the Gandhian workers e.g., the philanthropologist like Thakkar Bapa who started Ashram Schools for tribals is some part of Gujarat and Maharashtra. Another social movement with significant bearing was the one by Godavari Parulekar among the Warlis of Thane district in 1940s. Considering the tribal situation which presents an extremely varied socio-economic condition, demographic features and the degree of exposure to outside world, the efforts of Christian missionary and social workers were very meagre and could not lead to significant educational progress among tribes, which is evident from 1931 census where the percentage of literacy among tribes was only 0.75 as against 7.5 percentage of literacy of the total population in the country. However, with the independence, the policy of tribal development had undergone a qualitative change.

**Approach After Independence: Second Phase**

Contrasted with the British policy, the Government of India's important concern which moulded its policy was the welfare and socio-economic upliftment of the tribal people. The policy accorded high sense of respect and recognition for the tribal culture and traditions and strongly opposed to any kind of interference by outside agencies which are likely to contribute to the destruction of the tribal art, culture and so on. This has evinced in the five fundamental principles of tribal development evolved by Pandit Nehru, the former Prime Minister of India. These are:

*(i)* People should develop along the lines of their own genius and we should avoid imposing anything on them. We

should try to encourage in every way their own traditional arts and culture.

*(ii)* Tribal rights in land and forest should be respected.

*(iii)* We should try to train and build up a team of their own people to do the work of administration and development. Some technical personnel for outside will, no doubt, the needed, especially in the beginning. But we should avoid introducing too many outsiders into tribal territory.

*(iv)* We should not over-administer these areas or overwhelm them with a multiplicity of schemes. We should rather work through, and not in rivalry to, their own social and cultural institutions.

*(v)* We should judge results, not by statistics or the amount of money spent, but by the quality of human character that is evolved". (Elwin 1960).

The above principles of tribal development were envisaged in the Constitution through various statutory measures to uplift them and thereby to bridge the gap between tribals and others in socio-economic development. The architects of the Constitution were well aware of the disadvantaged condition of tribals due to their unique socio-economic and geographical constraints. Hence various articles have been provided with the object of promoting and safeguarding the interests of the scheduled tribes. The constitutional provisions have envisaged various measures ranging from the recognition of their social customs, customary rights over land and forest etc., to their upliftment by educational and economic development. To say briefly, Article 46 promises that "The states shall promote with special care and educational and economic interests of the scheduled tribes and protect them from social injustice and all forms of exploitation". Thus at the general level the safeguards are of the two kinds: *(a)* protective, and *(b)* ameliorative and concessional.

The constitutional safeguards, when analysed, convey the concern of the nation in regard to the scheduled tribes in terms of their educational and economic betterment, their protection from social, injustice and exploitation as found in various manifestations of discrimination and prejudices, and development of their general way of life. The creation of scheduled and tribals areas, preference in admission to educational institutions and public services, are some of the mechanisms which tend to fulfil the objective of the constitution.

At this juncture there was a lot of debate and arguments and ——higher priority over economic development or the other way. One group felt that unless tribal population are equipped properly with positive attitudes and understanding, economic development can not reach them. For this, education should become a crucial instrument to play a vital role for their total development. The other group just made the reverse argument, canvassing that unless the people have minimum economic stability they cannot go for education. After all, they cannot wait for many years to reap the fruits of education. Therefore, education without economic development is an ideal but not a practical approach and economic development without education is highly risky and unsuccessful. Therefore, it was planned that both should go hand in hand complementing each other.

**Community Development Approach**

The phase between 1947-1952 has witnessed structural change in total administration of the country. An era of special efforts for the socio-economic development of tribals indeed decisively began only from 1952 onwards.

In the beginning, the general administration itself was assigned this risk, but gradually in some states separate developmental administration set-up was established. Even today the administration system varies from one state to another. They have either exclusive or multiple developmental departments.

The early fifties witnessed some important structural changes in the administration system while during this period planned economic development was adopted as the national policy in India. The tribal communities, like all other constituent groups in the country, were expected to equally partake in the development process. Keeping in view the disadvantages they have to face, special provisions were provided for tribes to overcome their socio-economic constraints.

During the first five year plan the Community Development approach was adopted. However it became clear very soon that the entire tribal population cannot be covered by with a single model. The study team on Social Welfare and Welfare of Backward Classes (Government of India, 1959) led by Shrimati Renuka Ray reviewed the tribal scene in the late fifties and remarked in their report that while each aspect of development was important in its own place in actual operation no rigid order of priority was universally applicable. The Committee took note of the fact that the felt needs of tribal communities vary from community to community. The team recommended: *(a)* economic development and communication, *(b)* education, *(c)* public health as the overall order to priorities. However they stressed that the programmes should be integrated with each other; and the degree of emphasis on each of them be determined by systematic survey of needs and possibilities in each area.

**Integrated Development Approach**

Keeping in view the recommendations made by the committee and to eliminate the limitations and weaknesses of community development approach, a massive programme of integrated development was initiated by organising 43 special Multipurpose Tribal Blocks during the second five year plan in areas with tribal concentration. Such programmes incurred an expenditure of Rs. 0.642 crores which formed a part of Rs. 493 crores spent on tribal welfare during the second five year plan. Top priority was given to the promotion of education followed by communication, agriculture, animal husbandry and health care. Inspite of according high priority to education the progress was very slow. While allocating funds education was clubbed under social services, except in those 43 special Multipurpose Tribal Blocks and educational development of tribes was treated synonymous to rural development. Therefore, no special efforts were made either to provide educational facilities or incentives to tribes. However the concessions which were in vogue could benefit the upper crust of tribal communities and thus created a gulf among tribal communities. This phenomenon has affected mostly those tribals living in areas where their population size is similar. The schematic budgetary system adopted during this period hindered education as other social service sectors absorbed larger quantum of funds and education remained nominal and only marginal.

# 4

# Design of the Study

## Introduction

In spite of all the efforts still the tribal education has not shown any marked improvement. There are drop-outs, absenteeism and stagnation. To examine these aspects at the micro level the study has been undertaken with certain objectives which are stated as follows:

### *(a) Objectives*

The main objectives of the present study is focused on the impact of educational programmes on the social—cultural and economic conditions of the tribal households, and also to examine the problems and constraints in the implementation of such Programmes in the selected district. More specifically the objectives of the study are as follows:

1. The assess the existing pattern of education and educational facilities available to the schedule tribes.
2. To find out the bottlenecks, problems and constraints coming in the way of successful implementation of educational programmes. Such as absenteeism.
3. To suggest suitable corrective and remedial measures for effective implementation of the Educational Programme in the study are for achieving the desired results.

### *(b) Study Area*

Visakhapatnam district is one of the North-Eastern districts of Andhra Pradesh situated within the geographic coordinates of 17° 14′ and 18° 32′ of northern latitude and 18° 6′ and 83° 32′ of eastern longitude. The district is bounded by Vizianagaram district on the north, East Godavari on the south, Koraput of Orissa on the West and Bay of Bengal on the east.

According to 1991 Census, total literates (excluding the population in the age group of 0–6 years) is 1262458 persons. Of these, 789044 are males and 473416 are females. In the rural areas of the district 470583 persons (328044 males and 142539 females) are literates and in urban areas 791875 persons (461000 males and 330875 females) are literatures. The rate of literacy of these population to the total population, excluding 0–6 years age group according to 1991 census are shown below:

**Table—4.1 Distribution of Literates Aged 7 Years and Above by Sex and Area in the Year 1991.**

| | *Persons* | *Males* | *Females* |
|---|---|---|---|
| Total | 45.51 | 56.13 | 34.60 |
| Rural | 28.54 | 39.65 | 17.35 |
| Urban | 70.38 | 79.70 | 60.51 |

The study was taken up in Visakhapatnam district of Andhra Pradesh, being one of the tribal concentrated districts in the State. Among the 23 districts in the Andhra Pradesh, Khammam district with 24.5 per cent of tribal population ranks first, followed by Adilabad with 16.55 per cent, Visakhapatnam with 13.74 per cent and Warangal 12.73 per cent to the respective total population. This district is chosen because it is having many advantages like political awareness, transportation and infrastructural network and the like. The district is also bound by tribal concentrated areas protecting the tribal culture ethos, customs, traditions, etc. Because of its ideal location, the State Girijan Cooperatives Corporation of the Government of Andhra Pradesh had its headquarters at Visakhapatnam to extend all necessary assistance including marketing to the tribals. Therefore, the Visakhapatnam district ranking third among tribal concentrated districts in the State was found to be more ideal for undertaking the present study. Therefore, it has been decided to take Visakhapatnam district for the study. Since it is not possible to cover all the tribal concentrated mandals (11 tribal mandals) in the district it has been decided to select one mandal based on the following criteria.

## Visakhapatnam District

The population of the district is 32.85 lakhs as per 1991 Census and this contribute about 4.9 per cent of population of the state while the geographical area of the district *viz.*, 11.161 sq. kms. The district has a density of population of 294 per sq. kms. Agency area shows lesser number. The district has a workforce of 10.10 lakhs constituting about 39.2 per cent of the population besides the marginal workers to the tune of 1.09 lakhs.

Among main workers, the cultivators constitute 41.3 per cent, agricultural labourers 21.0 per cent and the balance of 37.7 per cent engage in primary, secondary and tertiary sectors.

There are 12,62,458 literates forming 38.42 per cent of total population of the district. Among the literates, males literates constitute 56.13 per cent while female literates form 34.60 as per 1991 Census.

The literates among schedule classes account to 50.217 forming 24.82 per cent of scheduled caste population. The male, female ratio of scheduled caste literates is 2:1 ratio.

The male female ratio of scheduled tribe literates is 5:1 ratio.

## Section of Mandals

Paderu Block has been selected from Visakhapatnam District, it being the oldest block in the wake of community development programmes and its clear primacy in respect of educational facilities among eight samithis in agency.

For selection of one mandal in the district, two criteria have been adopted and they are as follows:

1. Proximity to the Integrated Tribal Development Project office;

2. Availability of infrastructural facilities particularly to education.

By adoption of the above criteria, one mandal namely Paderu has emerged as the ideal mandal for conducting the study.

The ITDA headquarters is located at Paderu because of its central location in the tribal track of the district. Paderu because of its central location, and location of various sectoral Departments, including ITDA exclusively meant for development of tribal population is socially and culturally well developed because of symbiotic relationship with the plain non-tribal population officials, traders etc., Paderu Mandal is selected.

Paderu, the headquarters of the taluk of the same name, is situated at a distance of about 74 kms. from Visakhapatnam. Paderu is a broad picturesque and rich valley, with an altitude of over 900 metres above the sea level. There are a good number of hill stream, locally known as Giddar in this area and they provide irrigation facilities. Paderu is an Agency area, which is backward in all respect. There is much potential development due to the construction of the railway line.

**Selection of Villages**

Further, down in the selected 12 villages with the primary upper-primary and high schools were selected in the block which has high concentration of tribal population. The selection of villages was done in such a manner that the following conditions are met.

1. The village so selected should cover a wider area included interior.
2. The sample of villages should as well as roadside villages.
3. It included predominantly. These sample villages provide representation to the major tribal communities of the region.
4. The sample includes the villages where teachers are tribals.

To fulfil the above conditions the selection of study villages will be done as follows—

1. Road-side villages with exclusive tribal population.
2. Road-side villages with tribal and non-tribal population.
3. Non-road-side villages exclusively with tribal population.
4. Non-road-side villages with tribal and non-tribal population.

## Selection of Sample

Therefore, it has been decided to study 50 households in selected mandal. The households have been selected on the basis of simple random sampling method.

## Students

The tribal pupils studying in Primary and Secondary Schools were selected from 12 centres. The tribal students were found in considerable numbers in these centres because of the availability of the hostel facilities. All the available tribal pupils studying in the Primary and Secondary classes in these centres were interviewed.

## Teachers

46 teachers teaching in the both primary and secondary schools were selected.

## Parents

Similarly parents were also selected randomly from the selected 12 schools where their children were studying.

## Variables

In order to gather the data regarding the I.T.D.A activities and its impact on socio-economic conditions of tribals, all the important variables involved in this study have been identified. The relationship between these variables is indicated and the pattern of measurement of the qualitative variables is also explained.

The following are the variables employed in this study:

### *(a) Independent Variables*

All demographic, social, and economic attributes of sample respondents are treated as independent variables, *(a)* Demographic variables: (1) size of households and (2) Literacy level, *(b)* Social Variables: (1) proportion of nuclear and joint families, (2) Tribes compositions in sample households; *(c)* Economic Variables: (1) type of house, (2) pattern of land ownership and income, (3) and occupational structure.

### *(b) Intervening Variables*

The I.T.D.A. Programmes and political activities are taken as intervening variables.

### *(c) Dependent Variables*

The impact of development programmes on socio-economic conditions are the dependent variables. By impact, we mean the positive changes in educational attainment and other related aspects of the beneficiaries.

## Data Collection

Both secondary and primary data were collected. The primary data was collected by the scholar himself for a period of three months. The main activities were the field work collection of all relevant information from ITDA, Paderu and social facilities like education and selection of one Mandal to canvass schedules.

## Tools and Techniques

The required information was collected through various types of scheduled meant for students, teachers and heads of households.

The tools of data collection include a household schedule, observation and unstructured interviews. The household schedule comprised seven sections. The first section included only the identification questions, to elicit the background information of the head of the household such as name, age, tribe etc. The second section included family members, age, education, marital status and primary and secondary occupation.

The third section deals with I.T.D.A. and other beneficiary oriented developmental programmes. The technique of participant observation was employed to gather data on interactions with developmental functionaries and peoples participation in developmental activities and their behaviour and attitudes etc. With special reference to educational programmes only.

To avoid stereotype, unreliable responses, and to get valid information, this researcher held as many informal and extended interviews as possible with elderly persons and resourceful people of the villages. Discussions were also held with officials such as Project Director ITDA Dy. Inspector of schools extension officials of education etc., to generate data regarding their opinions toward educational developmental activities in the villages. The experience reveals that friendly talk, outside trips, gossiping are some of the best means of collection of information. All the information thus collected was counter-checked with reliable persons and other available records in doubtful cases.

## Analysis of Data

The data thus collected were of two types, qualitative and quantitative, the quantitative data that were collected through the household schedule were transferred to I.B.M. Sheets after carefully editing the schedules. All the data were analysed and tables were prepared with the help of computer.

The qualitative data gathered through interviews and observation were recorded in field diaries. Sometimes the observed data were also recorded on schedules. These data were thoroughly edited before incorporating in the thesis.

## Chapterisation Scheme

The chapterisation of the Thesis is as follows:

### *Chapter—I: Introduction*

It deals in depth the various tribal protective measures, development strategies, constitutional and legislative provisions, educational development programmes for the benefit of tribals, both in pre and post-independence periods of the country.

### *Chapter—II: Review of Literature*

Comprehensive review of literature of tribal education in general and tribals of paderu Mandal in particular is discussed.

### *Chapter—III: Approach to Tribal Development*

In this Chapter approach before independence, community development approach, integrated development approach, sub-plan approach have been discussed.

### *Chapter—IV: Design of the Study*

The chapter deals with the methodology consisting of the objectives of the study, sampling, variables, tools and methods of data collection, analysis, chapterisation and limitations of the study.

### *Chapter—V: Profile of Tribals in Andhra Pradesh*

### *Chapter—VI: Profile of the Respondents and Enrolment*

The chapter is focused on the educational facilities and differential growth of literacy of the study area is discussed along with the socio-economic life of students, teachers and parents and it also focussess on the educational facilities and differential growth of literacy of the study area along with detailed analysis of enrolment pattern at the primary and secondary level.

### *Chapter—VII: Impact of Education*

### *Chapter—VIII: Absenteeism—Wastage—Stagnation*

This chapter deals with the problems of absenteeism, wastage and stagnation of the selected schools in the study area and the reasons for the same in primary and secondary schools are discussed.

### *Chapter—IX: Alternative Strategies of Development of Tribal Education—Non-formal Education*

This chapter deals with the students, teachers and parents attitudes and aspirations towards tribal education.

### *Chapter—X: Findings, Summary and Conclusions*

The chapter deals with the alternative strategies of

development of tribal education with specific emphasis on non-formal education.

## ANNEXURES

## BIBLIOGRAPHY

### Limitations of the Study

#### Primary Data

The primary data were collected through survey method by administrating a household interview schedule to the head of the households. The respondents have generally provided information by recollecting from their memory. In spite of all the efforts made to elicit correct information by careful probing during interview, it would be wrong to assume that lapse of memory on the part of the respondents was fully overcome in regard to the minute details. Therefore, the outcome of the analysis of primary data is within the limitations of the responses for various questions in the schedule.

Another important limitations is that the data were mostly collected for five years. However, the data relating to Absenteeism, stagnation and wastage varied year to year. The data for five years therefore, cannot claim to represent the actual picture of the mandal with absolute accuracy with the passage of time.

Secondary Data

As regards the information from secondary sources most of the information were collected from I.T.D.A Paderu alone.

These informations have been supplemented by reference of a number of books, official reports from the centre and state, journals and other relevant matters, both published and unpublished, for purposes of properly planning the tribal problems of the study area in comparison to plain areas in the district and the state.

## PADERU BLOCK AND VISAKHAPATNAM DISTRICT PROFILE

### Introduction

Visakhapatnam District is a coastal district with two distinct regions of contrasting ecological and topographic characteristic features, one with the plain landscape extending from the sea coast up to the foot hills of the Eastern Ghats with moderate temperature and the other covered by the thick forests a top elevated Eastern Ghats with cool temperature inhabited by the Tribal people.

## Area and Population

The Geographical area of the district is 11,167 sq. kms. of which the agency tract covers 6298 sq. kms i.e., 56.4 per cent of the total Geographical area of the district.

Visakhapatnam district consists of 3 Revenue Divisions, 14 Taluks and 19 Panchayati Samithis, out of which the Paderu agency division consists of 3 Taluks and 8 Panchayat Samithies.

The total population of the district, as per 1981 Census, is 25,76,474 with a density of 230 per sq. kms while the population in the Agency area is 3,57,140 with a density of 56 per sq. kms.

## Topography

The range of Eastern Ghats forming the hilly region of Visakhapatnam District with an average altitude of about 900 Metres is dotted by several peaks exceeding 1200 metres. The highest mountain named Sankaram Scales 1515 metres high. The entire hilly region is divided into 3 Taluks Viz., Paderu, Chintapalli and Araku and covering 8 Panchayat Samithies Viz., Paderu, Pedabayalu, Araku, Munchangiputtu, Ananthagiri, G. Madugula, Chintapalli and Koyyuru.

## Rainfall

The normal rainfall for the district is 1038.7 K.M. and that for the Agency areas is 1163.6 K.M.

## Schedule Tribe Population

The Schedule Tribe population in the district is 3,54,127 (as per 1981 Census) which works out to 13.74 per cent of the district population. Of them 3,16,048 which works out to 89.2 per cent live in the Agency areas.

## Integrated Tribal Development Agency, Paderu

The Integrated Tribal Development Agency, Paderu, Visakhapatnam District, a Society registered under the Societies

Registration Act. 1860 on 20 . . 75 started functioning from 4.12.75. The objectives of the Integrated Tribal Development Agency are to plan, programme and execute schemes aiming at Socio-economic Development of the tribals in the Agency areas. The Project area comprises of 8 Tribal Development Blocks, Viz., Paderu, Pedabayalu, Araku, Munchangiputtu, Ananthagiri, G. Madugula, Chinthapalli and Koyyuru and 86 villages in the plains areas adjoining the Tribal Development Blocks and having 50 per cent or more or Tribal population, covering a total population of 3,57,140 of which, ,116,048 belong to Scheduled Tribes (As per 1981 Census).

## General Information Regarding Tribal Sub Plan Area of Visakhapatnam District

| | |
|---|---|
| 1. *No. of Blocks Covered* | 8 Tribals Development Blocks and 86 Villages adjoining the plains areas of Narasipatnam, Madugula and Chodavaram Panchayat Samithis. |
| 2. *Name of the Block Covered* | |
| Tribal Development Blocks: | 1. Paderu, 2. Araku, 3. Pedabayalu, 4. Munchangiputtu, 5. Ananthagiri, 6. G. Madugula, 7. Chintapalli and 8. Chodavarm |
| 3. *No. of Villages:* | 3,521 Villages. |

| | | | As per 1971 Census | As per 1981 Census | % increase |
|---|---|---|---|---|---|
| 4. | *(a)* | Total population | 3,30,152 | 3,57,140 | 8.2 % |
| | *(b)* | Population of Scheduled area | 2,80,717 | 3,16,048 | 12.6 % |
| 5. | *(i)* | No. of Ashram Schools | | | 71 |
| | *(ii)* | No. of Hostels:- Boys | | | 25 |
| | | Girls | | | 10 |
| | *(iii)* | No. of Junior Colleges: | | | 3 |
| | *(iv)* | No. of High Schools | | | 13 |

*(Table Contd.)*

| | | |
|---|---|---|
| *(v)* | No. of U.P. Schools | 14 |
| *(vi)* | No. of Primary Schools | 344 |
| *(vii)* | No. of Adult Education Centres | 300 |
| *(viii)* | No. of Technical Training Schools | 1 |
| *(ix)* | No. of Boarders in Ashram Schools Hostels | 9039 |
| *(x)* | No. of Residential Polytechnic | 1 |

**Table—4.2 Tribe-Wise Population in Visakhapatnam District**

| *Sl. No.* | *Name of the Tribe* | *Population as per 1971 (Census)* | *Projected population (1981) Census* |
|---|---|---|---|
| **1** | **2** | **3** | **4** |
| 1. | Bagatha | 71,305 | 84,179 |
| 2. | Chenchus | 64 | 75 |
| 3. | Gadabas | 12,251 | 14,463 |
| 4. | Jatupus | 154 | 182 |
| 5. | Kammara | 15,375 | 18,151 |
| 6. | Konda Doras | 58,202 | 68,710 |
| 7. | Konda Kapus | 25,103 | 29,365 |
| 8. | Khonds | 30,804 | 36,365 |
| 9. | Konda Reddies | 672 | 793 |
| 10. | Kotia-Bentho Oria | 15,840 | 18,151 |
| 11. | Koya or Gond | 5,057 | 5,970 |
| 12. | Kulia | 143 | 169 |
| 13. | Malis | 1,638 | 1,934 |
| 14. | Manne Doras | 4,289 | 5,063 |
| 15 | Mukha Doras | 10,898 | 12,866 |

*(Table Contd.)*

| 1 | 2 | 3 | 4 |
|---|---|---|---|
| 16. | Nayaks | 1,137 | 1,342 |
| 17. | Porja | 12,357 | 14,588 |
| 18. | Reddi Doras | 4,862 | 5,740 |
| 19. | Savaras | 114 | 134 |
| 20. | Valmikis | 24,146 | 28,505 |
| 21. | Yanadis | 95 | 112 |
| 22. | Yerukulas | 3,187 | 3,762 |
| 23. | Un specified | 2,277 | 2,689 |
| | **Total** | **2,99,970** | **3,54,127** |

# 5

# Socio-Economic and Demographic Profile of the Respondents

In this Chapter an attempt is made to analyse the socio-economic and demographic profile of the same studied *viz*. students, teachers and parents.

## I. Students

***Age***: 44 per cent of the total students were in the age group of 16-18 years and 25 per cent of the students were in the age group of 11-14 years and 2 per cent of students were in the age group of 19-23 years.

***Sex***: In respect of sex, male students were in majority (92 per cent) and the rest 8 per cent of these were females.

***Tribal distribution***: Bhagathas constituted 39 per cent, Valmikis formed 34 per cent and 27 per cent students belonged Konda Dora tribe.

Of the total 150 students, students belonging to 7th standard formed 44 per cent, students of Xth class formed 34 per cent and students who belonged to primary level constituted 22 per cent.

***Managements***: Students who belonged to Government Institutions formed 69.00 per cent. 15.00 per cent of students belonged to schools managed by IIDA and 16.00 per cent of students belonged to schools managed by Zilla Parishads.

## Subsidiary Occupation

80.00 per cent heads of households did not have any secondary source of subsidiary occupation. 10.00 per cent had business, 5.00 per cent were also contractors, and 2.00 per cent were agriculturists. The percentage of heads of households who did not respond were quite negligible (3.00 per cent).

***Income***: 55.00 per cent of students stated that family income of their parents ranged from Rs. 500-3000 per year, 43.00 per cent of students were not aware of their parents income. Income which ranged from Rs. 6000-7000 their percentage was quite ineligible (2.00 per cent).

***Status***: Nearly 55.00 per cent of students mentioned that their father had no special status in their tribal society 27 per cent were Munsifs, 10 per cent belonged to Muthadar's family, 4 per cent each belonged to post of president in youth club and membership at block panchayat.

An attempt was made to find out the students opinion on religious beliefs and customs. Nearly 65 per cent of students opined that individual initiative and efforts along with Gods grace are necessary to achieve any thing in life.

***Decision making***: Majority of students (80 per cent) had the view that their parents were main decision makers in the family matters, followed by relatives, elder brother and uncle (19 per cent) mother and sisters, and their decision is taken into account to the extent of 1 per cent only.

***Selection of Life partner***: In case of selection of life partner nearly 70 per cent of students stated that parent decision is not final perception of students about their life partners was ascertained and furnished in the following table.

Most of the tribal students intended to have their life partner from their communities as they suspected that girls from plain areas might get averted to tribal way of life.

Problems of adjustments with curriculum, homework, teachers and colleagues.

**Table—5.1 Perception of Students in Selection of Life Partners**

| *Sl. No.* | *Categories* | *Percentage* |
|---|---|---|
| 1. | Good character | 35.00 |
| 2. | Beautiful, educated good at household works | 40.00 |
| 3. | Did not respond as they are too shy | 9.00 |
| 4. | Wealthy | 1.00 |
| 5. | Same tribe | 1.00 |
| 6. | Did not mention | 14.00 |

***Level of Interaction*:** Majority of students (86 per cent) revealed that there was no conflicting relation, 79 per cent of students knew each other and their communities.

An attempt was made to whether there was any basic factor in making the friendship. Nearly 61 per cent opined that there is no any valid reason for making friendship—Educational institution is like home and is above caste and creed differences.

The pattern of response obtained on this aspect are presented in the Table—5.2.

**Table—5.2 Reasons for Making Friendship as Perceived by Students**

| *Sl. No.* | *Categories* | *Percentage* |
|---|---|---|
| 1. | Advise | 27.00 |
| 2. | No specific reason given | 26.00 |
| 3. | Relative, Classmate, room-mate | 11.00 |
| 4. | Welfare oriented | 10.00 |
| 5. | Affinity of tribe area, kinship | 7.00 |
| 6. | Good Characters | 8.00 |
| 7. | More intelligent, industrious in their studies | 4.00 |
| 8. | Tribal Students never come close | 3.00 |
| 9. | Helpful in crisis | 3.00 |

Opinion about the teacher: When students were asked to give their opinion about the teachers they gave following responses.

**Table—5.3 Perception of Students towards Teachers**

| *Sl. No.* | *Categories* | *Percentage* |
|---|---|---|
| 1. | Favourable | 93.00 |
| 2. | Teaching is good | 81.00 |
| 3. | Solving their difficulties sympathetically | 4.00 |
| 4. | Bad, unnecessarily interfere in hostel matters, careless in teaching bad treatment to students | 7.00 |

Studies done by scholars like Singh (1981), Desai and Patel (1981), Joshi (1981), Rath and Misra (1974) contradicts findings of the present study of the research scholar.

Singh (1981) observed that due to overcrowded classes, teachers failed to pay proper attention to these students, and Desai and Patel (1981) reported that attitude of teachers towards tribal children was not healthy. Joshi (1981) also reported that heads of the tribal families expressed that teachers did not show any favourable attitude towards their children. It was observed that majority of the teachers had no special training for working in the backward areas. Rath and Mishra (1974) also confirmed that majority of ST students felt themselves neglected by the teachers on the other hand Pathak (1981) found that 55.00 per cent of the ST students expressed positive attitude whereas 33.75 per cent had negative attitude towards the teacher. Similar to this observation Shah (1989) reported that Scheduled Tribe students did not feel any problem in adjusting to their teachers. They expressed that they never experienced any influence by their teachers.

***Syllabus:*** In regard to the syllabus of different classes students opined that some portion of Mathematics, English and General Science subjects at VII, Xth classes needs to be reduced as it is heavy. Education in our country has remained elite oriented and is designed to meet the requirements of average ability. Thus in an educational system which is alien to the tribal life and culture it is found that tribal children experience considerable difficulties in their studies. Findings of the studies done by Pratap (1971), Solanki (1977) and Srivastava (1982) confirmed the findings of present study of the research scholar. Pratap (1971) and others have also reported that curriculum of Ashram schools which have been specially created for tribals was almost similar to that of other primary schools, except for the teaching of crafts. Similarly, Solanki (1977) observed that textbooks did not properly reflect the special needs of tribal children. Srivastava (1982) reported that the pressing problems areas for the tribal students were curriculum teaching procedure and adjustment to school work.

***Languages known*:** Almost all students were aware of Telugu language including reading and writing 4.00 per cent of them expressed difficulty in expressing in English, all these belonged to private, panchayat and T.W. and ITDA management schools though majority were in class 7th and 10th their inability to read and write in English would certainly be treated as a handicap.

In the order of liking language 85.00 per cent students expressed that they have special liking for Telugu followed by General Science, Physics, Botany and Zoology (33.00 per cent), English (21.00 per cent) and Social Studies (11.00 per cent).

With regard to reason for liking the subjects students responses refer Table—5.4.

Time devoted to studies. Nearly 75.00 per cent of students opined that they are spending 1 to 4 hours per day, rest of the students did not had any regular timings for their studies.

Studies done by Nayar (1995), Lakhera (1987) confirms the findings of the present study of the research scholar whereas studies done by Rajagopalan (1974), and Shah (1989) contradicts findings of the present study. Regarding the home work Nayar (1975) found that ST students usually gave 3-4 hours to complete their homework and studies. Rajagopalan's (1974) study contradicts this finding. He reported that domestic work seemed

**Table—5.4 Reasons for Liking the Subjects by Students**

| | *Responses* | *Per cent* |
|---|---|---|
| 1. | Easy | 42.00 per cent |
| 2. | Monetary gain | 12.00 per cent |
| 3. | Career prospects | 8.00 per cent |
| 4. | Mother tongue | 6.00 per cent |
| 5. | Useful in day to day life | 7.00 per cent |
| 6. | Ambition to learn | 9.00 per cent |
| 7. | Status symbol (To learn English) | 6.00 per cent |
| 8. | Did not give any options | 10.00 per cent |

to come in their way of education. Most of the students felt difficulty in completing their homework due to lack of guidance/ help available in the family. Similarly, Lakhera (1987) observed that only a small proportion of students were found to be regular in completing their homework, tasks assigned by their teachers. On the contrary Shah's (1989) study revealed that tribal students of senior basic and secondary levels either studying in tribal schools or in general schools did not experience serious problem in completing their homework.

With regard to special hobbies nearly 57.00 per cent of students had interest in playing Kabaddi, Volley Ball and Kho Kho, 19.00 per cent of students did not had any hobbies. 4.00 per cent each were interested in reading gardening 3.00 per cent of students were interested in watching films, physical exercises and singing 5.00 per cent each, hunting 1.00 cent.

***Level of assimilation***: Students responses in relation to difficulty in following one or more subjects are as follows:

| | |
|---|---|
| English | 67.00 per cent |
| Mathematics | 61.00 per cent |
| General Science | 42.00 per cent |

Study done by Shyamlal and Singh (1981) supports the findings of the present study of the research scholar.

Singh (1981) found that a majority of ST students felt problems due to poor handwriting in learning of English and Mathematics and due to lack of textbooks. However, a small proportion complained about the partial biased attitudes of their colleagues also.

Shyam Lal reported that a major proportion of students felt problems in learning English (67.3 per cent in and mathematics (29.4 per cent). Thirty eight per cent of students blamed the teachers for their low quality teaching.

The various problems expressed by them are presented in Table—5.5.

**Table—5.5 Nature of Educational Hardship as perceived by Students**

| | *Nature of Problem* | *Per cent Age* |
|---|---|---|
| *(i)* | In reading and writing | 28.00 per cent |
| *(ii)* | Syllabus was new and | 25.00 per cent |
| *(iii)* | Teaching is not done properly | 13.00 per cent |
| *(iv)* | Foreign Language | 11.00 per cent |
| *(v)* | Negligence on their part and poor standard at primary level | 13.00 per cent |
| *(vi)* | Lack of sufficient staff | 1.00 per cent |
| *(vii)* | Did not respond | 9.00 per cent |

Interaction between students and teacher has a direct bearing on relationship pattern. Most of students (70.00 per cent) had said that they meet teacher the 19.00 per cent of students did not specify any reason. 4.00 per cent of students did not find any strong desire to meet, 3.00 per cent of students were shy, 31.00 per cent of students met teacher to solve their difficulties in mathematics, 15.00

per cent in English, 4.00 per cent in Telugu and 3.00 per cent each in science and social studies. ST students usually hesitate to go to their teachers for guidance and help. This indicates the problem of adjustment between teachers and ST students.

***Inspection***: Nearly 62.00 per cent of students viewed inspection as necessary, 38.00 per cent of students said that inspection by authorities is not useful, 18.00 per cent of students opined that official visit the school as a part of their duties, without having an impact on the development of an institution and pupils progress. 16.00 per cent of students suspected about the seriousness of officials in checking the hostel management. Nearly 3.00 per cent of students opined that official made only false promises. 1.00 per cent of students stated that official were not sympathetic towards tribal students.

***Aim of Education***: Nearly 67.00 per cent of students expressed that better employment was their perceived need towards their studies. 19.00 per cent of students said to gain knowledge they pursue studies. A desire to enhance their status was stated by 4.00 per cent of students. Doing social work was mentioned by 2.00 per cent.

***Urban Contacts***: Nearly 77.00 per cent of the students visited urban centres at least once. About 59.00 per cent of the students expressed reluctance in setting down in urban centres, 66.00 per cent of students mentioned that educational tours to new places have helped them in widening their horizon, and in meeting new people.

***Availability of Primary School***: In exploring the factors that influence the students choice of institution certain issues were taken into consideration they are the distance at which institution is located; the reputation of the institution and the special facilities offered, 45.00 per cent of students said that they choose school because facility was available at their native place. 51.00 per cent studied in other villages, 3.00 per cent in other blocks. 35.00 per cent of students selected primary school because school is nearer to their place of stay. 9.00 per cent of students selected schools due to their relatives, 15.00 per cent of students selected schools due to hostel facility and 4.00 per cent of students selected schools due to good teaching, 34.00 per cent did not specify any reason.

***Vacation:*** With regard to vacation 47.00 per cent of students expressed that they wanted to go back to their villages. 25.00 per cent of students wanted to meet their parents. 24.00 per cent of students wanted to assist their parents in agriculture, 3.00 per cent of students expressed that they need to meet their relatives and friends, quite negligible per cent of students (1.00 per cent) wanted to help villagers in management of diary.

***Extra curricular activities:*** 53.00 per cent of students did not involve in any extra-curricular activities 45.00 per cent of the students participated in debates on various topics like rural and urban life, politics is not for a student, is pen or plough which is great, students indiscipline etc., few students participated (2.00 per cent) in sports, NCC, Scouts, and in gardening as their extra curricular activities.

The term co-curricular and extracurricular have been used as almost similar or synonymous. Studies done by Sachchidananda and Pathak confirms the findings of the present study of the research scholar whereas studies conducted by Desai, Pandoor, Lal Salma contradicts the findings of the present study.

Co-Curricular activities provide a situation where hierarchy does not exist. Recognition should normally depend upon performances and achievements. Participation of ST students in co-curricular activities is markedly uneven. Desai and Pandoor (1974) Lal Salma, (1980) Singh and Shah (1985) reported that SC/ST students participated actively in the co-curricular activities and without any hesitation. Dubey and Singh (1974) et al. also showed that there was adequate participation of STs in co-curricular activities; Shah (1985) reported that all the students (ST as well as others) were getting equal and adequate encouragement from their teachers to participate in different co-curricular activities and ST students participated actively in all the activities. But, several other researchers have reported low participation of SC/ST students in the co-curricular activities; Sachchidananda (1975) also reported that, in general, SC/ST students did not take much interest in co-curricular activities. Pathak (1981) pointed out that a majority of

St students 55.75 per cent never took part in any co-curricular activities.

*Occupational aspirations:* Students were interviewed with a view to know their occupational aspiration. Among those who indicated to become teachers, (42.00 per cent). Tahasildar, Engineer, contractor, Bank Manager (16.00 per cent) Doctors, (9.00 per cent) Collector, (5.00 per cent) Business and trade, (3.00 per cent) less than 2.00 per cent wanted to be agriculturists, social workers, 23.00 per cent of students did not respond.

*Educational aspirations:* The educational aspirations of school students mentioned are as follows:

| | |
|---|---|
| Degree level | 57.00 per cent |
| Matriculation | 19.00 per cent |
| MBBS, B.E., LL.B., | 17.00 per cent |
| Post Graduation | 7.00 per cent |

*Tribal Culture and their:* 58.00 per cent of students stated that their culture is too traditional, 10.00 per cent students opined that improvement is essential in their traditional practices and values with changing times, 28.00 per cent of students supported their traditional practices and values and they want to continue with them.

Negligible percentage of students (4.00 per cent) opined that they are making all efforts to change their family members, kinsmen and villagers to be free from their blind beliefs and to follow new methods for their welfare.

## Impact of Education

An attempt was also made to findout any change, if any, in their thinking and behaviour pattern due to impact of education, 39.00 per cent of students indicated that there is change in their thinking pattern. 23.00 per cent of students opined that their is change in style of speaking, 14.00 per cent of students stated that there is change in their dress and dietary pattern, 7.00 per cent of students don't believe in fatalism, 17.00 per cent of respondents did not respond

***Exposure to mass media:*** Since mass media is a powerful source in communicating ideas, it is of vital value of find out the level of mass media contact among students.

The pattern of responses obtained on this aspect is presented in the following table:

**Table—5.6 Students Exposure to Mass Media**

| *Sl.* No. | *Frequency* | *Movie* | *Listening Radio* | *News paper* |
|---|---|---|---|---|
| 1. | Daily | | 50.00 | 12.00 |
| 2. | Weekly once | 23.00 | | |
| 3. | Weekly twice | 3.00 | 7.00 | 19.00 |
| 4. | Once a month | 32.00 | | |
| 5. | Once in 3 months | 3.00 | – | – |
| 6. | Yearly once or twice | 5.00 | – | – |
| 7. | Rarely | 4.00 | 25.00 | 35.00 |
| 8. | Once in life time | 2.00 | | |

Films with fights, were, liked by majority of the students, listening to film songs (in radio) were preferred by many students (50.00 per cent). Advertisement on employment and politics were much favoured items in the news by the majority of students.

**Politics Vs. Students**

To the question whether students are politicized at all. Do they hold membership in any political party. What is the nature of the political activities in which they are involved? Do they do any regular party work? Do they attend political rallies or meetings take up their own grievances at a political level. The following data provide some information on these.

81.00 per cent of students, reported that they never participated in any procession and rallies of any political, party and nearly 15.00 of students stated that they did take part in Telugu Desam

Party (TDP) campaign in last general election in Andhra Pradesh. Nearly 2.00 per cent of campaigned in favour of congress party in last election of the state and 2.00 per cent students participated actively in samithi president elections. 58.00 per cent of students reported that they had no affiliation with any party, and 89.00 per cent of students never supported nor worked for any political party.

In response to the question who is their favourite leader their responses are given in Table--5.7.

**Table—5.7 Perception of Students Towards their Favourite Leader**

| | *Categories of Leaders* | *Per cent age* |
|---|---|---|
| 1. | Nehru family | 61.00 per cent |
| 2. | N.T. Rama Rao | 17.00 per cent |
| 3. | Local MLA | 2.00 per cent |
| 4. | Dr. Ambedkar | 1.00 per cent |
| 5. | Health Minister | 1.00 per cent |
| 6. | Sarpanch | 1.00 per cent |
| 7. | Did not specify | 17.00 per cent |

With reference to liking for their leaders 52.00 per cent of students expressed that their leaders helped the poor, and showed more sympathy towards tribals. Their administration was good (19.00 per cent). Acted well in films (3.00 per cent), helped for reservation in jobs and seats (8.00 per cent) in educational institutions.

***Problems*:** 10.00 per cent of students stated that their elders had certain problems in obtaining caste certificate from Revenue Office (Tahasildar) and transfer certificate from school.

***Scholarship*:** When asked to State whether they consider the scholarship is useful, the overwhelming majority of the students (91.00 per cent) said that they consider the facility very useful as it had created more interest among tribal parents to send their children to schools.

A large majority of students complained about the inadequacy of the scholarship. In some of educational institutions, deduction from the scholarship amount became regular, for want of attendance in the institution. The findings of the present study undertaken by the research scholar is in confirmation to the findings of the study undertaken by Shah, Nayar, Rajagopalan, Rath and Misra, Parvathamma and Sachchidananda. Shah (1989) reported that majority of the tribal students of both middle and secondary levels were found dis-satisfied with amount of scholarships. The findings of Nayar, (1975) Rajagopalan, (1974) and Rath and Misra (1974) were that majority of tribal students appreciated the government sponsored programmes meant for their benefit but nearly 90 per cent of the respondents had shown dissatisfaction with the amount of scholarship they were receiving; Chitnis (1974) also found that scholarship was not adequate for the needs of the tribal students. Similarly, Parvathamma and Sachchidananda showed that although awareness about the reservation facility in jobs and educational institutions was present for the tribal people, they were not satisfied with the amount of scholarship and its disbursement. Lakshmanna, Desai and Solanki also reported similar findings.

About the timely supply of scholarship 56.00 per cent of students informed that it is being received on time 41.00 per cent of students were not aware about amount of scholarship they are supposed to receive.

## Ashram Schools

With response to the question of satisfaction of hostel facilities students reaction are being presented in the following Table—5.8.

The present study of the research scholar confirms the findings of the study done by Srivastava and George whereas findings of Sachchidananda, Desai, Nayer, Rajagopalan, Rath and Misra, Lakshmanna were contradictory to the findings of the present study. Sachchidananda (1975) suggested that separate hostels for

Adivasis should be constructed, whereas George (1975) concluded that the system of eparate hostels for SC/ST was unhealthy. Srivastava (1970) observed that there was a shortage of space, furniture, medical care, recreation facility and above all conducive atmosphere for studies in hostels; but Desai (1988) reported that hostel facilities were inadequately utilised by SC/ST students; similarly, Nayar. (1975) Rajagopalan, (1974) Rath and Mishra, (1974) and Lakshmanna (1975) reported that only a small proportion of ST students was in the hostels, as majority of them were ignorant of the hostel facility. Singh (1974) identified that hosteilers among SC/ST students were more studious than day scholars.

**Table—5.8 Perception of Students Towards Hostel Facilities**

| | *Types of Responses* | *Per cent age* |
|---|---|---|
| 1. | Inadequacy of accommodation | 58.00 per cent |
| 2. | Food supply was not satisfactory | 50.00 per cent |
| 3. | Supply of books were prompt | 61.00 per cent |
| 4. | Lack of supply of note books in time | 53.00 per cent |
| 5. | Insufficient supply of lights | 61.00 per cent |
| 6. | Lack of adequate supply of stationary and clothing | 52.00 per cent |

About the role of Warden 38.00 per cent of students mentioned that hostel management and stock verification is their main task, 15.00 per cent opined that supply of ration is their main work. For 12.00 per cent of students their security was main work of Warden. For 9.00 per cent of students Warden is drawing officer.

11.00 per cent of students mentioned that Wardens were merely interested in their personal gain rather than their well being.

About the implementation of educational programmes 32.00 per cent of students informed that measures were not effective 11.00 per cent reported delay in supply of books, clothes, etc., 3.00 per cent felt—inadequate supply of stipend, 6.00 per cent faced problems in getting hostel seat, clothing, trunks, blankets, 1.00 per cent of students mentioned about lack of adequate teacher (for mathematics subject).

***Developmental Programmes*:** In the initial stages they had high hopes on govt. developmental programme, but in due course of time only few tribal elites, president and secretary of gram panchayats were benefitted. They are completely neglected officials did not extend any help to them.

**Problems**

Other problems mentioned by students are presented in Table—5.9.

**Table—5.9 Various Problems mentioned by Students**

| | *Problems* | *Per cent age* |
|---|---|---|
| 1. | Lack of degree college at Paderu | 16.00 per cent |
| 2. | Lack of supply of books, clothes at intermediate level | 8.00 per cent |
| 3. | Poverty | 1.00 per cent |
| 4. | Lack of primary school at every village | 1.00 per cent |

Teachers were not serious about their profession and were on leave frequently.

85.00 per cent of students felt that working hours could be from, 9.00 a.m. to 12.30 p.m. and 2.00 p.m. to 4.30 p.m. with regard to holidays 82.00 per cent of students demanded changes in the present set up, 3.00 per cent opined to declare local tribal festivals as holidays.

## II. Teachers

To examine the social and educational background of teachers, their understanding of tribal culture and interaction with the community their attitude towards tribal children, and society, their willingness to work in tribal areas, their perception about educational problems and their suggestions, etc. information has been collected and presented in the following pages.

In substantially different and diverse tribal culture the social background of teachers assumes special importance. The teachers' interaction with community and students depends on his/her understanding of tribal culture and life. Most of the teachers (95.00 per cent) in tribal areas being non-tribals lack proper understanding of tribal culture and life and they feel hegemony of their social background. Instead of considering tribal culture as different and equal, the non-tribal teachers label them as inferior.

However, the distinct difference in dress, values and behaviour of tribals is a strange situation for teachers. Similarly, for most of the tribes, the teacher is the first outsider to come into contact who represents different cultural ethos. One can imagine the cultural gulf that exists between the teacher and the tribal society.

Due to slow progress of education among the tribes, trained and educated tribal manpower is not available for various jobs including teaching. Secondly, most of the educated tribals either occupy the lowest position in hierarchy or migrate to non-tribal areas in search of better opportunities. Therefore, teachers from non-tribal areas were appointed. In fact, this problem is universal in all tribal concentrated areas in the country. However, in 1986 the State (Andhra Pradesh) adopted an innovative policy to enhance access to primary education and the pace of educational development in tribal areas by opening single-teacher schools Grameena Vikas Kendras (GVKs) in all school-less tribal habitations and only tribal youths been appointed as teachers by relaxing the qualifications. Those who had studied upto X standard and above were recruited.

The policy of recruiting only tribal youth helped to increase sharply the proportion of tribal teachers. However, still most of the teachers working in primary, middle and Ashram Schools run by different managements belong to non-tribal groups.

## Educational Qualifications

The findings of the present study by the research scholar is in conformity with findings of Haddad.

The educational qualifications and experience of teachers are some of the indicators for the quality of teachers. Although highly qualified persons need not necessarily be more efficient or committed, still there seems to be a "bracket" of knowledge and skills that teachers must possess for teaching different subjects at different levels below which they can not teach effectively (Haddad, 1985).

With regard to educational background of these primary and secondary school teachers taking the sample as a whole 31.00 per cent and non-graduates and 30.00 per cent graduates, 22.00 per cent are matriculates and 5.08 per cent are post graduates, 12.00 per cent are non-matriculates.

## Linguistic Background

The linguistic background of teachers has a crucial role in their interaction with the students and community. All the teachers belonging to non-tribal group have Telugu as their mother-tongue which is the regional language and also the medium of instruction. The tribal groups in block and district speak Telugu but the dialect-vocabulary and accent is different from Telugu spoken by non-tribals. The non-tribal teachers admit that it is problem to understand and converse in tribal dialect. The teachers who belong to local tribal groups have advantage in interacting with the students and parents in their accent.

Telugu was the mother tongue of 59.00 per cent of teachers, and 38.00 per cent of teachers had acquaintance with English. A few others (3.00 per cent) were familiar with Oriya Language (to teachers who were nearer to Araku Mandal).

## Tribal Language and Medium of Instruction

In 1956, the Indian Constitution through Article 350A recognised the need to provide facilities for primary education in the mother tongue to linguistic minorities. However, today, almost four decades later, education is being imparted primarily in the 15 official languages that are listed in the English. Schedule' of the Constitution as well as in English Languages of communities such as the Scheduled Tribes do not figure in the Schedule and remain outside the precincts of the school.

The denial of schooling in the mother tongue to children from tribal communities gives cause for concern in view of the growing volume of research that highlights the crucial role played by languages, of the home in processes of early learning. The poor response of tribal children to formal education and their high rates of attrition, especially in the first few years of schooling, assume significance in this context.

Information on the quality of education is limited largely to the physical facilities for schooling that are available to children. Data from the All India Education Surveys reveal that primary schools in rural areas have relatively poor infrastructures. There are a large number of schools that have 'kutcha' buildings, inadequate number of classrooms and lack library facilities and basic amenities such as drinking water arrangements and toilets within the premises. Blackboards, chalks and dusters are also in short supply. However, as compared to rural areas in general, tribal habitations are relatively poorly served with facilities for schooling. For instance, while 51.4 per cent of rural habitants have primary schools, this is so in only 45.4 per cent of tribal habitations (NCERT 1986: 116-36). Again, while 30 per cent of rural primary schools are 'single teacher schools', they predominate more in backward tribal areas (India 1988:300).

The academic attainment of children in specific skills that they are expected to acquire in primary school is yet to be systematically tested. Studies which have been conducted suggested that the average student has poor reading abilities, does not master content area in mathematics and performs poorly in science (Kurien 1974: Jalaludin 1991). Passing reference that is made to tribal students in some studies emphasises poor levels of comprehension and reading ability among children (Srivastava 1992:135). Of critical importance to the learning process is the language of communication in schools and the medium through which school knowledge is imparted. The child's access to subject areas in the curriculum depends on a minimal level of proficiency in the language used for instruction within the school. The data that are available from awareness among teachers about the linguistic validity of non-standard languages as well as demonstrate their scope and flexibility. Teachers need to recognise that the freedom of children to use languages with which they are most comfortable can facilitate the general process of learning and contribute to specific abilities in reading and writing, and their the knowledge of more than one language (including what are called dialects) can improve the linguistic and conceptual abilities of children. The debilitating effects that negative attitudes to language can have for children from minority communities also require special emphasis. Miller quotes Edwards who insists that ". . priority should be given to sensitisation of teachers to the relationship between language attitudes and social stereotypes and to the danger that these may be translated into reality" (Miller 1983).

At an all-India level, data reveal that 98.3 per cent of primary schools were single medium schools. In 96.9 per cent of rural schools, the media of instruction were the 15 languages listed in the English Schedule. While 0.6 per cent of schools have English as the medium, only 2.5 per cent were using "other Indian languages", a category that comprised as many as 24 languages (NCERT 1986)! While the first language introduced in school is usually assumed to be the medium of instruction this is not always the case. Only 27 languages are introduced in primary schools as first languages as compared to 43 that are observed to function as media of instruction. In as many as 97 per cent of rural schools, the first languages introduced at the primary stage are the languages included in the Eighth Schedule (NCERT: 1986).

The situation pertaining to the language of instruction and communication (by teachers) in schools gives cause for concern. It is known that of the 1,64,129 predominantly tribal habitations in the country, 45.4 per cent had the facility for primary school within them while 87.6 per cent had access to schooling within 2 km. (NCERT 1986: 22). The NCERT figures on school languages suggest 'hat in only' a negligible number of these habitations, mainly in north-east India, is the language of instruction that which is spoken in the homes of tribal children.

As regards textbooks in tribal languages, it has been noted that initiatives are being undertaken by the Central Institute of Languages, Hyderabad and NCERT, New Delhi. The number of languages in which textbooks are primers actually have been published, the extent to which they are made available to schools, and the manner in which these are being utilised by teachers and pupils are anybody's guess. Such information is not clear from reports such as that of the Commissioner for Linguistic Minorities, Srivastava has observed that the paucity of literature and textbooks in tribal dialects, will for the time being come in the way of teaching through the mother tongue' (1992).

The foregoing discussion suggests that tribal children in India are by and large being imparted primary education in languages that are not their spoken languages. Further, it also appears that systematic efforts are yet to be made to prepare the ground for schooling in tribal languages. Why is it important that tribal children be given education in their own languages at least in the early years of schooling?

## Why Education in Mother Tongue?

Broadly two kinds of perspectives are advanced to advocate the use of mother tongues or home languages as media for instruction in early education as well as to encourage linguistic diversity in schools. The first stems from a recognition that mother tongues are not merely speech varieties but are languages that provide social and emotional identify to individuals, express the essence of their cultures, and give them a sense of rootedness (Pattanayak 1990: ix). Schooling in the language of the child reflects respect for her and an appreciation of her culture. The exclusion of mother tongues from school hence is seen as "harmful to the child's self-esteem" (Edwards 1984: 81). According to Pattanayak children are thereby reduced to "minorities in their own homes" (1987: 71).

Research on bilingualism offers a number of insights that are relevant for the education of tribal children. Studies have shown that bilingual children have greater cognitive flexibility, greater social sensitivity and greater adeptness at creative thinking (Wiles, 1985: 92). The learning strategies of such children, for instance problem solving are found to be highly developed. It is emphasised that the "sense making strategies" that bilingual (and multilingual) children acquire, as well as the social skills they possess (seen in the ease with which they shift across and within languages in different contexts), are strengths that should be supported by the school system (Edwards 1984; Miller 1983; Wiles 1985). Most tribal communities in India re-observed to be bilingual and multilingual, though they usually have one language for 'in group' communication (Singh and Manoharan 1993: 21). Out of 623 tribal communities analysed by the ambitious People of India Project, "80.26 per cent were bilingual, in some cases trilingual and multilingual". Thus, children from these communities who have acquired or are acquiring more than one language are also likely to have highly developed linguistic and social skills which need to be recognised and strengthened with the classroom.

Linguistic diversity is today beginning to be seen by scholars as a pedagogic resource that can engender learning within classrooms rather than act as an impediment to education (Wiles 1985). Encouraging children to talk using languages they are most comfortable with as well as their own cultural experiences is seen to facilitate expression and communication of ideas, and to motivate reading and writing. The assumption is that in such an environment, children will be better able to practise linguistic and conceptual skills which can enlarge their repertoire and also aid second (dominant) language learning. They will have "access to as wide as possible a range of language . . . which will allow them to form/hypothesise about words and structures. They must also have realistic opportunities to communicate with teachers and peers so as to test the validity of the rule systems they are developing" (Edwards 1984: 85). While this perspective underlines the pedagogic relevance of home languages or mother tongues in early learning, it also suggests that an early imposition of the dominant language and an abrupt termination of the home language in school would be detrimental to the development of children's learning abilities.

## Willingness, Attitude and Awareness of Teachers

Effective functioning of a school depends to a large extent on teachers, their willingness and positive attitude and understanding to live and work in tribal villages. The attitude of the teacher also is moulded by many factors like personal interest, job satisfaction, facilities provided, etc. It is very important on the part of the teacher to understand and appreciate the culture of the tribes so that he might suitably motivate the children for education. The intimacy between the teacher and community can be provided only when teachers live in the village they work. In fact, earlier studies (Sachchidanda, 1967, Srivastava, 1967, Ambasht, 1970, Ratnaiah, 1978, Chaudari, 1982, Sujatha, 1987) have pointed out that the teachers hardly reside in the village. They stay in nearby town or road side village and commute daily. But in the present study, it found that the primary school teachers live in the same village where they are working and the remaining teachers commute daily from nearby places. If the villages are situated in the interior areas and inaccessible, it is more difficult for teachers to stay outside and commute daily. Lack of proper transport facilities also make the teachers stay in the same village.

Some of the teachers also discussed the general problems of the community with the tribals. Since most of the teachers (40.00 per cent) stay in village, obviously it helps to have interaction between the teacher and the society. Studies done by Sachchidananda, Srivastava, Ambasht, Ratnaiah, Choudhari, Sujatha contradicts the findings of the present study. The job chart of teachers expects them to play the role of a bridge between community and government.

The effectiveness of an organisation not only depends on the interaction of the school with environment, but also on the understanding of each other. Being an outsider, the teacher also forms certain perceptions and attitude towards tribals based on his experience and interaction, which has important bearing on his functions.

Both the tribal and non-tribal teachers have expressed more than one opinion about the personality characteristics of tribal people. The teachers' perception has to be understood in relation to their values and cultural background. Therefore opinions are tabulated:

In general, the tribal teachers tend to have advantage they can easily identify with their fellow men as well as understand their ethos. Even the tribal community feels confident to trust the tribal teachers. Therefore, except for a few, all the teachers felt that the tribals are friendly and helping. In case of non-tribal teachers, less than half of them have bad experience of friendliness of tribes. Although the teachers express their understanding of different behavioural aspects of tribes, in reality, it may also be true that the teachers themselves may not identify with the community and have preconceived assumptions. The educated tribal youth seem to like to share both tribal traits as well as other values. Blaming the tribals as lazy and superstitions seems to be mostly based on biased views of teachers. The tribal social customs and rituals are relevant to their socio-economic and ecological context which seems to others as superstitious or blind faith. For instance, after harvesting the crops, the Kondareddi tribals celebrate a festival on new moon day to have a community meal in which all members of the family take part. They believe that those who do not eat on a new moon day will fall sick. The parents come to Ashram School to ask children to join the celebration. The teachers do not realize the social value of the ritual and simply feel that they are superstitious. It is not to argue that the tribals are not superstitious, but all their beliefs need not be considered so.

The inter-tribal social hierarchy, illiteracy and tradition, limited social interaction due to ritual status keep distance between the tribal teachers and the community. And also some of the tribal groups who are better educated and more modern have some prejudice like non-tribals against the backward tribals. For example, Valmiki tribe in Vizag district occupies lower ritual status than Kondareddi tribe, but they are mostly educated. If a teacher belongs to Valmiki tribe the Kondareddies do not even like to give a house to teacher and do not treat him as equal. Similarly, the Valmiki teachers feel that the Kondareddies are lazy and superstitious. As such, the general belief that a tribal is better suited than the non-tribal teacher may not always be true.

It is important to examine what motivates teacher's willingness to work in tribal areas and the reasons for this unwillingness.

In addition to salary, all the employees in tribal sub-plan area in Andhra Pradesh get 40 per cent of basic pay as an extra allowance to work in inaccessible and difficult area. This incentive is offered to compensate the facilities foregone and to attract the employees to work in tribal areas. The extra allowances seems to be an attraction for a large percentage of non-tribal teachers (95.00 per cent) to serve in tribal area.

## Teacher's Attitude Towards Tribal Students

A number of studies highlighted relation between expectations labelling and failure (Rist, 1970). Although teachers in affluent and poor areas could be equally poor in their performance, children in the affluent school learn in spite of poor teaching, whereas in other schools, children would not learn because of poor teaching. In one of the studies (Leacock, 1971) on Black American children, it was shown that academic expectations and attitude of teachers based on the social class origin and race of the children were crucial for high performance of children.

To internal function of school system particularly the teaching-learning process depends on how the teachers perceive the tribal children and understand their capabilities. Mere presence of school and teacher would not facilitate the child's learning, particularly in the context of first generation learners.

An attempt is made to examine the teacher's understanding of tribal students, their interests, problems etc.

Increasingly majority of non-tribal teachers (95.00 per cent) are of the opinion that the present content and curriculum are adequate and suitable to tribal children. But among the non-tribal teachers, many have a different view and made different suggestions about what should be the content and the text-books. More than one-fifth of non-tribal teachers pleaded for need-based education for tribal children. Some of them felt that unless the text books are well designed with illustrations and diagrams the students would not be able to follow the class room teaching. Quite interestingly, more non-tribal teachers felt the need to introduce the tribal culture and life in text-books.

To a large extent, understanding of children's interest is true. Visit to any school shows that the children are very active while playing, and very passive in class room.

The instruction offered in institutions of elementary, secondary and higher secondary education broadly follows the pattern in vogue in non-tribal areas, without any serious attempt to link it to the culture-specific. The pedagogic tools used are generally those evolved in the urban areas or for non-tribals. Lack of innovative and imaginative pedagogy needs to be blamed for low interest of tribal students in education.

On the other hand, the tribal children lack home support for their academic work as most of their parents are illiterate and on the other, the passive teaching in class room in monotonous and boring for them. According to teachers (both tr bal and non-tribal) the tribal children face difficulty in some subjects like English and Mathematics. But some of the teachers reported that even Telugu language is difficult for tribal children because of limited and different vocabulary they have in their dialect.

Except the class room teaching, no attempt is made by the teachers to compensate lack of educational support at home say by organising remedial coaching. While suggesting the need for introduction of tribal culture and life in school curriculum, some teachers indicated () that it should be incorporated in lessons or in environmental education, in story forms or as examples.

A constant criticism about the present day teacher-training is that it is not keeping pace with changes that occurred in curriculum and development in pedagogical science. The training methodology orients the teachers for teacher learning and to teach children of urban and similar cultures. Teaching the poor, disadvantaged and isolated groups cannot be same as the other. But no attempt is made at training level to orient the teachers to face different cultural situations.

According to (95.00 per cent) of non-tribal teachers, special training is needed to teach tribal children. All the tribal teachers who are untrained also feel that training in pedagogy is essential for effective class room teaching.

The experience of teachers shows that a large number of teachers both among tribal and non-tribals lack interest, and they find teaching the tribal children difficult. However, among the tribal teachers 31.00 per cent had reported that it is easy to teach tribal children, while only 23.00 per cent of non-tribal teachers felt the same. More than one-tenth of teachers among both the groups had expressed that teaching tribal children is like teaching any other. From this it is clear that the present teaching methods and students' learning capabilities are not in consonance with each other. This, infact, indirectly reflects the teachers' inadequacies in their training. This may be one of the reasons why majority of teachers felt (95.00 per cent) the need for special training to teach tribal children.

Both tribal and non-tribal teachers admit that they could not give individual attention to children because they have to handle multiple classes and different age-group children.

Many of the teachers not only seemed to attribute their pupils' learning difficulties to home background or to "mental deficiencies" as they called them, but also believed that there was nothing they could do about these difficulties.

## Educational Problems and Measures

On the basis of experience and interaction with tribals the teachers understand to some extent the relevant reasons for educational backwardness of tribes. The teachers expressed more than one problem that constrains their education. Interestingly the views of teachers belonging to tribal community differ from non-tribal teachers.

How do the teachers analyse the reasons for educational backwardness of tribes? Most of the teachers belonging to non-tribal group exclude themselves from owning the responsibility for educational problems, and hold the parents' ignorance and lack of interest as major reasons for educational backwardness. Secondly, these teachers also attribute the educational backwardness more to poverty than to school system. However, an interesting aspect is that the teachers belonging to tribal community had different views and understanding of the problems. They consider the schools system and the teachers have an important role to play in educational development. The routine rules rigid school hours and requirement of academic support at home generally discourage children to come into the folds of education. Similarly, the teachers' authoritarianism hardly makes the school attractive. By and large, children learn from others what they are or are not capable of doing and the way in which this concept is, internalised (i.e., the meaning each person gives to the outsiders information) substantially affects the success of their learning efforts. The teachers usually single out children by calling them dullards, cannot learn fast, no amount of help can make them educated etc. But there is sufficient evidence to show that the teachers' attitude their performance and success of children are interrelated. The non-tribal teachers often comment on tribal children in discouraging terms.

Poverty and opportunity cost of children were recognised by both tribal and non-tribal teachers that affects the education of tribes. The parents cannot afford to spare the child because each child in the home contributes directly or indirectly to the family economic sustenance.

Highest percentage of teachers among both the groups favoured the most, among all the measures, mid-day meals expecting children to pay attention to studies with empty stomachs is ridiculous if not cruel.

Non-tribal teachers suggested that the pedagogy should be suitable to psychology of tribal children and should be easier for tribal children to follow class room teaching. The measures suggested by teachers show that there is a need to strengthen the existing system as well as to offer more support in the form of mid-day meals. The teachers suggestions also imply the relationship between education and economic development. While the non-tribal teachers view more measures for family and economy, the tribal teachers recognise and attach equal importance in improving the school inputs, pedagogy along with poverty alleviation.

**Summary**

Teachers play a very crucial role in educating the tribals for whom education is a new phenomenon. An empirical study conducted by Dr. K. Sujatha in tribal sub-plan areas of East

Godavari and Warangal districts in Andhra Pradesh shows that majority of (86.75 per cent) teachers working in tribal areas are non-tribals. The present study by the research scholar also showed that majority of teachers are non-tribals (95.00 per cent).

However, the recent policy decision to appoint tribal youth as teachers had helped to increase the proportion of tribal teachers. Most of the teachers working in tribal areas are young and less experienced. The attitude and understanding of teachers about tribals and students differs among the tribal and non-tribal teachers. The teachers belonging to tribal community have advantage to have close interaction and communication with community as compared to non-tribal teachers. The choice and reasons for working in the tribal areas vary between the two groups of teachers.

While extra allowances and nearness to native place encourages non-tribal teachers to work in tribals areas, tribal youth would like to work in tribal areas as they can be in their native place. The two groups of teachers perceive the constraints for slow progress of education differently and suggested various measures.

**Social Background**

Out of total number of sampled teachers is 46, 35 were males and the rest were females. The majority of these teachers were non-tribals (95.00 per cent) and the rest 5.00 per cent of teachers were tribals.

Among male teachers Hindus were in the largest number, Telugu is the mother tongue of the overwhelming majority.

**Experience**

45.00 percent had five or less than 5 years of experience, 25.00 per cent were 6 to 10 years, 16.00 per cent 11-15 years, 9.00 per cent were between 16-20 years and 5.00 per cent were above 20 years.

Teachers with varied professional background (qualifications, experience etc.,) are more or less uniformly distributed in all the different types of institutions, (Government, Tribal Welfare, Private, etc.,)

## Teacher Perception about the Area and Tribal People

55.00 per cent of teachers liked the place due to easy way of life, few did not like due to lack of basic amenities (like medical, transport, education, entertainment, electricity, drinking water etc.).

47.00 per cent of teachers stated that tribals are good. Majority of tribal communities are cooperative except Valmikis, and 37.00 per cent of teachers treated them as bad, drunkard, uncivilized, illiterate, innocent.

76.00 per cent of teachers opined that tribals are obedient, 20.00 per cent of teachers stated that behaviour of tribals is degrading not submissive before officials, uncivilized, non-co-operative.

## Teacher Opinion Towards the Intelligence of Student

64.00 per cent of teachers stated that tribal students are dull and their comprehension capacity is low. 20.00 of teachers mentioned that tribal students are intelligent on par with others, but they are not vocal, and introverted and fearful by nature, 6.00 per cent of teachers opined that their intelligence is at average level. This reveals that fairly large number of teachers considered tribals, as inferior in intelligence.

Negligible per cent of teachers mentioned that tribal culture and life need to be in corporated in preparation of syllabus.

## Role of Inspecting Authorities

82.00 per cent of teachers mentioned that visits of DEO, DIS, DTW, PO, ITDA to schools and hostels are necessary for functioning of schools, negligible per cent of teachers stated that officials are not serious about their work, they do it as ritual, corruption has also cropped these days in the academic field also, to do favour officials take bribe.

## Methods Used in Assessing the Intelligence of a Tribal Students

Performance in tests and other examinations, question and answer method were highly preferred by 67.00 per cent of the teachers, 13.00 per cent of teachers preferred giving assignment, 20.00 per cent of teachers mentioned that it is difficult to assess intelligence of tribal students.

## Students Attention Towards Studies

Nearly 62.00 per cent of teachers opined that the students took their assignments seriously and are punctual in their home work. Negligible per cent of teachers mentioned that as tribal students don't have inherent desire or curiosity towards classroom teaching so teacher has to be strict.

## Teacher Views on Content and Curriculum

27.00 per cent of teachers felt that syllabus was relevant, 25.00 per cent of teachers viewed it as impracticable, 50.00 per cent of teachers mentioned that syllabus is too high which becomes difficult for tribal students to comprehend because of their low grasping capacity 16.00 per cent of teachers expressed that there should be separate syllabus for tribals, because of their low comprehension level.

*Salaries:* 84.00 per cent of teachers expressed that they are satisfied with their pay. 64.00 per cent of teachers did not offer any suggestions for enhancement of their pay. A negligible percentage of teachers mentioned that housing and medical aid were to be provided to teachers.

With reference to service conditions (29.00 per cent teachers of private, tribal welfare, and ITDA schools were dissatisfied they emphasised that heir service condition should be improved on par with teachers of government schools.

Negligible percentage of teachers stated that their services were not regularised, and probation is not declared even after service of two year in agency area.

Their appointment is made by DEO, DIWO was the controlling authority but this payment was made by BDO.

## Opinion About the System of Transfer

62.00 per cent of teachers expressed need for transfer 31.00 per cent of teachers wanted transfer to plain areas. 7.00 per cent of teachers wanted transfer to road side villages. 5.00 per cent of teachers to native places, 4.00 per cent to upper primary schools, 2.00 per cent to district headquarters, 2.00 per cent depending on wives transfer their place of option will be intimated.

60.00 per cent of teachers did not have place to stay where they are working. This mean that they were daily commuting to their respective schools from other places.

### Option About the Job

The teacher happened to work in tribal schools due to different reasons. For a majority of teachers, their teaching career started in tribal area as their first appointment rest 25.00 per cent tried for jobs in banks, govt. etc., and they were not successful and thus entered teaching job in the agency as a sort of last resort.

Nearly 69.00 per cent of teachers never wanted change in their profession, 42.00 per cent of teachers stated that they joined teaching job as it was a Government Service (which is permanent). For 22.00 per cent teachers compulsion was main reason. For 21.00 per cent of teachers it is a native place, 15.00 per cent of teachers mentioned that getting job in tribal area is easy.

### Training to Work in Tribal Areas

96.00 per cent of teachers mentioned that they did not receive any special training, only 2 teachers (4.00) out of 46 teachers got trained in special English training in State Institute of Educational Research and Training (SCERT) for 6 days.

### Opinion

47.00 per cent of teachers mentioned that due to lack interest among students poverty and illiteracy of parents, there is poor enrolment of tribal students.

### Opinion About the Vacation

74.00 per cent of teachers stated that the existing holidays and working hours were convenient, teacher expressed that climate and culture and local festival of tribals need to be taken into account while deciding holidays. Vacations could be in rainy and harvesting season (June-August), Summer vacation needs to be reduced as it is more now.

## Views on Syllabus and Text Books

44.00 per cent of teachers were satisfied about the text books for primary school level, and 36.00 per cent of them were dis-satisfied as syllabus for Social Studies upto VIII standard is very high and for Mathematics also syllabus is too high.

3.00 per cent of teachers opined that tribal culture should find place in their syllabus. A convent type of education from first standard might improve the base of the education, local tribal dialect had to be evolved with local Telugu words.

Text books needs to contain more illustrations, with more stories.

## Opinion About the Attitude of Tribal Parents

Nearly 44.00 per cent of teachers mentioned that tribal parents have favourable attitude towards their children, 25.00 per cent teachers did not express any view.

20.00 per cent of teachers stated that parents are irresponsible, and always grumble about hostel warden, and facilities available in hostel remaining 11.00 per cent of teachers opined that parents think that once boy or girl is admitted in the school the entire responsibility depends on the teacher.

## Home Work by Teachers

When asked to specify the time teacher spend on their home work every day 47.00 per cent of then would spend 1-2 hours, 12.00 per cent said that home work was not necessary, 11.00 per cent each spend 2-3 and 3-4 hours per day.

This analysis reveals that serious attention was not being paid by teacher in the preparation of the subject.

27.00 per cent of teacher mentioned that they did not have any hobbies, 17.00 per cent mentioned sports, 15.00 per cent stated general reading, negligible per cent of teachers mentioned social services, playing cards, drinking, drawing, singing as their hobbies, their number is very minimal.

**Opinion of Teachers on the Service in the Agency**

73.00 per cent of teachers were desirous continuing their service in tribal areas, 7.00 per cent of teachers stated that there is no question of individual choice in government service, wherever they are transferred they have to serve. 16.00 per cent of teachers stated that their teaching career started in tribal area and they had a strong conviction to serve in the agency area, 4.00 per cent of teachers stated that tribals ignore services rendered by teachers so they opt for transfer.

**Influence of Childhood Days on Mental Make up of Tribal Student**

82.00 per cent of teachers confirmed that there was a greater scope of ones childhood days, his family and societal influence in influencing the individual personality.

Nearly 56.00 per cent of teachers said that poverty is the sole factor for the low mental calibre of tribal students, economic status of pre-family, hereditary and environment in which tribal child is brought up would lead to the mental state of that child.

**Teachers Views on Policy of Reservation**

About 58.00 per cent of them accepted its relevance, with this provision parents are coming forward to send their children to schools, 6.00 per cent of teachers opposed the idea of reservation, according to them it was wrong as the country believes in democratic, secular and social pattern of society.

**Views on Scholarship**

74.00 per cent of teachers stated that scholarship is necessity to the students due to poverty of tribal parents, 49.00 per cent of teachers stated that there was no proper interaction between them and parents. Parents whose wards were studying in private schools use to meet parents on shandy day (to get permission to take their children to shandy places).

## Types of Job for Tribal Students as Visualised by the Teaching Community

55.00 per cent of teachers stated that choice of job is left to the students. 29.00 per cent of teachers mentioned that due to reservation of jobs in government services students can try for the post of Engineer, Revenue Officer, BDO, Doctor etc.

## III. Parents

Tribal parents were contacted to know their perception and practice towards education and educational programmes. In order to get this information, apart from general information, we recorded the aspects included such as objective behind educating their children, his preference for rural or urban life, attitude towards tribal and non-tribal teachers, methods of inducement to their school going children, frequency of interaction with the teachers and other difficulties in the process of implementation of various development schemes in the field of tribal education, the religious beliefs and practices and their value-orientations.

***Age:*** More than half of the respondents (28.00 per cent) were in the age group of 26 to 30 years. However 22.00 per cent of them were in the age group of 46-50 years. These results to some extent. Suggest that the respondents belonged to young and middle age group. The findings of the present study by research scholar contradicts findings of study done by Joshi.

Joshi (1980) observed that 85 per cent of the father's (were below 45 years of age).

***Tribe:*** A higher percentage of respondents (62.00 per cent) belonged to Bhagathas tribe followed by Valmikis (14.00 per cent) and Kondadoras (12.00 per cent) Porja, Kummari, Gadabha, and Nookdora tribes constituted two per cent each.

***Occupational Structure:*** Twenty per cent of households are engaged in two occupations to supplement their main source of living. Since the main occupation cannot (agriculture) sustain the members of the household throughout the year, about four minor (subsidiary) occupation like business (20.00 per cent) collection of minor forest produce (2.67 per cent) contractor (5.33 per cent) and agriculture (2.00 per cent) were also mentioned by the respondents.

## Number of Members in the Family

The number of members in the family included husband, wife, children and other dependents.

The size of the family is also one of the indicators development. Among tribal communities smaller size families are most common because of prevalence of nuclear type of family unlike J.F. system in most of the rural areas in the country. The family size among the simple household in Paderu mandal is as follows:

There were 28 households with the family size between 3-5 members, and 20 families upto 2 members and 2 households between 6-9 members. The findings of the present study of the research scholar contradicts the findings of Singh's study.

***Land:*** The average land holding size among the sample households in the study area is 1.80 acres. Inspite of Governmental efforts for elimination of Podu cultivation, 44 households among the sample households are reported to have Podu lands.

## Income

Even though every member of tribal family works still it is difficult for them to make both ends meet. Their economic means are always hand to mouth. They take loans from their masters to meet their basic needs and these are adjusted against their pay.

There were 8 households in Paderu with an income of Rs. 6,400/- and 42 households were below the poverty line category.

With respective socio-economic conditions of tribal students Singh reported that the majority of them belonged to agricultural class. Their family size varied from 5 to 8 members in a large number of cases. Approximately 30 per cent parents were below the poverty line. Similarly, Chitnis mentioned that a higher proportion of ST students came from disadvantaged home and most of them belonged to rural occupations. On the other hand, Desai and Pandoor reported that by and large, the SC/ST students came from average economic status families, and they believed that their status was still lower than that of their colleagues belonging to other cases.

Further, Nayer concluded that economically, ST Students were in more comfortable position than the SC students, which was however, contradicted by Pathak and Shah and Patel. They found that the income of the SC parents was more than that of ST parents. These investigators felt that although there was some improvement in the status of ST students, yet, on the whole it continued to be inferior. Sachchidananda had supported the finding that a large number SC/ST students felt that their status had improved but not to the extent of the caste Hindus.

## Religion

Respondents those who are interviewed belonged to both Hindu and Christian religious communities. Of the total 50,96.00 per cent of them were Hindus, and the rest 4.00 per cent were Christians. Although Telugu, Kutia and Gadaba languages had been the mother tongue of different communities, Telugu was being used by all of them as a medium of communication.

## Age

All the respondents were in the age group of 20-60 years. Further analysis revealed that about 28.00 per cent of them belonged to 26-30 years and about 22.00 per cent in 46-50 years. In other words, the sampled parent respondents were represented mainly from the young and middle age groups. Joshi (1980) observed that 85.00 per cent of the fathers were below 45 years of age. This finding of Joshi contradicts the finding of the present study of the research scholar.

## Sex

Of the total, 92 per cent of them were male, 8 per cent females. The respondents represented from the Bhagatha, Valmiki,

Kondadora, Porja, Kummari, Gadaba and Nukadora tribal communities. Bhagathas (62.00 per cent) Valmikis (14.00 per cent) and Kondadora (12.00 per cent) constituted the major percentage of the sampled respondents.

## Occupation

Analysis of the respondents on the basis of their occupations revealed that about 88.00 per cent of them thrived on agriculture as their main occupation. The rest 12.00 per cent eked out on agriculture labour, government service and other activities. Collection of minor forest produce had been treated as the subsidiary occupation of many of our respondents.

## Education

Considering the literacy particulars of the respondents, it was found that out of 50, half of them were illiterates. Among 50.00 per cent literate tribal parents, 46.00 per cent of them studied upto primary level and 4.00 per cent upto upper primary level. The low level of educational standard of the respondents tends to reveal the general backwardness of the area. The findings of the present study of the research scholar contradicts the findings of studies done by Joshi (1980), Pathak, Lakshmanna and the study of SCERT, Solanki and Parvathamma. Joshi observed that 95.00 per cent of mothers had practical no education in schools. Pathak found that 42 per cent parents were educated but only 9.00 per cent had education above intermediate level; similarly, Lakshmanna (1975) concluded that 28.3 per cent fathers were high school pass and 14 per cent had received college education. On the contrary, in the study by the SCERT (1979) it was reported that the distribution of parents according to levels of education was primary—12.3 per cent, middle school—9.8 per cent, high school—7.5 per cent, higher education—2.5 per cent and illiterates about 60 per cent. Similarly, Solanki (1977) reported that 45 per cent of ST students came from families having educated parents; Parvathamma concluded that even among the current generation, many of the SC/ST children do not come for education. On the whole, eventhough the educational status of the tribal families is progressing continuously, as compared to higher castes the position is extremely unsatisfactory.

## Formal Position

Social position has been generally an indicative of special status of an individual in a society. By virtue of their formal positions, they are more accessible to the new ideas. It is found that the aspiration level of these sections is reasonably high compared to the other groups. The much mentioned social positions in the tribal area and Muthadar, village headman, Record Keeper (Karnam), religious head, Agency guruvu (Barki) Village panchayat member and sangham president. However, the positions of Muthador, Karnam, and headman have no relevance now as the post of Mathadar had been removed with the abolishment of Muthadar system in tribal area. And in regard to the posts of Karnam and village headman, the present government had removed these posts as a policy measure in the entire state and so is with the tribal areas. As far as the present respondents are concerned, 80 per cent of them had no any formal status. The remaining stated that they had some position or the other.

## Belief System

Religion has been an important component in tribal way of life. They start any activity with some religious practice. When parent respondents were asked about the existence of God, about 98.00 per cent of them said 'yes' and fully subscribed to the idea that every event in life would happen as a result of one's fate.

## Value Orientations

Tractor in place of plough could be more effective in agriculture. This was in innovation of modern technology. People should change values with changing times. It was found that in the modern values, there was free play of corruption in every act of life which was absent in the traditional set up. With the impact of modern values, without any discriminatory attitude among tribals and their identities. All of them were moving and working together. Modern values were good, it did not force anybody to spend money lavishly on any social functions with the result of modern values, the tribals had been showing care about their health and hygiene. The poor and the suppressed tribals had to work and suffer for nothing as far as the old values are concerned. Now those days had gone. All were alike. The difference could also be discerned between the aged and the young, the old would go in for traditional values and the young would like modern values. Tradition had been since generation, everything was cheap in those days, and in the old order there were severe punishment for the culprit, the degree of punishment had lessened in the modern set up. Some evinced interest to have old and new values with them. Tribal had to change their attitude according to the necessity. In the olden days, the tribals were used to observe some religious principles and practices at the initiation a house construction. Now the tribal was prepared to occupy the house, allotted to him by the Government as there was no room for inquiring into the sentiments of a allottee.

Total Children in the Family

With reference to the number of children, 20 of them stated that they did not have boys, 18 of them told one boy each, 12 of them told 2 boys each. Out of 50 respondents, 34 of them informed that they did not have female children at all. However, 10 families had one girl each, 4 families, 2 girls each, and 2 families 5 girls each. Analysed according to school going age groups, the figures revealed that, out of 50, 5 of them had no school-going children at all. 32 respondents had one boy each, 10 families 2 boys each, 3 families 3 boys each.

## Reasons to Dropout and Wastage

Coming to the 'wastage' in the case of school going children, 35 of them stated that no single boys had never discontinued from studies. However, there were 3 in 2 families in which 1 and 2 boys respectively had dropped out from the schools.

In regard to girls incidence of drop out rates was much less to the boys among the families of our parent respondents as 47 respondents stated that there was no drop out from the schools, in 2 families 1 girl each and in one family 2 girls had discontinued their studies. Further probing in this matter revealed out of our 50 sampled respondents, about 46.00 per cent of them did not come out with any specific reason. 14.00 per cent of them told that it was due to young age. 40.00 per cent of the parents stated the various reasons for drop out such as disinterest of students, financial constraints, ill health of child, economic necessity, non-availability of schools of a higher level in and around their villages and sudden demise of mother.

## Inducement Method Used by Parents

It was found that tribal students at lower level were not punctual in attending the schools, because of various reasons. The higher the level of educational standard, the lesser the rate of absenteeism among the students. About 30.00 per cent of them never had an occasion to induce their children as they were regular. 70.00 per cent of the parents tried and used to give caution, proper advice, beating, offering money for the inducement of school going children whenever the latter become indifferent in attending school.

## Parents' Visit to Schools

Periodicity of visit to school by parents for inquiring the performance of his child in the achievement of education is positively correlated with the intensity of interest shown towards the education of a child. But in the case of tribal parents, visiting school, interaction with the teacher has been an usual practice. It was found that about 76.00 per cent of them stated that they never visited and participated in any formal functions. When they were asked whether the schools were working well or not, 82.00 per cent of them expressed their satisfaction. In regard to the Telugu language as the medium of instruction, about 72.00 per cent had no objection. But 24.00 per cent insisted on English as the medium of instruction at high school and college level as the English language had its advantages in the society.

## Conclusion

Spread of education in any community, by and large depends on various factors such as universal provision of school, universal enrolment of pupils and universal retention of pupils in the school till the completion of their prescribed course. A closer analysis of all the variables listed above reveals the difficulties and disparities in educational attainments among tribals from three sets of structural constraints i.e., the ecological, the socio-economic and the internal elements of the school system.

# 6

# Profile of Tribals in Andhra Pradesh

In this Chapter an attempt is made to analysis the socio-economic and demographic profile of the tribals in Andhra Pradesh.

## Tribal Population Profile

Scheduled Tribes form 5.9 per cent of the total population of Andhra Pradesh. There are 33 Scheduled Tribes with a population of 31.76,001 as per 1981 Census. Of these more than 50 per cent live in a contagious belt of inaccessible hilly and forest areas extending from Adilabad district in North Telangana area of Srikakulam district in north coastal Andhra (via) Karimnagar, Warangal, Khammam, West Godavari, East Godavari, Visakhapatnam and Vizianagaram districts. While these areas form the exclusive habitat for 30 scheduled tribes, three tribal groups-Lambada Yerukala and Yanadi—live in both these hilly areas and plain areas. 93.78 per cent of total tribal population live in rural areas.

The largest concentration of tribal population is in Khamman district where they form almost ¼th of the total population followed by Adilabad and Visakhapatnam with a small percentage in East and West Godavari. Three districts have shown a great increase in tribal population over the decades.

These are Medak with an annual growth of 6340, Nizamabad 1495 and Nalgonda 3904.

## Tribal Development Issues and Perspectives

### Issues

Of the 538.16 lakh Scheduled Tribe population in India, the Scheduled Tribe population in Andhra Pradesh is 31.76 lakhs which constitutes 6.15 per cent of the total population of Andhra Pradesh. The 33 scheduled tribes in Andhra Pradesh form a very large component in the entire South India.

Based on the spatial distribution and the level of development, the Scheduled Tribe Population in Andhra Pradesh can be categorised into five groups as detailed below:

*(a)* Tribals living in areas of concentration covered by 8 ITDAs in the districts of Srikakulam, Vizianagarm, Visakhapatnam, East Godavari, Khammam, Warangal and Adilabad.

*(b)* Smaller but compact pockets of tribal concentration outside ITDA areas covered by 41 MADA areas.

*(c)* Tribal population living in 17 smaller clusters.

*(d)* Areas inhabited by primitive and isolated tribal groups; and

*(e)* Dispersed tribal groups living in rural areas.

An analysis of the situation of the tribal population and their status on the various development indicators points out that this population lags behind in almost every area of development. The community is characterised by higher death rates, low age of marriage, high fertility, high infant mortality rates and lowered life expectancy than the general population.

Nutritional levels of most of the tribal population is low with dietary intakes often being far below required levels. The dependence of the communities on certain form of livelihood such as collection and sale of minor forest produce etc., makes wage earning difficult during certain period of the year resulting in enforced starvation.

The poor nutritional levels, in turn, lower the resistance of the tribals and when coupled with the hazardous environmental conditions and poor sanitation, make them more prone to infection and ill-health. The inaccessibility of their habitations and the non-availability of health infrastructure results in chronic illness and higher mortality rates.

As in the case of health and nutrition, the literacy levels among the tribal population is the lowest in the state. Female literacy stands at a low 4.3 per cent. There has been no substantial increase in the literacy of the female tribal population over the past 3 decades and the present rates of their enrolment and retention in school does not hold out great hope for an improvement in the coming years without drastic interventions.

Poverty and perpetual indebtedness are a reality in the life of the tribal community. The majority of the tribals do not own agricultural land or have marginal land holdings which do not produce enough for sustenance. Many tribals work as agricultural labourers, and are also engaged in the collection and sale of minor forest produce. The extreme poverty conditions often force them to take loans given by traders and middle-men who in turn charge high rates of interest or buy their produce at extremely low rates. Often the tribals are not able to return the loan and lose possession of their lands. Caught in the bind of poverty and indebtedness, they are unable to break out of the cycle of undernutrition and disease. Education which would help them to combat the exploitation and improve living conditions has not reached them to any appreciable extent. The government is keenly aware of the situation of the tribals and has special schemes which encourage children going to school, but these have yet to make substantial difference.

## Perspectives

What is needed is a multi-pronged programmes that will help increase the economic, health and educational levels of the tribal population!

In order to implement the programmes in an integrated fashion, the ITDAs have been established in the 8 districts where there is a large concentration of tribals.

Experience in the past has shown that tribal children who study in residential schools have a greater chance of completing school possibly because of the greater attention paid to them in the school. At present the number of schools for girls are far less than those for boys. This lacuna is to be addressed in the new plan. 25 Ashram schools and 10 residential schools exclusively for girls are being planned. The provision of hostels, new school building and incentives for education will continue under the state plan for tribal development.

Since many of the schools and other incentive schemes in the tribal areas are administered by the ITDA, the Education Department has no specific programme. The provision of non-formal centres in SC and ST areas will continue as in the previous plan.

## Educational Status

### Literacy

The educational status among tribal population across the country continues to remain a cause for concern and Andhra Pradesh is no exception. Very often it is difficult to get educated persons among the tribal community to fill the posts in the various community based projects such as ICDS and Adult Education. The tribal communities are often caught in a circle of low education—low availability of locally educated people—dependence on outsiders who are either disinterested or exploitative which in turn serve to slow down the process of educating the community.

Andhra Pradesh being one of the educationally backward states in the country, it is not surprisingly that the levels of literacy among the more disadvantaged sections of the society are still very low. Literacy rates among the tribals is one of the lowest which in turn is reflected in the educational status of the district where they form a sizeable proportion of the population. Among the tribal population, the literacy rates of women is almost dismal and cause for much concern.

The table below compares the literacy rate among tribal men and women across two decades. As can be seen there has been no appreciable increase in the literacy level of tribal men and women, especially women over the last three census period. The increase of literacy in women over two decade has been only half of that of men and even now stands at a dismal level of 3.4 per cent.

The literacy rates of Scheduled Tribes in Andhra Pradesh when compared with the general population and the literacy rates in the country show that the literacy at 7.82 per cent is approximately 25 per cent of Andhra Pradesh figures (29.90 per cent) and around 21.5 per cent of that of the country (36.23 per cent).

A district based comparison of tribal literacy in the eight tribal districts shows inter district variation. Literacy is highest among the East Godavari tribals and lowest in Adilabad. This trend is in keeping with the literacy trends in the general population.

A comparison of the Literacy rates among the 33 scheduled tribes reveals that as per 1981 census, the maximum number of illiterate population (less than 2 per cent literacy) are among Khonds living in the tribal areas of Visakhapatnam district. The comparative literacy rates are presented below.

**Table—6.1 Literacy Ranges of Scheduled Tribes—1981**

| *Sl. No.* | *Literacy Range* | *Number of the Sub-Group* |
|---|---|---|
| **1** | **2** | **3** |
| 1. | 0–2.0 per cent | 1. Khond |
| 2. | 2.1–4.0 per cent | 2. Kolam, 3. Mukha Dora, 4. Porja, 5. Reddy Dora, |
| 3. | 4.1–6.0 per cent | 6. Gond, 7. Konda Dora, 8. Naik, 9. Rona-Rena |
| 4. | 6.1–8.0 per cent | 10. Gadaba, 11. Konda Reddy, 12. Koya, 13. Manne Dora, 14. Savara, 15. Lambada, 16. Yanadi |
| 5. | 8.1–10.0 per cent | 17. Andh, 18. Bagata, 19. Chenchu, 20. Jatapu, 21. Kammara, 22. Kotia-bento-Oriya, 23. Malis |

*(Table Contd.)*

| 1 | 2 | 3 |
|---|---|---|
| 6. | 10.1–12.0 per cent | 24. Kulia |
| 7. | 12.1–14.0 per cent | 25. Hill Reddi |
| 8. | 14.1–16.0 per cent | 26. Pardhan, 27. Yerukala |
| 9. | 16.1–18.0 per cent | 28. Thoti, 29. Gond |
| 10. | 18.1–20.0 per cent | 30. Bhil, 31. Konda Kapu, 32. Valmiki |
| 11. | 20+ | 33. Kattunayakan |

Among the tribal population there are clear inter regional and inter tribe variations in literacy levels. Tribals settling in Urban area have a slightly higher rate of literacy as can be seen in the Table—6.2 below:

**Table—6.2 Tribal Literacy Rate in Urban and Rural Areas**

| *Area* | *Females (per cent)* | *Males (per cent)* | *Total (per cent)* |
|---|---|---|---|
| Urban | 14.1 | 31.5 | 23.3 |
| Rural | 2.7 | 10.7 | 6.8 |
| Tribal | 2.4 | 10.6 | 6.6 |
| **Total** | **3.4** | **12.0** | **7.8** |

## Enrolment

The following chart shows the enrolment particulars among tribal children over the school period. It is clear that dropouts in the first five year is a serious problem with almost 71.8 per cent children dropping out. Approximately 75 per cent of the girls drop out in the first five years. It is interesting to note that there are only about 14,150 girls studying in the high school. It is important that special efforts be made to follow-up these girls and utilize them for community development programmes.

Literacy rate being so low, it is evident that educational levels among the children will be correspondingly be low. Though there has been considerable effort to improve tribal status on education through the provision of schools, residential facilities, incentives, etc., enrolment figures still leave much to be desired.

**Table—6.3 Enrolment Particulars of STs in Andhra Pradesh 1990-91**

| *Stage* | *Class* | *Boys* | *Girls* | *Total* |
|---|---|---|---|---|
| Primary | I | 1,12,050 | 71,001 | 1,83,057 |
| | | (61.21) | (38.79) | (100.00) |
| | II | 76,142 | 47,519 | 1,23,661 |
| | | (61.47) | (38.43) | (100.00) |
| | III | 57,144 | 40,356 | 97,500 |
| | | (58.61) | (41.39) | (100.00) |
| | IV | 44,210 | 22,948 | 67,158 |
| | | (65.83) | (34.29) | (100.00) |
| | V | 33,930 | 17,706 | 51,636 |
| | | (65.77) | (34.29) | (100.00) |
| | Sub-Total | 3,23,476 | 1,99,536 | 5,23,012 |
| | | (61.85) | (38.15) | (100.00) |
| Upper Primary | VI | 23,353 | 10,077 | 33,430 |
| | | (69.86) | (30.14) | (100.00) |
| | VII | 20,543 | 8,700 | 29,246 |
| | | (70.24) | (29.76) | (100.00) |
| | Sub-Total | 43,896 | 18,780 | 62,676 |
| | | (70.04) | (29.96) | (100.00) |
| High School | VIII | 15,070 | 5,507 | 20,577 |
| | | (73.24) | (27.68) | (100.00) |
| | IX | 12,878 | 4,928 | 17,806 |
| | | (72.32) | (27.68) | (100.00) |
| | X | 10,955 | 4,550 | 15,105 |
| | | (72.53) | (27.47) | (100.00) |
| | Sub-Total | 38,903 | 14,585 | 53,488 |
| | | (72.73) | (27.27) | (100.00) |
| | Grand Total | 4,06,275 | 2,32,901 | 6,39,176 |
| | | (63.56) | (36.44) | (100.00) |

Source: Director of School Education, Govt. of Andhra Pradesh, Hyderabad. (Figures in the parenthesis indicate percentages).

There are many reasons for the low enrolment of girls. Parents believe that investment in girls is not rewarding. Further, early marriages in the tribes is a great obstacle in the development of education among girls.

A factor to be kept in mind is that in tribal areas, enrolment and attendance vary significantly. Studies have shown that only 20 per cent of the enrolled pupils attend schools and that too irregularly. There may be two reasons for this. Enrolment figure itself may be exaggerated or alternatively may be due to other factors as irregularity of teachers, disinterest among parents, frequent festivals, children going to work, family responsibilities, etc. Irregular attendance finally leads to drop-outs.

If enrolment and retention rates continue at present level the problem of low literacy among tribal and lack of trained manpower as well as lack of awareness, poor health etc., which are associated problems, will be with them for the next two decades.

**Government Programmes**

The tribal children upto six years of age receive pre-primary education through a network of ICDS scheme covering supplementary feeding of nutritious food, immunization, health check-ups and nutrition education. There are 1977 Anganwadi Centres in the states catering to 1,52,888 children between the ages of 6 months-6 years.

Besides the normal incentives like scholarships, free supply of dresses, books etc., there is a special emphasis on girl education. Government of India and State Government share expenditure equally for construction of buildings for educational institutions for girls. Government of Andhra Pradesh has also opened six residential schools exclusively for tribal girls.

There are 121 girls hostels with a strength of 9,231 students and there are 6 girls residential schools with a total strength of 990 students.

In addition there are 423 Ashram Schools functioning in the tribal areas which caters to 40,069 children. Free boarding, books, uniforms, toiletries are provided to these children, most of whom are in the primary sections.

In order to tackle adult literacy, the government has started a number of adult literacy centres. Approximately 13 per cent of the total Adult Education Centres in the State Cater to the tribal population covering about 2032 villages/hamlets.

## Conclusion

The education scenario in tribal population of Andhra Pradesh is a cause of great concern are requires careful area based planning with all out efforts to improve adult literacy, universal enrolment and better retention. Non-formal education centres need to be established to tribal hamlets which do not have schools. It is also important to maintain contact, with the small number of girls who do reach high school to use them as models for other girls in the community.

**Table—6.4 Enrolment Ratio in Classes VI—VII (1993-94) Scheduled Tribes**

| | | *Classes (VI—VII) (11-13 Yrs.)* | | |
|---|---|---|---|---|
| *Sl. No.* | *Districts* | *Boys* | *Girls* | *Total* |
| 1 | 2 | 3 | 4 | 5 |
| 1. | Srikakulam | 36.30 | 11.78 | 23.97 |
| 2. | Vizianagaram | 33.41 | 12.18 | 22.79 |
| 3. | Visakhapatnam | 40.96 | 14.24 | 27.77 |
| 4. | East Godavari | 33.07 | 23.54 | 28.31 |
| 5. | West Godavari | 39.73 | 26.82 | 33.29 |
| 6. | Krishna | 43.97 | 21.00 | 32.67 |
| 7. | Guntur | 40.07 | 16.42 | 28.42 |
| 8. | Prakasam | 39.37 | 16.31 | 28.01 |
| 9. | Nellore | 24.52 | 15.31 | 19.96 |
| 10. | Kurnool | 54.53 | 18.03 | 36.72 |

*(Table Contd.)*

| 1 | 2 | 3 | 4 | 5 |
|---|---|---|---|---|
| 11. | Anantapur | 52.24 | 20.45 | 36.78 |
| 12. | Cuddapah | 54.65 | 22.36 | 38.87 |
| 13. | Chittoor | 48.82 | 27.81 | 38.50 |
| 14. | Hyderabad | 105.86 | 75.95 | 91.42 |
| 15. | Ranga Reddy | 41.51 | 17.72 | 29.98 |
| 16. | Medak | 41.25 | 6.65 | 24.21 |
| 17. | Nizamabad | 32.64 | 6.12 | 19.12 |
| 18. | Mahabubnagar | 26.71 | 5.74 | 16.37 |
| 19. | Nalgonda | 37.03 | 7.99 | 22.79 |
| 20. | Warangal | 36.35 | 11.25 | 24.04 |
| 21. | Khammam | 35.24 | 14.87 | 25.26 |
| 22. | Karimnagar | 33.55 | 8.59 | 21.16 |
| 23. | Adilabad | 50.94 | 17.37 | 34.33 |
| | Andhra Pradesh | 38.83 | 14.90 | 27.02 |

Source: DSE.

**Table—6.5 Rural and Urban Population India Vs. A.P.**

| *S. No.* | *India/A.P.* | *Rural population (in lakhs)* | *Urban population (in lakhs)* | *per cent of urban population to total population* |
|---|---|---|---|---|
| 1. | India | 6286.91 | 2176.11 | 25.73 |
| 2. | Andhra Pradesh | 486.21 | 178.87 | 26.89 |

**Table—6.6 Distribution of Scheduled Tribes population 1991 India Vs. A.P.**

| *S. No.* | *India/A.P.* | *Scheduled Tribes population* | *per cent of St population to total population* |
|---|---|---|---|
| 1. | India | 67758380 | 8.08 |
| 2. | Andhra Pradesh | 4199481 | 6.31 |

*Source:* EFA—NIEPA.

**Table—6.7 Literacy Rates of Andhra Pradesh (Caste Wise)**

| *S. No.* | *Caste* | *Male* | *Female* | *Total* |
|---|---|---|---|---|
| 1. | ALL | 55.13 | 32.72 | 44.09 |
| 2. | SC | 41.88 | 20.92 | 31.59 |
| 3. | ST | 25.25 | 8.68 | 17.16 |

*Source:* State Council for Educational Research and Training (SCERT).

**Table—6.8 Drop—Out Rates—General (1993-94)**

| | | *Classes I—IV* | | |
|---|---|---|---|---|
| *Sl. No.* | *Districts* | *Boys* | *Girls* | *Total* |
| **1** | **2** | **3** | **4** | **5** |
| 1. | Srikakulam | 66.06 | 76.74 | 70.87 |
| 2. | Vizianagaram | 70.29 | 79.19 | 74.32 |
| 3. | Visakhapatnam | 63.67 | 71.96 | 67.46 |
| 4. | East Godavari | 52.79 | 61.05 | 56.85 |
| 5. | West Godavari | 64.93 | 71.09 | 67.91 |
| 6. | Krishna | 64.20 | 68.19 | 66.10 |
| 7. | Guntur | 63.59 | 71.16 | 67.21 |
| 8. | Prakasam | 72.33 | 80.03 | 75.82 |
| 9. | Nellore | 70.24 | 75.80 | 72.77 |
| 10. | Kurnool | 74.24 | 79.76 | 76.49 |
| 11. | Anantapur | 70.51 | 77.47 | 73.53 |
| 12. | Cuddapah | 67.12 | 75.71 | 70.92 |
| 13. | Chittoor | 57.19 | 62.79 | 56.52 |
| 14. | Hyderabad | 35.02 | 29.51 | 32.22 |
| 15. | Ranga Reddy | 62 11 | 60.11 | 61.51 |

*(Table Contd.)*

| 1 | 2 | 3 | 4 | 5 |
|---|---|---|---|---|
| 16. | Medak | 70.76 | 74.16 | 72.05 |
| 17. | Nizamabad | 68.56 | 69.27 | 68.83 |
| 18. | Mahabubnagar | 77.36 | 75.54 | 76.70 |
| 19. | Nalgonda | 68.16 | 73.96 | 70.60 |
| 20. | Warangal | 70.71 | 70.61 | 70.67 |
| 21. | Khammam | 69.55 | 73.05 | 71.04 |
| 22. | Karimnagar | 63.71 | 69.91 | 66.36 |
| 23. | Adilabad | 64.46 | 59.65 | 62.89 |
| | Andhra Pradesh | 65.98 | 70.25 | 67.81 |

*Source:* DSE.

**Table—6.9 Drop—Out Rates—Scheduled Tribes (1993-94)**

| | | *Classes I—VII* | | |
|---|---|---|---|---|
| *Sl No.* | *Districts* | *Boys* | *Girls* | *Total* |
| 1 | 2 | 3 | 4 | 5 |
| 1. | Srikakulam | 86.04 | 93.84 | 89.20 |
| 2. | Vizianagaram | 79.97 | 91.45 | 85.22 |
| 3. | Visakhapatnam | 84.42 | 83.99 | 84.31 |
| 4. | East Godavari | 88.96 | 89.57 | 89-55 |
| 5. | West Godavari | 82.28 | 88.01 | 84.90 |
| 6. | Krishna | 68.32 | 83.55 | 75.36 |
| 7. | Guntur | 83.04 | 91.15 | 86.45 |
| 8. | Prakasam | 84.83 | 92.06 | 88.18 |
| 9. | Nellore | 86.86 | 91.53 | 89.07 |
| 10. | Kurnool | 73.64 | 87.37 | 79.09 |
| 11. | Anantapur | 74.59 | 86.88 | 79.66 |

*(Table Contd.)*

| 1 | 2 | 3 | 4 | 5 |
|---|---|---|---|---|
| 12. | Cuddapah | 75.88 | 84.13 | 79.04 |
| 13. | Chittoor | 72.73 | 80.89 | 76.25 |
| 14. | Hyderabad | 22.08 | 38.31 | 29.53 |
| 15. | Ranga Reddy | 74.61 | 84.03 | 78.41 |
| 16. | Medak | 81.46 | 94.07 | 85.25 |
| 17. | Nizamabad | 86.62 | 94.76 | 89.03 |
| 18. | Mahabubnagar | 88.34 | 94.77 | 90.27 |
| 19. | Nalgonda | 86.68 | 93.10 | 88.51 |
| 20. | Warangal | 82.25 | 92.49 | 86.39 |
| 21. | Khammam | 81.87 | 87.99 | 84.21 |
| 22. | Karimnagar | 85.13 | 93.89 | 88.26 |
| 23. | Adilabad | 70.04 | 84.49 | 75.34 |
| | Andhra Pradesh | 82.06 | 89.20 | 84.72 |

*Source:* ESE

Pupil teacher ratio at the all India level was 42 and 37 in 1990-91 at the primary level respectively. It was 53 in Andhra Pradesh at Primary level and 47 at the Middle level/Sr. basis school. Here also there are large interstate variation. It was 15 in Sikkim and at the Uttar Pradesh level Mizoram and Manipur with 14 had the best ratio where Karnataka had the worst ratio of 54.

# 7

# Impact of Education

As examined, the existing facilities and its requirement, it is found that there is wide gap in the educational facilities. This is clearly revealed as 14.74 per cent of the villages were only covered by schools at present. It is also found that the educational infrastructure such as teaching aids, laboratories, libraries, etc., at these schools are either inadequate or altogether absent, in some Dhebar (1961) and Ruth (1981) have hinted the need of equipment in schools of tribals areas. There is a provision to keep the medicines at schools and hostels to treat the ailing students in emergency, but the system of operation has not been found so effective. The syllabi of Xth and Intermediate levels have been treated as too heavy specifically in subjects like Mathematics, Science and Social studies. The single teacher schools (74.6 per cent of primary schools) are more in number and they have peculiar problems to run them properly. The average strength of primary school is 27.58 for 78 primary schools with 2,014 as the total enrolment. The enrolment in seven upper primary schools is 1,370, average works out to 196.7 pupils per schools. Out of the four high schools, the total enrolment is 2328. The average enrolment is 282. The enrolment figures reiterate that the majority of the schools have excess of strength with no corresponding improvement in infrastructural facilities. The incidence of drop-out among the students at higher standards is so severe due to their socio-economic conditions such as poor economic conditions ignorance and reluctance of parents, family environment and unhappy school atmosphere as also found from the studies done by Srivastava (1969) and Joshi (1982).

It is felt that the environment in which the tribal children were brought up at times act as a deterrent to the development of their education. Srivastava (1968) commented that the tribal child who lives in an isolated and untouched with the currents of modern civilization can hardly assimilate the information about the nation. It would not create any attitude towards formal education. Sitting in the four walls of an institution is supposedly as a punishment for them.

However with the introduction of (Residential) Ashram schools/hostels and other package of incentives have made a substantial change in the attitude of tribal parents towards formal education. But they are dissatisfied with the way in which the incentives are being implemented. The importance of proper implementation of various facilities meant for the development of tribal education has also been emphasized by Singhi (1979) in his study. Tribal parents are resistant towards the policy of the Government to impose restriction of admission of locals (a boy or a girl) into a hostel or Ashram school, when this facility was located at one's village.

The location and communicational limitations have a direct bearing on the little or no interest of supervising authorities to visit the interior places. At times it becomes a great hindrance to the timely supply of provisions and other commodities to these places. In such situations, teachers more often become irregular. To overcome those problems Tippo (1979) has visualised the need to committed and efficient teachers to work in tribal areas. Tribal areas suffer from adequacy of transport, housing, and lack of higher education and health facilities. In such situation teaching staff lose interest to continue their stay in tribal areas.

The beliefs and values have been always a guiding force for the attitude and behaviour of a particular social group. Once these cultural elements institutionalised in their social milieu and they acquire meaning and become functional at a particular point of time. These values at times resist people to adopt and absorb new ways and orientations, in the attempts of their change and development. Likewise the value orientations of tribals in the area under study are reflected as deterrents in the extension of formal education into the following areas:

1. Agricultural activity
2. Traditional tribal hierarchy
3. Attitude towards girls' education
4. Weekly market (shandy)

As agricultural activity is family oriented and mostly it is at subsistence level, every family member has to contribute his/her mite in pooling the family resources. As for the opinion of the majority (75.60 per cent) of the tribal parents and (80.00 per cent) teachers, the school going tribal children sometimes have to assist their families in various agricultural operations. The daily wage for a worker per day in Coffee plantation is Rs. 8.00, it is so attractive for the tribal parents to make their children as wage earners in the process, they miss their classes.

There exists tribal hierarchy among different tribal communities. It is found that around 55 per cent of tribal students follow the traditional norms in the cultivation of friendship with the fellow students, although the new system of formal education advocates the values of equality and secularism. It is however, observed that these traditional norms lose its importance when he or she reaches the higher education.

The 'gender issue' is much predominant in their value orientations. About 95 per cent of the tribal parents are of the opinion that they show extra care for upbringing of their daughters. Physical movements need to be curtailed, once the daughters attain the stage of puberty. As a result, the girls' education as compared with boys, has been a low profile.

'Shandy' the weekly market plays a pivotal role in the lifeways of tribals. As for the opinion of the majority (65.80 per cent) of teaching staff, the school going children abscond and miss their classes and some times they return along with their parents to their villages on Shandy days. In this process, the tribals students will become irregular in attending the schools.

As examined, the level of change among the students is inversely related to their level of educational standards. With the rise in education and age and increase in physical and social mobility, this outlook gets changed on many aspects of life. The change in their attitude is directly related to the new socio-economic values in the society. According to them, change is inevitable. A few of them have informed that they have started educating the illiterate tribals to take to modern methods in observance of health and hygienic habits. It indicates that they clamour for change.

Although the students at primary school prefer to make friendship with the students those belong to their communities and their villages, they change their attitude and treat the traditional behaviour as meaningless, when they enter into high school and above levels. The secular traits like intelligence, nature of hard working, helpful attitude and leadership are considered important for the students to come closer. This implies that the impact of formal schooling is to develop in them to adopt the modern values in place of their traditional values. To them the school has been turned out an agent of change. Ambast (1970) and Mutatkar (1976) came out with a view from their studies that formal education would act an agency of change.

Exposure to mass media has become a part of their life. Students seek to enjoy in witnessing cinemas mostly during vacations. Although the students belonging to interior villages are used to visiting cinemas, frequency is more among the students studying at Paderu and Hukumpet. Videos run twice a day at these places. Next to cinema, radio and newspaper have been playing an important role in educating and entertaining the students. News, songs and politics are treated to be their interesting features. Reading of Newspaper has been confined to the students of Xth and Intermediate classes. There is a significant association between the periodicity of reading newspaper with its availability and the level of educational qualification of the student. Mostly the students intend to look Newspaper for advertisements, employment news and political aspects.

There is no political activism among the students. However a few students participated in processions and rallies and attended meetings of different political parties such as Congress (I), Communist Party, BJP and Telugu Desam in the Agency Area. This has happened only on the advice of their elders but not on their initiative.

Changes have also percolated into the role relations of family. Although the parents play a dominant role, the adolescent boys and girls do go against the decision of the parents, in case their consent is not properly sought about the issues concerned to them.

Although the education has made inroads into the social life of students, its degree of influence and impact is dissimilar between the two sexes. However, the blind beliefs and practices are very much persistent in the area of religion in some quarters, the students rejected the concept of fatalism and accept the human endeavour as the prime determinant in shaping the destinies of people.

The same trend has been witnessed in the case of stagnation among the students. Although the rate of enrolment in different levels of educational institutions has been so high, there is no corresponding improvement in the infrastructural facilities. Nevertheless the Ashram school sand hostels are flooded with exceeding number of students sans with necessary accommodation, working equipment and other facilities. Single teacher schools and the schools located at interior areas are beset with peculiar problems.

Although there is no persistent resistance from the tribal parents to send their children to schools, there are some physical, socio-economic and cultural constraints that impede the extension of education. Policy limitation for admission of tribal children into Ashram schools and hostels are also causing much discouragement to many of the tribal parents. There is a change in the attitude and behaviour of students about the different aspects of life situation. It is shown that there is a greater accent on their socio-economic development. And their aspirations have increased, modern values have set in, and attachment to certain traditional values has started declining. But the tribal parents display their helplessness as the educated children are not getting employment after education.

The evaluation of Integrated Tribal Development Projects. Conducted by Programme Evaluation Organisation, Planning Commission Govt. of India, New Delhi in February 1987 reports that in Paderu block due to increased educational facilities as tangible signs of impact of the ITDPs in 82-83 as compared to 1975-76. The nontangible signs which according to them were:

*(i)* increased social and economic awareness amongst the tribals;

*(ii)* acceptance of modern technology and approaches to development by them;

*(iii)* going in for jobs and professions which were totally new to the tribals; and

*(iv)* increased consciousness of their ethnic cultural position in the society.

However, according to the Project Officer, side by side with the emergence of the positive, non-tangible signs mentioned, certain other non-tangible signs had become discernible which were of a negative character. There were:—

*(i)* The emergence of a feeling of superiority amongst the educated tribals vis-a-vis other tribals and the rise of a class amongst tribals themselves who exploited other tribals.

*(ii)* A certain degree of root-lessness amongst the educated tribals, especially those who had got their education in the christian missionary schools and governmental welfare hostels and who would not like to return to their tribal moorings but at the same time did not find jobs and employment openings of the white-collor variety; and

The two important reasons identified by selected Project Officers for these negative non-tangible signs of impact were *(a)* that the rate of exposure of the tribals to non-tribals cultural environment was faster that what the tribals could absorb and *(b)* the spread of education amongst the tribals (mainly because of missionary schools) was faster than the growth and opening up of new employment opportunities for them. Both these developments were reported to be contributing to a socio-economic undercurrent of restlessness amongst the tribals. In view of these reported tendencies of social unrest among the tribals it may be worthwhile to re-examine the nature and type of educational facilities to be provided to the tribals had as to whether the focus of education amongst tribals could be shifted and greater emphasis placed on imparting of technical training in suitable crafts and trades so that when tribal boys and girls come out of these schools they get locally absorbed instead of having to face an environment totally new to them and where in they may take a long period to adjust and settle down.

In 1969 Naik produced an important book on the impact of education on the Bhils (Research Programmes Committee, Planning Commission, New Delhi). Working on data from the Dhar and Jhabua districts of Madhya Pradesh, he traced the impact of education on family and kinship, leadership, occupational patterns and community obligations. He demonstrated that different facets of life are differently affected by education. People are not attracted to education if it does not bring quick economic advantages. It has promoted greater adherence to the traditional code of the community and encouraged greater participation in panchayati raj as well as reformist movements.

Srivastava (Education and Modernisation, Patna University, 1968) dealt with education and modernisation among the Munda and the Oraon of Ranchi. For modernisation he selected mobility, empathy, rationality, participation, achievement motivation and communication as the basic indices. On each of these indices, the scores have been calculated. The study has been enriched by case studies and careful use of statistics. The role of education as an important factor of modernisation has been sought to be examined against the background of a control sample.

Another significant doctoral work on tribal education in Bihar has been done by Toppo herself a tribal (Education Then and Now among the Oraon). She has analysed the traditional mechanisms of education, modern school system run by the government and the missionaries and their impact on the tribals in Ranchi district.

Education is one of the mediators between the tribal social system and factors of change. In the long run, it enables children to adjust to the demands of modern life. The pattern of this adjustment covered family health, social and emotional aspects of Adivasi students in Ranchi district (Nomani 1965) which has been analysed on the basis of 200 samples drawn from male and female students. Not much difference was found in the adjustment of male and female students. College boys are superior to school boys in the matter of family adjustments. However, social adjustment with outside elements were not very satisfactory.

The role of education in promoting the occupational mobility of the tribals (Nambissan, 1983) has been examined in respect of Bhils of Rajasthan. The author took care to take into account the nature and magnitude of inequality of educational opportunity between tribal and non-tribal community. It was seen that compared to the Brahmin households the tribals were educationally backward and with better economic status and easier access to the school. The economic constraints were most acute in the age group 12 to 16. People who were exposed to outside influence through entering into service had entered professions having higher status. Education become viable in respect of educational mobility only after completion of middle school. It is necessary to analyse the tribal situation in the context of changes taking place in and around the tribal areas.

Education has been hailed to be the most important instrument, say, even the weapon, in this struggle of the tribal people against exploitation, domination and expropriation including land alienation. Education also equips them from developing self-management and self-regulation competency. There has been the right emphasis on spread of education among the Scheduled Tribes by the State, especially since independence. Literacy has definitely improved from census to census, though some unexpected findings make us sit up for further concerted effort. For example, Prof. Roy Burman points out that between 1961 and 1971 out of 258 districts, where the tribal people constituted one per cent or more of the population, in 36 districts the literacy rate had actually declined; in 69 districts it had increased only nominally (less than 0.02 per cent), and in 153 districts it had increased substantially (more than 0.02 per cent). He notes the alarming fact that the States where the literacy rate had registered a fall are ones where tribals had been in cultural contact for a long time. Then he comes across a 'spectacular fact':

Some of the tribes, which had shown a decline it literacy rates during 1961-71, has also registered a rapid spread of higher education. For instance, while in the case of the Bhumij of Bihar, the literacy rate declined from 11.81 per cent in 1961 to 10.36 per cent in 1971, the percentage of matriculates and above among the literates went up from 1.3 to 4.06. The incongruence between the spread of literacy and that of higher education among many tribes seems to be a function of incipient (or, crystallised among some) stratification within the tribal communities. (Roy Burman, 1985: view in brackets added).

The intra-tribal differentiation of access to educational opportunities is in addition to the inter-tribal differentiation of access to educational opportunities, scholarships, admissions in professional institutions, and based upon this differentiated access to education, also inequities access and eligibility for job opportunities, although legally all the Scheduled Tribes have equal access to job and educational opportunities. The tables given will provide the lee-way we have to make up in the field of education among the Scheduled Tribes. (Tables IV and V). It will be clearly seen from the tables given that in enrolment ratio in 1986-87 of girl students among the Scheduled Tribes population, Rajasthan (30.83) and Karnataka (21.42) are among the lowest, and Madhya Pradesh (52.88), Bihar (52.70) and even West Bengal (57.03) had not yet fared well in the enrolment ratio of girls. It is interesting to note that in Assam (109.65), Sikkim (117.29) and, above all, in Daman and Diu and Goa (188.51) the enrolment ratio of girls in 1986-87 has gone beyond hundred and in one Union Territory, it has almost doubled in proportion among the Scheduled Tribes.

**Table—7.1 Literacy Rates—1971 and 1981 Scheduled Tribes in TSP States/Union Territories**
***(States/UTs Ranked by Total ST Population)***

| *Name of State/UT* | *1971* | | | *1981* | | |
|---|---|---|---|---|---|---|
| | *Persons* | *Males* | *Females* | *Persons* | *Males* | *Females* |
| | *(1)* | *(2)* | *(3)* | *(4)* | *(5)* | *(6)* |
| Madhya Pradesh | 7.62 | 13.5* | 2.18* | 10.68* | 17.74* | 3.60* |
| Orissa | 9.46* | 16.38 | 2.58* | 13.96* | 23.27* | 4.76* |
| Bihar | 11.64 | 18.45 | 4.85 | 16.99 | 26.17 | 7.75 |
| Maharashtra | 11.74 | 19.06 | 4.4.21* | 22.29 | 32.38 | 11.94 |
| Gujarat | 14.12 | 21.83 | 6.15 | 21.14 | 30.41 | 11.64 |
| Rajasthan | 6.47* | 12.03* | 0.49* | 10.27* | 18.85* | 1.20* |
| Andhra Pradesh | 5.34* | 8.33* | 2.13 | 7.82* | 12.02* | 3.46* |
| West Bengal | 8.92* | 14.49* | 3.09* | 13.21* | 21.16* | 5.01* |
| Assam | 26.03 | 34.62 | 17.16 | Census not held | | |
| Karnataka | 14.85 | 21.71 | 7.67 | 20.14 | 29.96 | 10.03 |
| Tripura | 15.03 | 23.60 | 5.76 | 23.07 | 33.46 | 12.27 |
| Tamil Nadu | 9.02* | 13.34* | 4.48* | 20.46 | 26.71 | 14.00 |
| Manipur | 28.71 | 38.64 | 18.87 | 39.74 | 48.88 | 30.35 |
| Kerala | 25.72 | 32.01 | 19.40 | 31.79 | 37.52 | 26.02 |
| Uttar Pradesh | 14.59 | 22.51 | 15.58 | 20.45 | 31.22 | 8.69 |
| Himachal Pradesh | 15.89 | 26.25 | 5.53 | 25.93 | 38.75 | 12.82 |
| Sikkim | STs not specified | | | 33.13 | 43.10 | 22.37 |
| A & N Islands | 17.85 | 24.14 | 11.10 | 31.11 | 38.43 | 23.24 |
| Goa, Daman & Diu | 12.73 | 20.33 | 5.08 | 26.48 | 33.65 | 18.89 |
| India | 13.30* | 17.63* | 4.85* | 16.35* | 24.52* | 8.05* |

Including Non-TSP States/UTs

**Table—7.2 Literacy Rates 1971 and 1981—General Population in TSP States/Union Territories (States/UTs Ranged by Total ST Population)**

| *Name of State/UT* | | *1971* | *1981* | *1991* | *(7 Yrs. & above)* | |
|---|---|---|---|---|---|---|
| | | *Persons* | *Persons* | *Persons* | *Males* | *Females* |
| Madhya Pradesh* | (12.0) | 22.14 | 27.87 | 43.45 | 57.43 | 28.39 |
| Orissa* | (5.9) | 26.18 | 34.23 | 48.55 | 62.37 | 34.40 |
| Bihar* | (5.8) | 19.94 | 26.20 | 38.54 | 52.63 | 23.10 |
| Maharashtra* | (5.8) | 39.18 | 47.18 | 63.05 | 74.84 | 50.51 |
| Gujarat* | (4.8) | 35.79 | 43.70 | 60.91 | 72.54 | 48.50 |
| Rajasthan* | (4.2) | 19.07 | 24.38 | 38.81 | 55.07 | 20.84 |
| Andhra Pradesh* | (3.2) | 24.57 | 29.94 | 45.11 | 56.24 | 33.71 |
| West Bengal* | (3.1) | 33.20 | 40.94 | 57.72 | 67.24 | 47.15 |
| Assam* | (2.2) | 28.15 | Census not held | 53.42 | 62.34 | 43.70 |
| Karnataka* | (1.8) | 31.52 | 38.46 | 55.98 | 67.25 | 44.34 |
| Tripura | | 30.98 | 41.12 | 60.39 | 70.08 | 50.01 |
| Tamil Nadu | | 39.46 | 46.76 | 63.72 | 74.88 | 52.29 |
| Manipur | | 32.91 | 41.35 | 60.96 | 72.98 | 48.64 |
| Kerala | | 60.42 | 70.42 | 90.59 | 94.45 | 86.93 |
| Uttar Pradesh | | 21.70 | 27.16 | 41.71 | 55.35 | 26.02 |
| Himachal Pradesh | | 31.96 | 42.48 | 63.54 | 74.57 | 52.46 |
| Sikkim | | 17.74 | 34.05 | 56.53 | 64.34 | 47.23 |
| India | (52.3) | 29.45 | 36.23 | 52.11 | 63.86 | 39.42 |
| Tribal Majority States | | | | | | |
| Arunachal Pradesh | | 11.29 | 20.79 | 41.22 | 51.10 | 29.37 |
| Meghalaya* | (1.1) | 29.49 | 34.08 | 48.26 | 51.57 | 44.78 |
| Mizoram | | 53.79 | 59.88 | 81.23 | 84.06 | 78.09 |
| Nagaland | | 27.40 | 42.57 | 61.30 | 66.09 | 55.72 |

*Note:* * refers to States with more than one million STs in 1981. Figures in brackets refer to ST population in 1981 in millions.

**Table—7.3 Enrolment Ratios at Primary Level (Class I—V or 6-11 years) of ST Students 1984-85 to 1986-87 and of All Students as in 1986-87 in TSP States/Union Territories**

| *Name of State/UT* | *(States/UTs ranked by Total ST Population)* | | | | | |
|---|---|---|---|---|---|---|
| | *Enrolment Ratios ST Students* | | | | | |
| | *Boys* | | | *Girls* | | |
| | *1984-85* | *1985-86* | *1986-87* | *1984-85* | *1985-86* | *1986-87* |
| Madhya Pradesh | 86.5 | 98.49 | 99.02 | 40.8 | 48.93 | 52.88 |
| Orissa | 98.6 | 107.11 | 106.86 | 47.7 | 49.41 | 52.68 |
| Bihar | 107.8 | 116.25 | 106.33 | 54.3 | 59.91 | 52.70 |
| Maharashtra | 150.2 | 118.52 | 122.83 | 101.9 | 81.05 | 86.13 |
| Gujarat | 132.4 | 124.50 | 134.79 | 86.8 | 87.55 | 95.91 |
| Rajasthan | 81.7 | 104.21 | 103.85 | 21.9 | 29.83 | 30.83 |
| Andhra Pradesh | 147.3 | 119.67 | 124.85 | 87.9 | 69.69 | 74.18 |
| West Bengal | 73.6 | 93.43 | 93.72 | 46.9 | 64.90 | 57.03 |
| Assam | 92.3 | 127.58 | 127.77 | 69.7 | 110.55 | 109.83 |
| Karnataka | 132.7 | 72.71 | 28.82 | 100.8 | 55.11 | 21.42 |
| Tripura | 133.0 | 159.54 | 156.78 | 82.3 | 103.37 | 101.75 |
| Tamil Nadu | 112.2 | 102.43 | 107.24 | 91.3 | 82.45 | 82.78 |
| Manipur | 144.0 | 177.63 | 170.06 | 116.0 | 143.15 | 137.31 |
| Kerala | 124.5 | 120.44 | 23.09 | 119.03 | 112.41 | 113.65 |
| Uttar Pradesh | 14.1 | 109.29 | 111.28 | 9.1 | 72.43 | 73.49 |
| Himachal Pradesh | 156.7 | 102.22 | 111.00 | 82.8 | 66.10 | 74.89 |
| Sikkim | N.A. | 148.01 | 145.02 | N.A. | 113.82 | 117.29 |
| A & N Islands | 119.9 | 97.02 | 93.51 | 91.1 | 81.54 | 77.22 |
| Daman & Diu (incl. Goa) | 208.3 | 186.25 | 211.99 | 175.7 | 168.24 | 188.51 |
| **Total** | **100.49** | **109.77** | **109.62** | **56.16** | **62.17** | **63.79** |

*Source:* Selected Educational Statistics, Department of Educational, Government of India.

**Table—7.4 Enrolment Ratios at Primary Level (Class I—V or 6-11 years) of ST Students 1984-85, 1986-87 and of All Students as in 1987-87 in TSP States/Union Territories**

| *Name of State/UT* | *Enrolment Ratios ST Students* | | | | | |
|---|---|---|---|---|---|---|
| | *Total ST Students* | | | *Enrolment Ratios all Students 1986-87* | | |
| | *1984-85* | *1985-86* | *1986-87* | *Boys* | *Girls* | *Total* |
| Madhya Pradesh | 64.5 | 74.33 | 76.58 | 117.29 | 75.81 | 97.12 |
| Orissa | 74.1 | 78.33 | 80.00 | 111.74 | 78.04 | 95.04 |
| Bihar | 81.9 | 88.37 | 79.82 | 107.45 | 52.75 | 80.41 |
| Maharashtra | 126.9 | 100.23 | 104.95 | 126.24 | 108.90 | 117.79 |
| Gujarat | 110.3 | 106.45 | 115.78 | 125.99 | 97.97 | 112.29 |
| Rajasthan | 52.8 | 68.23 | 68.49 | 109.56 | 46.73 | 79.14 |
| Andhra Pradesh | 118.5 | 94.87 | 99.73 | 116.37 | 86.87 | 101.65 |
| West Bengal | 60.7 | 79.20 | 74.97 | 134.94 | 96.52 | 115.84 |
| Assam | 81.4 | 119.36 | 119.10 | 97.19 | 82.78 | 90.22 |
| Karnataka | 117.2 | 64.00 | 25.17 | 104.45 | 85.92 | 95.30 |
| Tripura | 107.4 | 131.89 | 129.72 | 139.21 | 85.82 | 112.96 |
| Tamil Nadu | 102.1 | 92.63 | 95.25 | 138.25 | 122.36 | 130.61 |
| Manipur | 129.8 | 160.58 | 153.87 | 127.82 | 105.78 | 107.20 |
| Kerala | 122.0 | 116.88 | 118.44 | 108.58 | 105.78 | 107.20 |
| Uttar Pradesh | 11.7 | 91.98 | 93.67 | 96.49 | 53.41 | 76.22 |
| Himachal Pradesh | 117.5 | 84.43 | 93.67 | 118.87 | 103.25 | 11.16 |
| Sikkim | N.A. | 131.12 | 131.24 | 141.30 | 115.18 | 128.42 |
| Daman & Diu (incl. Goa) | 192.0 | 177.35 | 200.34 | 135.67 | 123.10 | 129.43 |
| **Total** | **79.07** | **87.00** | **87.17** | **111.83** | **79.21** | **95.96** |

*Source:* Selected Educational Statistics Department of Education.

N.A.Means not Available.

States (Arunachal Pradesh, Meghalaya, Mizoram and Nagaland) had made substantial progress in literacy as compared to 1981. Mizoram has attained the second highest literacy, among females, next only to Kerala. Nagaland has recorded higher literacy among the total population, among males and among females than the all India average. Except Arunachal Pradesh, which started rather late in the development process, all the other tribal majority States have higher female literacy than the all India average. Not to be outdone, Arunachal Pradesh has made spectacular progress in the 1981-91 decade by outstripping Bihar and Uttar Pradesh in both total literacy and females literacy. Though in the field of higher education, the Nishis and Miris are yet to catch up with the Apa Tanis, their progress was nevertheless remarkable compared to the Gonds and other tribal groups of peninsular and central India. (Von Furer-Haimendort, 1985).

One major factor contributing to lower level of education and literacy is the large scale of drop-outs, even at the primary level, among the Scheduled Tribe pupils as compared to all the pupils taken together.

**Table—7.5 Primary Level Drop-outs in 1983-84 (in per cent)**

| *State* | *ST Pupils* | *All Pupils* |
|---|---|---|
| Bihar | 76.52 | 66.34 |
| Orissa | 73.38 | 42.81 |
| Maharashtra | 71.87 | 51.50 |
| Gujarat | 71.28 | 47.84 |
| Madhya Pradesh | 67.39 | 51.84 |
| Rajasthan | 63.32 | 48.93 |

*Source:* Ministry of Welfare (1989: 52).

Moreover, several research projects sponsored by the Ministry of Welfare, Government of India, have brought out the dismal findings which are, unfortunately, based on well known trends:

1. The impact of education has not been felt, as it has not led to employment or self-employment.
2. The infrastructure available in schools in the TSP areas is grossly inadequate.
3. Coverage of population and area by schools is inadequate.
4. Economic factors are primarily responsible for preventing the ST children from going to schools.
5. Even within the STs, drop-outs are higher among the lower socio-economic strata.
6. The teachers are not sufficiently trained and motivated.
7. Agriculture and other vocations should form a part of the curriculum.
8. Proportionately, ashram/residential schools attract a large number of children as compared to normal schools.
9. The ST parents are often unaware of the potential benefits of education.

Added to these problems, we have to consider the question of the medium of instruction which is a great deterrent to retention of enrolled children, even if the parents are motivated to send their children to school. Similarly, there is the problem of cultural dissonance between the primers and textbooks for the young children at school and the cultural values, institutions and symbols in the tribal areas. Whenever the tribal people themselves have taken up the literacy drive in their own tribal medium—and sometimes also with a contrived script—as among the Santal with O1 Chiki script or among the Ho with a new script through the Adi-Samaj Organisation, the result has been always spectacular. The literacy and education movement merges with a cultural revitalisation movement. Among many tribal groups in central and eastern India, the educated elites, especially of the younger generation, have set up movement through registered or unregistered societies for such educational progress and amendment to their customary laws in line with the modern age. It is a pity that the government subsidies and encouragement do not reach these endogenous movements for educational development. (Mahapatra, 1982).

Professor Von Furer-Haimendorf has highlighted the differential progress achieved by the tribal groups in the North-Eastern States in general and in Arunachal Pradesh in particular, He elaborates:

The spectacular progress of Apa Tanis, Nishis, Sherdukpens and other tribes in Arunachal Pradesh within the past thirty years establishes beyond any doubt the capacity of Indian tribal populations to attain the same level of education, economic efficiency, and political maturity as any other ethnic group within the wider Indian society.

The fact that the enlightened policy of the Government of India vis-a-vis the hill-men of the north-eastern frontier regions could bring about so rapid a transformation of archaic and in some respect barbaric societies highlights the failure of the tribal policies of the governments of many of the Indian States. For some of these governments provides its aboriginal tribes with facilities similar to those available in Arunachal Pradesh, nor do they effectively assist them in their struggle for an existence free of exploitation and domination by powerful vested interests . . . The tribesmen of Arunachal Pradesh were fortunate that at the time when their isolation finally came to an end they benefited from a liberal policy framed by the distinguished a anthropologist Verrier Elwin and powerfully supported by the then Prime Minister, Jawaharlal Nehru. Thus tribes such as Apa tanis and Gonds—to take only two typical examples—stand today at the opposite ends of a spectrum which reflects the various possibilities for the development of tribal societies; while the Apa Tanis and clearly set on an upward path, the Gonds are threatened by apparently irreversible decline into their fortunes. (Von Furer-Haimendorf, 1985: 311-312).

Professor Sachchidananda adds another dimension of understanding of this enigma. He asserts:

In the north-east, education preceded development of their economy which even to this day continues to be in the pre-agricultural stage. In middle India economic development has precedence over education which remained neglected for a long time. The difference in the two areas is noticeable. The tribals in the north-east are ready for a leap forward in development based on the resources which have remained under their command. In contrast the tribals in middle India are suffering on account of the adverse impact of development processes and are facing disorganisation on being rendered resourceless. (Sachichidananda, 1992).

This spectacular progress of the North-Eastern tribal majority States is, however, fraught with some lopsided development, which may lead to frustration and disaffection among the more deprived sections.

## Dr. B.D. Sharma Prognosticates

The level of education in these States is quite high but in their case the opportunities in the tertiary sector have also been rising at a very fast rate. Therefore, their system has been able to accommodate the young people so far. However the growth in their case has been skewed, not balanced which has distorted their economies. The primary sector in all these States is quite weak and the secondary sector is almost non-existent. It is only the tertiary sector which has grown and become outsized. This cannot be a self-sustaining system. . . It cannot be replicated where big numbers are involved. . . In fact, this provides one of the biggest motive forces for demand for establishment of smaller politico-administrative units. It is obvious that this cannot be continued indefinitely and contradictions are bound to arise sooner than later. This is already happening, for example in Bihar where the tribal population is large and the new opportunities for the educated youth cannot be found in the tertiary sector. In their case the potential. . . While the gains of reservation have accrued to home communities who were first to take advantage of education, the other groups are not finding it difficult to move up. (Sharma, 1986-87: 1977-78).

Though it is difficult to isolate education as a factor in social change, we may observe social changes that may have occurred among the literate and educated tribals and attribute them to education. Such studies, attempting to examine the social changes among the educated tribals and assessing the impact of education are very rare. However, one can make some observations from the study conducted by the present research scholar:

### *(i) Change in Tribal Economy*

The modern economic processes have invaded the tribal economy. The tribal markets have linked with wider markets. Tribals now not only produce for themselves but also for sale in the wider market. In Andhra Pradesh federations of forest cooperatives have been established and the tribals have undertaken the sale of minor forest products like tooth-sticks, seasonal fruits, Kendu leaves etc. These tribes, in turn, by fashionable and luxury goods that reach their fairly. All these show that the tribal economy is changing.

### *(ii) Change in Policy*

The traditional political activity of the tribals was confined to the institutions like the council of tribal elders, village head-man and village panchayat. The head of the community at the clan, village and territorial unit level was generally accepted as the head of the group and was honoured and obeyed. His office was hereditary and all power was with him and his descendants.

The introduction of the statutory panchayat and panchayati raj in the post-independence period have reduced the power of these traditional tribal institutions and have opened up the political process for participation of the tribals at local, state as well as national levels. A tribal has now a right to vote as well as seek election at all these levels. This, along with community development programme for tribal welfare and development, have provided opportunities for specialization and leadership among tribals.

### *(iii) Change in the Tribal Culture*

Whatever change education may have brought in, it is reflected only in the outer forms of culture, whose vital parts still remain largely unchanged. In other words, whereas dress, modes of living, economy and even some of the less important customs have changed to some extent, there is hardly any change in the social values and ethical codes". (Naik).

Education has in some way influenced the amount of bride towards a decrease. The educated are found to accept a lower bride-price than the non-educated boys. There is also a gradual consciousness in the people's attitude towards getting boy's consent for marriage (instances of getting girl's consent are very few)" (Naik, 1969). Recent studies of the tribal scholar (Desai and Pondor, 1974) and college (Shah and Thake, 1978) students in Gujarat, however, reveal that in matters of mate selection, a large majority of them both accept parental authority even though it may be against their choice. Only one-fourth of them would marry a person not approved by their parents if the person is very good. More or less a similar situation is revealed in the studies of the tribal school and college students done in Andhra Pradesh (CRDS, 1975).

Education is an important instrument of special change and modernisation. However, only one study (Choudhury, 1985) in this review has been directly focused on the theme. The study covered tribes belonging to different economic settings in North Bengal.

Ar. effort was made to examine the effect of education on occupation, family, marriage, religion and political life. The study showed that education had effect on various aspects of tribal life to varying extent. Educated tribals had more modern attitudes towards occupation, family, marriage, religion and politics. The educated of all categories did not favour the joint family or participation in common endeavours but considered education as an important means of social improvement.

There are not studies focused on the process of detribalisation which sometimes results from the educational process. It is also seen that the type of education given to tribal students alienates them from their own family and home and induces some sort of inferiority complex. The denigration of tribal culture in the school atmosphere is something which has to be guarded against. In this connection, it is necessary to have the perception of the beneficiaries regarding the effective implementation of educational programmes and the impact it has made on the life and culture of the tribals. It is necessary to know the extent to which the social distance between tribals and non-tribals has been bridged through education.

Many studies have brought out the phenomena of drop out, wastage and stagnation. In some states, steps have been taken to reduce the incidence of these ills. The success or otherwise of these measures need to be assessed. The stage has been reached at least in some areas where tribal education does no longer-grapple with first generation learners since in those areas education has had long standing. Whether teaching learning methods in those areas should be the same as in the case of first generation learners has got to be examined at some length. Studies of the impact of adult education should be made in different states so far as in touches the tribals. In the same way, scholars should examine the impact of non-formal and continuing education on tribal at different stages of socio-economic development.

In our country there are many pastoral tribal groups. They move from one area to another according to the exigencies of the season. Special educational experiments have been in operation to make education accessible to their children. The success of these efforts needs to be examined.

Ranchi is the cultural home of the Scheduled Tribes. Lakra has examined the impact of education in the Ranchi district in his Ph.D. work. The result of education has been phenomenal among the tribals. It has reduced land alienation. The tribal standard of living has been elevated. A rather unhappy situation has arisen among the tribals as a result of education. It is that they have developed a fascination or rather fondness for the English language. In this process they are intentionally forgetting their own dialect.

Ambasht has examined the existing system of education in the tribal area of Ranchi district with a view to understand the problems of education and gain a sense of direction for future.

The impact of education was, however seen in a number of changes in additional and material aspects of their culture which they had adopted. In the ideational aspect, the formal education had changed the attitude towards the way of life, the social aspiration and tribal culture.

Naik who is credited to have worked extensively among the tribals of Gujarat and Madhya Pradesh, has examined the impact of education of the Bhils. He has taken up for his study the Bhils of Dhar and Jhabua. He has examined the influence of education on family kinship marriage, leadership and the community as a whole. One very important question which Naik has taken for discussion is who gets educated. His answer to this question is that it is the upper level of tribal society which gets higher education. Naik very analytically argues to try some alternative educational models to bring a change among these people.

Vimal Shah and Tara Patel of Gujarat University have examined the impact of education from a structuralist point of view. In order to assess the impact of college education on tribal social structure. The authors have raised the question: who goes to college? On the strength of empirical data they argue that the benefit of education such as post-matric scholarships and residence facilities have been cornered by the upper strata of the scheduled tribes and schedule castes. Structurally speaking, the benefits of higher education have gone in favour of the higher segments of the tribal groups.

# 8

# Absenteeism, Stagnation and Wastage

## Introduction

Inspite of several measures undertaken by government and voluntary organisations the problem of absenteeism, stagnation and wastage is on the higher side among tribals. An attempt has been made in this chapter to find out the reasons for low attendance, drop-out and wastage from teachers and parents point of view.

## Examination Result, Causes of Poor Attendance and High Wastage

Very few studies have been carried out on the examination outcomes of tribal and deprived students. The five ICSSR surveys conducted in 1973 in Assam, Gujarat, Bihar, Tamil Nadu and Karnataka concluded that over 60 per cent SC/ST students felt that their home environment mitigated against their achievement orientation, and home background factors become more important as one moved vertically to the higher stages of education. These were also the causes of early leaving/dropping out from the school poor examination results. Nayar (1975) and Shah (1989) confirmed that the number of repeaters in the class increased with the level of the class. Similarly, it has been reported that dropping out rate among STs was higher at primary level. It decreased with increase in the class of study. Phadke and Shukla (1980) reported that as compared to commerce, the drop out rate was higher for arts faculty. Desai and Patel (1981) found that the percentage of dropout among girls was significantly higher than among boys as the tribal parents in need of assistance in their household or economic activities, withdraw the female children from schools immediately. Several other researchers have pointed out that SC/ST girls came for education in a very low proportion. On the contrary, some other studies have reported that the rate of enrolment of girls as well as total ST students is increasing satisfactorily. However, patel studies the time series enrolment rates for the period 1964 to 1980 and showed that about 25 to 50 per cent of the tribal girls enrolled in standard I dropped out at the very next stage of primary education. Srivastava and Joshi (1981) conclude that inadequate schools and poverty in the tribal region, insufficient learning material, language difficulty, inadequate schools, ignorance of parents, child labour and parents compulsion were the causes responsible for the non enrolment as well as dropping out of ST students from the schools.

Thus dropping out is one of the major reasons for slow progress of education among tribes. The poor economic condition, household activities, inadequate schools and traditional prejudices are the main causes responsible for it.

## Absenteeism, Stagnation and Wastage Psychological and Educational Causes of Absenteeism

Our schools are not providing for the children the type of education in which the children are interested.

Apart from the data obtained through the questionnaire issued to the teachers, structured interviews with parents, through informal discussions and observations the research scholar could discover some more reasons for the absenteeism of tribal children from schools.

Retention of a student in a particular grade for more than one year on account of unsatisfactory progress results in stagnation.

Parents complained that the teachers did not care to call their children to school. It was impossible for the parents to check whether their children had gone to school or not, they leave their homes early in the morning for their work. As discussed earlier in connection with enrolment of children, if parents pressed their children a little harder for regular attendance to school, there was the risk of children running away from their houses and the village.

### Stagnation

Stagnation is one of the most difficult problems in the primary stage and especially in the case of tribes. It greatly hinders their educational progress and development. Absenteeism led to stagnation and both naturally contributed to wastage.

### New Education Policy (Government of Andhra Pradesh, 1971)

Formerly stagnation used to occur due to lower achievement in the annual promotional examinations. But as per the Government Order Ms. No. 1781 of 27th November, 1971, the Government of Andhra Pradesh in the Education Department took a policy decision to abolish the system of detaining students on the basis of annual examinations in all classes of the primary and secondary stages; (except in classes 7 and 10). This decision has been taken with a view to minimising the high incidence of stagnation leading to wastage, especially in the primary stage. The Government ordered that all students should be promoted to the next higher classes in accordance with the new evaluation procedure except in the 7 and the 10 classes, where common and public examinations respectively were to be concluded.

The non-detention system does not mean promoting failed students indiscriminately. But it really means remedying the conditions which give rise to the need to detain students. It also means adoption of a system of effective and continuous testing and consequent application of remedial measures, so as to render annual detentions unnecessary. Abolition of detentions does not mean absence of examinations. New procedures are adopted to make evaluation a continuous and integral part of the educative process.

### Policy of Evaluation of Primary Stage (Classes I to IV)

There are oral, written and practical informal tests conducted by teachers every month. The results of these tests are entered systematically in the process cards specially devised for the purpose. Home assignments and class work also will be considered as part of evaluation. There will be no examinations for these classes at the end of each academic year. The evaluation procedure at the Vth class include the following:

1. Adoption of the prescribed pupil cumulative record for all students.
2. Adoption of the prescribed progress card which may be communicated to the parents or guardians regularly.
3. Administration of teacher made tests at the end of teaching of each unit of syllabus, the results of which shall be incorporated in the progress card.
4. In addition to the above, at the end of each quarter for each subject, one formal examination will be conducted covering the syllabus completed during the quarter. The test material and the guidelines developed by the State Council of Educational Research and Training and adopted in all schools for conducting these formal examinations. The results of these quarterly tests are also entered in the pupil's cumulative records.
5. There will be non-detaining common external examinations at the end of class five at the mandal level. The results of this examination are also entered in the pupil's cumulative record.

**Minimum Attendance for Classes and for Tests**

A minimum attendance is prescribed for students at the Primary and Secondary stages. For Primary stage the minimum attendance required to be put in by every student is 80 per cent and for the Secondary stage it is 90 per cent, a condition of 10 per cent of absence for exceptional and unavoidable reasons like prolonged illness, bereavement etc., is given. The authority for such condonation will vest with the Head Master only. However, in case where a student's performance in all the prescribed tests and examinations is satisfactory the attendance required can be further reduced to 60 per cent. For the purpose of assessing the performance of the student the average of all the tests administered to the students for each subject is taken any test or examinations is compulsory. In case any student fails to take any test or examination for unavoidable reasons the teachers of the school can administer the test or examination again. The performance at these tests need to be taken into consideration for promoting the student to the next higher class. But attendance at these tests or those re-administered is compulsory requirement for promotion to the next higher class.

From the above discussion of the new evaluation and promotion policy of the Government of Andhra Pradesh which is applicable to the schools under the sample taken for this study, it is evident that the criterion for promotion to the next higher class has shifted from the pupils achievement in the annual promotional examination to attendance. It is obvious that even under the new so-called no-detention policy, there will be stagnation in primary classes, occurring now not for low achievement but due to absenteeism.

The extent of stagnation among tribal children studying in the primary schools sampled for purpose of this study has been calculated according to following two methods. Firstly, the percentage of stagnation in every class has been calculated taking into consideration the number of detained students with reference to the total number of students on the rolls. In the second method the stagnation index is calculated by counting the number of students detained in different classes from the same batch of pupils from classes I to V during the period 1979-80 to 1983-84. The formula for calculation of the stagnation index applied is

$$100X \frac{1 - \text{Total optimum years}}{\text{Actual used years}}$$

Optimum years refer to the total number of years prescribed for completing the stage of education, while actual years refer to the number of years actually taken by the students to complete the primary stage of education.

For example, a batch of 100 children is admitted into the first standard during a given year. The duration of primary stage of education is five years from 1 to 5 classes. It is assumed that each child normally takes five years to complete the primary stage of education. The total number of optimum years of 100 students is five hundred. But in actual practice all students cannot complete the programme with the prescribed number of years due to the factor of stagnation. Of the 100 students 20 may take five years, while another 20 may take six years, thirty may taken seven years, ten may take eight years and the remaining 20 may take ten years to complete the primary education. The actually used years for the entire hundred students will be:

$$= 20 \times 5 + 20 \times 6 + 30 \times 7 + 10 \times 8 + 20 \times 10 = 710$$

$$\text{Index of stagnation} = 100 \times \frac{1 - 500}{710} = 29.58$$

The index of stagnation has been calculated separately for roadside and interior schools and for boys and girls under each category.

As stagnation takes place only on the basis of attendance it naturally reflects absenteeism. The stagnation index for tribal children studying both in the Roadside and Interior village schools is presented in Table—8.1.

**Table—8.1 Index of Stagnation**

| *Category of school* | *Boys* | *Girls* |
|---|---|---|
| Roadside | 33.33 | 55.36 |
| Interior | 38.69 | 58.53 |

From the above index of stagnation it is seen that stagnation is more prevalent in the interior villages, especially in the case of girls. Even in the interior villages schools where stagnation is high, compared to roadside villages, the extent of stagnation is higher in the case of girls.

The above index gives a picture of a batch of students passing from class 1 to 5.

The second report of the commission for Scheduled Castes and Scheduled Tribes has dealt extensively with the problem of stagnation.

Data were collected from the teachers working in the schools situated on roadsides and the interior, for corroboration of the reasons for non enrolment of children in schools.

**Table—8.2 Opinion of Teachers regarding Non-enrolment of Children**

*(Per cent)*

| | *Reasons for non enrolment* | *Teachers* |
|---|---|---|
| 1. | Students not interested | 34.5 |
| 2. | Poverty | 25.00 |
| 3. | Illiteracy of parents | 22.5 |
| 4. | Cumbersome existing norms for the admission into Ashram schools | 18.00 |

Teachers blamed the parents accusing them of lack of interest in sending their children to school. Of course poverty the classical reason, takes the second place. The common reason given both by parents and teachers is that the children themselves are not interested in education.

## Reasons for Absenteeism

Apart from the analysis of the absenteeism among tribal children the reasons given by their teachers and parents throw more light on the socio economic factors.

In order to pinpoint the extent of stagnation at a particular grade/level in case of both the sexes a close study of this factor has been undertaken. For this purpose average stagnation figures for a period of five year in each class have been collected from both roadside and interior village schools.

From the above figures it can be seen that the extent of stagnation is the highest in the first standard decreasing in the second and third. It increases slightly in the fourth and fifth classes in both categories of schools especially in the case of girls.

**Table—8.3 Extent of Stagnation both in Roadside and Interior Villages—Class-wise**

| | *I* | *II* | *III* | *IV* | *V* |
|---|---|---|---|---|---|
| *Category* | | | | | |
| Roadside | | | | | |
| : Boys | 24.8 | 17.7 | 16.8 | 17.8 | 17.00 |
| : Girls | 28.4 | 19.7 | 17.0 | 20.6 | 19.00 |
| *Interior* | | | | | |
| : Boys | 32.5 | 30.3 | 28.0 | 23.0 | 23.0 |
| : Girls | 32.2 | 29.9 | 28.9 | 28.0 | 24.9 |

## Reasons for Stagnation

There are several factors influencing the high incidence of stagnation among tribal children in primary, upper primary, and high schools. In this connection teachers mentioned several reasons falling under three categories, namely socio-economic, psychological and educational.

*(a)* Irregular attendance due to domestic work.

*(b)* Irregular studies and absence of educational atmosphere at home due to the illiteracy of parents.

*(c)* Uncogenial habitation and environment.

## Psychological Factors

*(d)* Low receptivity of students.

*(e)* Indifference of students towards education.

## Educational Factors

*(f)* Ill-equipped school

*(g)* Poor teaching

*(h)* Curriculum alien to their life needs.

## Parents reasons for Stagnation

| | | (Per cent) |
|---|---|---|
| 1. | Lack of educational guidance and congenial atmosphere at home. | 40.00 |
| 2. | Irregular attendance due to help in the household work | 35.30 |
| 3. | Younger age | 14.00 |
| 4. | Irregular attendance of teacher | 11.00 |

## Educational Factors

5. Ill-equipped school.
6. Poor teaching.
7. Curriculum alien to their life needs.

The socio-economic factors are dominant in the reasons for stagnation followed by psychological factors and educational factors. These are, of course, the reasons stated by the teachers. They naturally, tend to defend their role in education and blame socio-economic and psychological factors as responsible for stagnation. Though the educational factor Irrelevance of the curriculum to the life needs comes as their last preference it is very important item and needs immediate attention of policy framers and educational planners.

Under each category the items have been arranged according to their relative importance. However, most of these factors are not exclusive, as often one factor operates in combination with other factors. But this classification is attempted to pinpoint the broad areas and individual factors regarded as constraints and which need suitable remedial action to reduce educational retardation. According to the general classification, the socio-economic factors take precedence over the rest. The subsistence level of living makes every member of the tribal household an economic unit and school age children are no exception. They supplement the family income, however meagre it may be. In case children are sent to school, parents not only lose the earnings of their children but also have to incur additional expenditure on their feeding, clothing and to a certain extent for education. It is the situation in which the parents usually take away children especially girls so as to keep them at home for baby sitting or to keep a watch on standing crops or to graze the cattle.

It is commonly observed that the tribal children sometimes bring their younger brothers and sisters to school as their is nobody at home to look after the kids, resulting in the distraction of their attention from studies. Also their home environment is not congenial for doing their home assignments. They do not have any proper place to sit in, lighting, have poor and little or no persuasion of parents to attend to their studies at home. Further, children, living in habitations near tanks and forests, and tempted to go to collect roots, tubers and berries or go fishing. Even the parents accepted the fact that the home environment is not congenial for study on the part of their children. They seldom enquire about the progress of their children's studies. Whatever is learnt during the school time is forgotten during terminal holidays due to lack of follow-up at home.

From enquiries with the teachers, it was revealed that they did not persuade the parents to send their children to school. It was stated that parents do not send their children's schools. This requires the teachers to enlighten the parents about the importance of education of their children.

**Reasons for Stagnation according to Parents**

Besides teachers the reasons for stagnation of tribal children at the primary, upper primary and secondary stage were ascertained from the parents also through a structured interview.

The following reasons are given by parents.

**Table—8.4 Reasons for Stagnation according to Parents**

*(Per cent)*

| | *Reasons* | *Parents* |
|---|---|---|
| 1. | Lack of educational guidance and congenial atmosphere at home | 40.00 |
| 2. | Irregular attendance due to help in the household work | 35.30 |
| 3. | Indifference and lack of interest in education on the part of children | 14.00 |
| 4. | Indifference on teachers towards their children's education | 11.00 |

Parents blame their children for indifference to and lack of interest in studies. On the other part they do not own any responsibility for stagnation, while a good number of them attribute to their irregular attendance to school to domestic pressures or even carelessness which all result in failure in the examinations. Irregular attendance remains the most important reason for stagnation, even in the context of the new policy of the Government of Andhra Pradesh. The factors of irregular attendance, irregular studies, absence of educational atmosphere and congenial physical facilities at home due to illiteracy of parents were corroborated by the teachers also. Teachers blame both the parents and children for their indifference, while parents blame both children and teachers for the same reason. So, both parents and teacher blame children alike. The indifference of teachers towards the education of tribal children, as claimed by the parents, may be due to several factors. Most important of these is the posting of the teacher to the interior village which is considered by him to be a curse. He does not feel at home, due to absence of communication and other facilities like housing, provision of healthcare, lack of facilities for higher education for his children, lack of recreation etc. So, he lacks enthusiasm for the education of tribal children as his attention remains diverted to his personal problems. Especially in the interior villages the teachers show a discriminatory attitude to the tribal children. Tribal children are employed to do odd jobs like cleaning vessels, washing clothes etc. for the teachers. So, a child born to a disadvantaged family also becomes a disadvantaged individual. In single teacher schools it is different for the teacher to pay sufficient attention to the behaviour problems of tribal children.

## Wastage (Dropouts)

In the foregoing sections of this Chapter the nature, magnitude and reasons of absenteeism and stagnation have been discussed. These two factors are mostly responsible for wastage at primary level. Wastage is the most important factor contributing to the slow progress of tribal education.

Why the parent is not checking this wastage? He/she is a victim of the socio-economic and cultural environment. He is dependent on the occasional help of the children at home and on the farm and this leads to absenteeism. Absenteeism leads to missing of lessons, lack of adjustment coaching or guidance for home work. This situation leads to stagnation. Frequent failures of students make the parents realise the futility of their children continuing in school which, really does not cater to their life needs. So the parent finally withdraws the child from the school and looks for some gainful occupation for him.

There are several approaches for the calculation of wastage: (1) The Hartog Committee (190) suggested the deduction of enrolment of the fifth grade from the enrolment of grade one done five years earlier, and to covert the difference into percentage. This approach does not take into account fresh admissions, double promotions and deaths. (2) Gadgil and Dandekar (1955) calculated wastage by taking a batch of students in the first standard in a given year following it up through the subsequent years till the last grade is reached, i.e., the fifth. The dropouts from the school before completing the final grade of primary education constitutes the case of wastage and the incidence of wastage is computed from the proportion of these dropouts of the initial enrolment in the first grade. (3) Chickermane (1962) introduced the concept of incremental gains in the learning outcome implying that earlier the student leaves the school in terms of classes, the more will be the extent of wastage due to that student in the process of moving from the beginning grade to the last grade of the stage of education under study. Thus the students leaving school in the fourth standard constitutes less wastage than the student's leaving school in the first standard. This method is criticised particularly while conducting study on the primary stage of education due to the intervention of the phenomenon of lapse into illiteracy which means that students who drop out in fourth or fifth standard are not very significantly different from those who drop out in first or second standard. But if wastage is viewed in terms of money, time and energy expended, the quantum of wastage is more in the former category than in the later. (4) There is another method which assumes that enrolment in the first to the fifth standards would be equally distributed in any given year and the rolls in all the standards are compared to that of the first standard. Any decrease from one standard to another is considered to be the extent of wastage. This method has its own limitations, because the number in the second standard is not the outcome of the first standard of the same given year. But it is the result of first standard of the previous year. The same limitation applies to other standards also. Another drawback is that it fails to take into consideration fresh admissions, double promotions and deaths in the succeeding grades. This method is utilised mostly to estimate the wastage on the basis of figures obtained from the Statistical Unit of the Ministry of Education.

Following the second method in this investigation the extent of wastage has been calculated separately from boys and girls of the primary stage, upper primary and secondary schools situated in the roadside village and interior villages.

The incidence of wastage among the tribal children at the primary stage ranges between 27.00 to 46.00 per cent. It means only to children out of 100 joined in class one pass out the fifth class. This presents an alarming situation.

**Table—8.5 Incidence of Wastage**

| | | *Boys* | *Girls* | *Total* |
|---|---|---|---|---|
| 1. | Roadside villages | 27.35 | 35.89 | 30.84 |
| 2. | Interior villages | 46.2 | 48.83 | 46.0 |

An attempt has been made to find out the class wise drop-out figures (Table—8.6) for both boys and girls to know exactly at what stage the incidence is high.

From the above table it is clearly seen that the incidence of wastage is on the top at the first standard itself among both boys and girls in both categories of schools. Incidence of wastage steadily declines from second class onwards.

The high incidence of wastage is consistent with the high incidence of absenteeism of stagnation, which naturally leads to wastage. The age of children at the fourth and fifth classes is crucial whether to continue in the school or settle in household work to help parents on full time basis.

**Table—8.6 Class-wise Incidence of Wastage in Roadside and Interior Villages**

| *Class* | *Boys* | *Girls* | *Total* | *Boys* | *Girls* | *Total* |
|---|---|---|---|---|---|---|
| I | 52.60 | 69.81 | ** | 52.60 | 75.86 | 60.00 |
| II | 40.48 | 49.32 | 38.5 | 46.6 | 55.60 | 40.48 |
| III | 25.40 | 20.72 | 27.1 | 26.8 | 34.74 | 27.33 |
| IV | 24.46 | 23.59 | 24.5 | *.70 | 25.00 | 22.46 |
| V | 19.57 | 13.79 | 21.6 | 25.0 | 39.57 | 31.30 |

## Causes for Drop-out

### *(a) Socio-Economic Condition*

The poor material circumstances of the tribals affect the enrolment of the children. The same conditions also force the tribal children to leave the school earlier without completing the prescribed course. Informal discussions with teachers and parents revealed that children may be sent to school between the ages of 6 to 8, because at this tender age, they may not be of much help at home. After the age of 9 or 10 to child becomes an economic asset because he can work at home or earn something outside. This is especially true to girls who assist their mothers at home. The child is, therefore, withdrawn from the school and thus becomes a drop-out. As Manning Nash correctly put it:

"Where school and work conflict in societies at this level of income, work always wins. Poverty coupled with familial agricultural production has the effect of drawing children out of school as they are useful in the fields".

Another reason for drop-out is that the tribals do not like to move far away from their villages. When the children are admitted into a hostel at a distant village, they may stay there for sometime but when they return to their village, they will be reluctant to go back and hence they discontinue their studies. The tribals would like to live in their own surroundings and closer to their villages. Thus if the hostels are far away from the tribal villages, the tribal children are more likely to discontinue their studies.

Early marriages are common among the tribals in this area. There are also wide variations in the ages of children joining the school. Sometimes the children join in the school at the age of 8 or 10 even. Such of these children discontinue their education as soon as they get married or whenever their help is required in the field or household. Generally the girls are withdrawn earlier than the boys. Hence the drop-out is higher for girls than boys.

***(b) Educational***

*(i)* Incomplete school: Another important cause for high incidence of drop-out in the tribal area is the inadequate schooling facilities. One third of the schools in this area are single teacher schools, where instruction is provided only for first one or two grades. There were 11 single teacher schools, 6 multiple teacher primary schools during 1983-85 in Paderu Mandal.

Though single teacher school per se is not the cause of wastage in education, the restricted instruction provided in these schools for the first time one or two grades only leads to wastage and stagnation. When the child completes his first or second grade in the local village school, he has either to go to another school at a distant village for continuation of his education at that tender age or discontinue his education. In most cases the tribals prefer the latter. Hence the drop-out is phenomenal at the end of first grade and second grade. The restricted instruction for one or two grades also sometimes leads to the repetition of the same grade by the pupils and thus cause stagnation in education. Thus incomplete school seems to be the most important cause for wastage and stagnation in the tribal area under study.

*(ii)* Malfunctioning of Schools and Hostels: The practice of sending on deputation the teacher from a single teacher school in a village to some other village also contributes to wastage in education. It was found that is this area some teachers from the single teacher schools were deputed temporarily from one village to another village for the reason that there was no significant student strength in the former village. When the teacher is thus shifted from a village, that village will not only be

deprived of the school but the few students who are studying in the local school will have to discontinue their studies; and again when the teacher is sent back, it becomes difficult for him to muster sufficient student strength in the school, for uncertainty prevails in the minds of both parents and students about the permanent existence of the school in their village.

*(iii)* Irregular Attendance: This has been found to be one of the most important contributory factors for the phenomenon of stagnation leading to wastage in tribal areas.

## Absenteeism

The problem of absenteeism is very serious in tribal areas. Whereas one sees a large number of pupils on rolls, the actual attendance is generally very poor. To ascertain the extent of absenteeism in the schools in the area, the average daily attendance in the sampled village schools was taken from last five years in each of the selected villages. It was found that the average attendance in all the schools was about ** per cent. The average attendance in ashram schools (**) was better than the other schools out that tribal children come to school at the time of serving midday meal especially during he lean period when they do not have sufficient food to eat in their homes.

To the question, how often do the parents meet the teacher to know about the progress of their children in the school, only 20 per cent responded 'often', whereas four per cent said only 'now and then', and 76 per cent said 'never'. This indicates that in tribal context parents neither take interest in sending the children to school not in knowing their progress in the school. On the contrary, the parents very often withdraw the children from school to help them in their household and agricultural work. The periodical withdrawal of the child from school develops in him the tendency of truancy and loss of interest in education, which culminates in drop-out.

## Seasonal Variations in Attendance

Attendance in the school was not found to be uniform throughout the year. It varied with the seasons. The research scholar was interested in analytically studying the variations in monthly attendance; but the attendance registers were so badly maintained in the schools that they did not depict a realistic picture. Hence the research scholar has to depend upon the reports of the teacher and on his personal observations. During the harvest season a large percentage of tribal children go to fields to look after the crops and to scare away the birds. This is a sport for the children during this season. A casual visitor to the area will find the young children standing on a wooden platform and scaring away the birds.

The children absent themselves on festival days. The total Gods and the numerous and hence there are many festival days on their calender. Some of these ceremonial. The tribals give much importance to the rituals and ceremonies. Hence it is difficult to make the tribal children (even the boarders of the hostels) attend the school on these occasions. Among the festivals the tribals in this area celebrate the Deepavali more profusely by organising dances for several days. On these days the tribal children inevitably absent themselves from schools. In general, it can be said that the economic cycle, ritual cycle and the attendance cycle roughly correspond with one another in the tribal region. But the school vacations do not correspond to the local conditions. The holidays and vacations in the region are given according to the uniform pattern prevailing in the non-tribal region all over the state.

Besides the festivals, there are shandies (weekly markets) which attract the tribal children. Generally the tribal parents go to the shandies and they take their children along with them. Hence the attendance in all schools of the neighbouring villages will be very thin on the shandy day.

Besides the students and parents, the teachers also have their share in absenteeism in tribal areas. We could not obtain a correct record of irregularity of the teachers in the village schools because there was both authorised and unauthorised absence in the interior villages. But from what was reported by the people in the villages informally and what was observed personally, it was found that irregularities in attendance of teachers who common in the interior village schools. During the period of field work, teachers in some of the village schools were found absent and it was understood that their absence was unauthorised. This irregularity on the part of the students and teachers has a cyclical effect in that, expecting one to be irregular the other would not be regular. Consequently, the schools remain closed for a number of days. In the roadside villages, however, the situation was better because of the fear of surprise visits of officials and also because a bigger number of students were regular than in the interior villages.

Attempt has been made to find out the incidence of absenteeism monthwise to examine the influence of climate conditions, agricultural operations.

More than average absence is noticed during, June, July, September, October, December and January. In June and July children attend the school fresh after enjoying a long spell of summer vacations gradually get themselves adjusted to school routine during these months.

September and October happen to be heavy rainy season resulting in difficulty for the tribal children to come to school crossing the stream on the way as they live in middle of the fields. The Dusserah festival occurs during the month of October, keeping the parents as well as children busy with other odd jobs besides transplantation in fields and children participating in the gaiety of festival by putting on different type of fancy dress. The real peak absence takes place in December and January when the parents are busy in the harvest of rice crop, followed by the most important festival called Sankranti.

For cross checking the monthly average attendance marked by the teacher an attempt has been made to compare the same with the attendance marked on inspection day and day on which surprise visits were made by the inspecting officer.

One notices incidence of absenteeism was more or less equal among tribal children on the road side schools on normal inspection or even surprise visit day.

But in the case of interior schools the incidence of absenteeism on normal day and annual inspection days is more or less equal though if shoots up on supervise visit day.

## Suggestions

After a close investigation and participation observation in the field, the following points are suggested for immediate attention of the administration in the interest of the education in tribal areas:

1. In the primary schools, at least one teacher should be preferably of the same tribe and locality in which the school is located so that they may have a sense of self involvement in the betterment of the school and in teaching the students whom they know from their very birth.
2. Holidays and vacations should be allowed during all local festivals and during sowing and harvesting seasons. Instead of giving holidays on every Sunday it should be given on the weekly day in non-Christian schools. The weekly holidays would be therefore vary from school to school.
3. At least in the lower primary stage the tribal children should be taught the medium of their own tribal language (dialect). This is possible only when the teacher himself knows both the language of the tribe as well as Hindi.
4. The teachers responsibility does not cease after the enrolment drive at the beginning of the school session. It should be made the duty of the teachers to visit the homes of children and to find out the reasons for their absence. Such frequent visits of the teachers will bring them nearer to the parents as well as the students.
5. Wastage is a phenomenon in which the number of students suddenly drops in higher classes. It is a natural that in the tribal areas, all students do not proceed to the higher classes and that they drop before reaching a particular stage in their educational career. Some of them give up studies as it does not interest them and others because of poverty. The fear from the minds of parents that their children will leave the home if they go in for higher studies, as they would not like to stay in their

father's occupation but would prefer to look for petty jobs in the town should be removed.

6. It is high time that a greater collaboration is worked out between anthropologists and educationalists. There is need to take up research projects both action and applied in these areas.

7. A new course of study must be designed for primary classes in tribal areas including their language and folktales so that they may not forget their traditional identity.

# 9

# Alternative Strategies of Development of Tribal Education: Non-Formal Education

The role of Adult Education in tribal areas is quite distinct from that in the other advanced areas of the country. It is, therefore, necessary that the approach and the very character of adult education should be especially defined for these areas. Many of the tribal communities have been living in isolation on account of socio-economic and geographical reasons. Their poverty and backwardness coupled with ignorance and lack of proper educational facilities have subjected them to all sorts of exploitations. However, the tribal communities are comparatively simpler and have been managing their own affairs under the traditional organisations. These organisations are non-formal and each member of the community is a participating member. They are governed by oral traditions interpreted by village elders, groups, Panchayats or the community as a whole. Their economic life has also been organised around the Central characteristics of self-sufficiency. The contact with modern economic system has been minimal but is increasing now gradually with the introduction of various programmes of economic development by the government. Many communities amongst them have not adopted the modern ideas of capital, credit, property etc. Generally, their economic rights and obligations are governed by conventions, oral agreements and mutual obligations. The formal system having the authority of law enacted by the State or the Central legislature do not have much meaning to them. Thus the tribal areas represent the meeting ground of two socio-economic systems which are organised on different principles, one traditional and the other modern.

In many tribal areas the cultural and physical isolation has been accentuated by the difference in the local tribal language and the regional language with the result that the point of contact between tribal community and the outside world gets reduced to a very few people. In most cases the contact points are middlemen, contractors, petty traders or the lower level functionaries of the forest, revenue and police administrations. In all these cases the contact is invariably a bad contact in which he is on the loosing end. His contact with the teacher, wherever schools exist, is also not a happy one. More often than not, the average teacher in schools in tribal areas is absent for better part of the year, disliking to stay with the community, has no knowledge of their social and cultural life, and in some cases works as an agent of their exploitation. His involvement in the village's social and cultural life and his expected role of village leadership are not be seen.

Keeping in view this situation, in tribal areas, the adult education programmes need be formulated in such a way that they provide a protective shield to the tribals against exploitation. These programmes should help them in building their inner strength and smoother the process of transition from obscurantism to enlightened modernism. As per recommendations of the Working Group on Adult Education for next Plan (1978-83), the programmes of Adult Education should:

*(a)* help them to acquire skills so that they may be able to negotiate effectively with the world around them and compete with outsiders in job situation and business dealings;

*(b)* it should assist them in acquiring appreciation of their vibrant culture and conserve their environment; and

*(c)* be interwoven with the rest of the developmental programmes being organised through integrated tribal development projects.

The objectives cannot be achieved by the small group of literates produced by the formal education system functioning in the tribal areas. The product of this system is too tiny to save the large illiterate masses from exploitation and help them in solving their problems of socio-economic development. The out-migration of educated young men further deprives these communities of the lasting benefits of education. There is, therefore, a need to provide intensive mass education to illiterate tribals through both the channels of formal and non-formal education. For this purpose, a new approach to adult education programmes will have to be adopted under which those elements of education have to be picked up which should create awareness in them and increase their absorption capacity for the new developmental programmes. A new curricula should be prepared for the adult education programmes for the tribal areas which should include, among others, a basic understanding of the cultural heritage of the community, an understanding of the economic processes set up by the Government for their economic development, knowledge about the institutional infrastructure with which they are supposed to come in contact, the rights and duties of a citizen, a greater understanding of the agricultural extension services and functioning of the cooperatives system and the basic elements of numerology, reading and writing. Within the vast tribal areas, the States will have to identify priority areas which should be in order of selection of extremely low literacy pockets in the first instance, then areas with large population of landless labourers and the regions where industrial and mining activity is increasing.

A note may be made of two important elements of this programme. There is a general apathy and indifference amongst scheduled tribes towards education. The provision of just facilities for education for them will suffice unless they are motivated to accept education. The process of removal of their indifference towards education is very important one, though a difficult one. Some of the organisations working in this field have found by experience that by providing extension services in their vocations help them in making them interested to know and acquire interest in reading and writing. The inculcation of imparting knowledge of 3 R's should not be taken up right in the beginning but in the first phase programmes should include items which help them in their vocations as well as such measures which reduce their economic exploitation. A provision of financial assistance can also help in removal of their initial inhibition. The second element which goes towards increasing the importance of this programme is its interdependence on the programme of universalisation of school education. The programme of achieving universalisation of education for school going children gets thwarted on account of indifference of illiterates adult parents. The non-attendance of younger ones in schools adds further to the illiteracy in the tribal areas. It is, therefore, very important that the programmes of adult education in tribal areas should receive the highest priority.

**Non-Formal Education**

A programme on Non-formal Education (NFE) for out of school children was started in 1980-81 in the nine educationally backward states including Andhra Pradesh were categorised as educationally backward based on the criteria of primary and upper primary enrolments and female literacy. In the Seventh Plan, Arunachal Pradesh was added to this list and now the scheme operates in these ten states which account for 75 per cent of the non-enrolled children in the age group 6-14 years. Girls formed 58 per cent of the out of school children and thus are expected to be the major beneficiaries of NFE programmes.

**Table—9.1 Out of School Children in India in 1981 (in Millions)**

| | *6-11 Years* | | *11-14 Years* | |
|---|---|---|---|---|
| | *Rural* | *Urban* | *Rural* | *Urban* |
| Male | 19.53 | 2.90 | 7.82 | 1.82 |
| Female | 25.21 | 3.53 | 11.99 | 1.70 |
| **Total** | **44.74** | **6.43** | **19.81** | **2.94** |

*Source:* Census of India, 1981.

According to the 1981 census, 51.71 million children in the age group 6-11 years were not enrolled in schools, of those 56 per cent were girls. In the age group 11-14 years, the number of out of school children was 22.75 million of whom 60 per cent were girls.

Rural girls accounted for 88 per cent of the out of school female children in the age group 6-11 and 11-14.

Setting up of NFE centres was visualised as a supportive system to the existing school system which was unable to meet the needs of children from hard core poor groups of population, among them girls working children, nomads, and children living in remote and separately populated difficult areas. Under this scheme assistance is given to the states and voluntary agencies for the setting up and maintenance of non formal education centres. The Central Government gives 50 per cent assistance to the states and 100 per cent assistance to voluntary organisations. Assistance is given for exclusively girls centres (since 1983-84) on 90 per cent basis. The scheme is in operation in the ten educationally backward states in all 274,000 NFE centres are being run. In addition to the government programmes, about 250 voluntary agencies run NFE centres, almost all of them on the pattern of government projects.

**Table—9.2 Enrolment in NFE Centres in 1986-87**

| *Area* | *Primary* | *Number of Upper Primary* | *Boys* | *Enrolment Girls* | *Total* |
|---|---|---|---|---|---|
| Rural | 111061 (93.72) | 6449 (89.96) | 1948193 (57.39) | 1446477 (42.61) | 3394670 (1100.0) |
| Urban | 7440 (6.28) | 720 (10.04) | 145800 (50.61) | 131358 (49.39) | 277164 (100.0) |
| Total | 118501 (100.0) | 7169 (100.0) | 2093999 (57.03) | 1577835 (42.97) | 3671834 (100.0) |

*Source:* Fifth All India Educational Survey, (1986) NCERT.

There were a total of 125,670 NFE centres in 1986-87 out of which 93.5 per cent were in rural areas enrolling 3.67 million children of whom only 42.97 per cent were girls. There were close to 1.5 million rural girls enrolled in NFE centres in 1986.

In 1986-87, there were a total 90988 villages having 110943 NFE Centres; of these centres 16867 were for boys, 15414 for girls exclusively and 78662 co-educational centres, in Andhra Pradesh

(11257). As is evident, the scheme is not uniformly implemented, with 50 per cent of the NFE centres in three states.

Only about 43 per cent of the girls in NFE centres at primary level in rural areas are between the age of 6-14 years. This raises the issue of looking for viable alternative channels of education for adolescent girls above fourteen years and linking of NFE with the condensed courses of the Central Social Welfare Board. It may be noted that, initially, the scheme was meant for children in age group 6-14 years, as it was felt that in several areas especially where no formal schools were available, NFE centres would be the only learning mode available for children, although now the strict policy is to open NFE centres in school less habitations on a priority basis.

The NFE programme has expanded without due regard to quality, equivalence, credibility and comparability in terms of inputs. There is a general lack of conviction about the whole programme. The states are not willing to commit resources. There is administrative neglect and lack of faith and commitment on part of the functionaries and the families of children who are supposed to benefit from the programme. There is little attempt to adjust the syllabus to the needs of the learner, who belong to the indigent groups of population. The quality of instructors leaves much to be desired as their professional preparations are weak. The instructor is under-paid and the learning materials, lighting arrangements and instructional equipment is much below the acceptable level. Incentives like a free meal, free uniforms and free books/textbooks etc. do not exist. More of ten than not, formal books and syllabi are covered within a few months by instructors and infrastructural facilities are also poor. The child is expected to attain primary/upper primary level academic competence. Nothing in the name of support services exists of NFE, nor any bid to make it into a multi-sectoral programme for convergence of various child care services and programmes for young girls. The isolation of majority of primary schools is bad enough, the isolation of an NFE centre especially in hamlets/habitations where there is no other development services available is worst.

The entire programme is being reorganised as follows:

(a) Area coverage: All agencies taking up NFE will ensure that all children in the area of their responsibility, regularly attend and complete primary education, either through formal or non formal centres.

(b) Comprehensive micro planning exercises will be undertaken to determine the need for NFE centres.

(c) Special attention will be paid to areas where children work under exploitative conditions.

(d) NFE centres, will also be opened in school less habitations.

(e) The comparability between formal and non-formal education would entail comparable outcomes in terms of minimum levels of competence as laid out for a particular level.

(f) Adequate technical resource support would be provided by revamping SCERTs and setting up state and district level resource centres.

(g) The honorarium of the instructor will be raised and the quality of his/her training improved.

(h) Voluntary agencies will be encouraged to be taken on a larger scale with greater flexibility.

(i) Management of NFE will be improved with separate structures at the state and district level with sufficient powers and honorarium etc., to the instructors.

(j) A clear preference will be given to women in the management and running of the NFE programme.

(k) So far the NFE system has mainly worked at the primary level. Attention will be paid to upper primary level now, with children having the option either to join the formal system or to continue through the open school.

(l) A proper system of monitoring and evaluation will be established to ensure the necessary quantitative and qualitative data become available for improvement of the programme (Ministry of Human Resource Development, Education for All).

It has perhaps to be admitted that there is still, continued lack of conceptual clarity as to whether NFE is only a short term intermediary strategy till such time as a formal school can be provided to all children or is an alternative independent parallel mode of learning for the young with adequate bridges to and from the formal. It is admitted frankly that India is not in a position to provide formal schooling to its 300 million children below 14 years and to over 210 million in the age group 6.14 years. In foreseeable future, it will not be possible to create a supply induced demand, i.e. open a properly equipped and staffed primary school in every neighbourhood. We are not supplying education in required measures and are not willing to deformalize the middle class loaded formal system to make it more flexible, receptive and sensitive to the needs of masses, is our failure. Infact, both the formal and non formal have failed to do one thing, i.e. capacity building among the young, capacity to work, capacity to live life to its fullest, capacity to care and share other people's concerns, and finally the capacity to face adversity and to be able to utilise opportunities when they come.

**Non-Formal Education for Girls (NFE)**

The programme of Non-formal Education was started in 1979-80 to provide education, comparable to formal schooling, to children in 6-14 age group who are unable to attend formal schools due to various socio-economic constraints. The programme mainly caters to disadvantaged group of children such as school drop-outs, working children, children in habitations without school, SCs/STs and girls who can not/do not avail full time schooling. Under this scheme, the Government of India provides financial assistance to States/UTs and NGOs as per the following pattern:

— Co-educational centres and administrative/resource support to States/UTs. 60%

— Exclusively girls centres run by States/UTs. 90%

— NFE Projects run by NGOs 100%

The programme NFE has been revised in 1993. As a special incentive to girls education, the ratio of number of girls centres to co-educational centres under NFE programme has been increased from 25:75 to 40:60. There are, at present, about 1.00 lakh exclusively girls NFE centres, out of the total of about 2.31 lakh centres, with annual enrolment capacity of about 25 lakhs children. During the first three years of 8th Plan, grants of Rs. 102.44 crores were released to 4 States/UTs for running exclusively girls NFE centres. The state-wise performance is given below:

**Table—9.3 Number of NFE Centres and the Girls Benefitted**

| *Name of the States/ Union Territories* | *Achievements upto 31.3.1995* | |
|---|---|---|
| | *NFE Centres for Girls* | *Girls Benefitted* |
| Andhra Pradesh | 12202 | 305050 |
| Assam | 5408 | 135200 |
| Bihar | 20000 | 500000 |
| Jammu & Kashmir | 249 | 6225 |
| Madhya Pradesh | 16795 | 419875 |
| Manipur | 520 | 13000 |
| Mizoram | 50 | 1250 |
| Orissa | 6618 | 165450 |
| Rajasthan | 7300 | 182500 |
| Tamil Nadu | 280 | 7000 |
| Uttar Pradesh | 29800 | 745000 |
| Chandigarh | 30 | 750 |
| **Total** | **99252** | **2481300** |

**Nutritional Support to Primary Education (NSPE).**

A programme of 'Nutritional Support to Primary Education, (Mid-day Meals) was launched on 15 August 1995 to give a boost to universalisation of primary education by increasing enrolment, retention and attendance and simultaneously impacting on nutrition of students in primary classes.

NSPE aims to cover, in phased manner, all the government, local body and Government-aided primary schools in all the States and Union Territories. To start with in 1995-96, the programme will commence in all the 2368 Revamped Public Distribution System (RPDS)/Employment Assurance Scheme (EAS) blocks and 40 Low Females Literacy (LFL) blocks. In state like Punjab which do not have EAS/RPDS blocks, the programme will commence in LFL blocks, i.e. blocks having female literacy rate lower than the national average. In States and UTs. Such as Goa, Delhi, Pondicherry and Chandigarh, which do not have RPDS or LFL blocks, primary schools in notified slums would be covered. In 1996-97, the programme will be extended to all the remaining 2005 LFL blocks having female literacy lower than the national average. In 1997-98, the programme will be extended to all other primary schools.

The Central Government will assist the local bodies authorities such as Panchayats and Nagarpalikas in implementing the programme by providing from the nearest Food Corporation of India (FCI) godowns wheat/rice (as may be required) at the rate of 100 grams per student per day free of cost. The local bodies will have the flexibility to organise the provision of cooked/pre cooked food by the schools or in association with the school parent-teacher committees, non-government organisations, women/DWCRA Groups and other organisations. They are also expected to decide the type of food to be provided subject to the food being wholesome and having a calorific value equivalent to 100 grams of wheat/rice per student per day. To ensure that this stipulation is adhered to both in letter and spirit, appropriate supervisory mechanisms will be established by the local bodies.

## Total Literacy Campaigns (TLCs)

Total Literacy Campaigns (TLCs) have been accepted as the most important strategy of the National Literacy Mission (NLM) for imparting functional literacy to 100 million persons in the target age group of 15-35. In addition to this identified age-group, the TLCs in individual districts have recently been covering children of the NFE age-group of 9-14 to the extent they are not covered under the Non-formal Education Programme.

The TLC has certain positive characteristics like being area-specific, time-bound, participative, delivered through voluntarism, cost-effective and outcome-oriented. Though the TLC emphasises the achievement of pre-determined minimum levels of literacy and numeracy, there are other activities linked up with TLCs, such as campaigns for universal enrolment and retention in schools, immunization, conservation of environment, the small-family norm, women's empowerment etc.

In the TLC campaigns women have invariably been the large majority of participants. On an average, two-third of the total learners in a district are women. The theme of empowerment of women is receiving special focus. As on March 1995, TLCs have taken up in 336 districts (with full or partial coverage), and PLCs in 134 districts. The total effective enrolment under TLC camps is 5.58 crores. Women covered under TLC is estimated to be 3.72 crore as on 14.5.1995 (No gender-wise break-up is available. Hence no statement is given).

Regarding attendance of tribal students in school Bihari (1969) reported that there were many S.T. children on the rolls who had never attended schools. Srivastava found that the attendance of S.T. adults at adult education centres was extremely low.

Bastia (1982) mentioned that in case of tribals attendance of male adult learners was better than that of female adult learners. Further Joshi found that teachers also perceived tribal students as irregular in attending the school.

Some researchers have gone beyond formal education and looked into the impact of adult education among the tribals. Both these studies (Lakshminarayan, 1983; Satyanarayan Rao, 1986), however, have been made in the state of Andhra. These studies bring out the problems of adult education and the response of tribal participants in the adult education programme. The performance of the participants was highly satisfactory in reading abilities, average for own writing abilities and below average for arithmetical abilities. One of the studies revealed a close association between participation in adult education and modernity levels.

The research scholar conducted a study in the year 1984 in the field of non-formal education among tribals, the details of which has been presented.

The study undertaken by the research scholar Yadappanavar (1984) in Paderu Block of Vizag District with the following objectives has revealed that:

1. To understand the learner's perception about adult education programme;
2. To examine the role of officials in Adult Education Programme;
3. To suggest alternatives for improving the implementation of the programmes; and
4. To find out the impact of Adult Education Programme in respect of three components, namely literacy, functionally and awareness, highlighted the need for the Adult Education Centres under Adult Education Programme to pay greater attention to improve their reading, writing skills and providing more information regarding occupational skills.

It may be desirable that in Adult Education Centres, female instructors should be present, so that, she is able to better motivate and sustain the interest of women learners. Sincere efforts should be made to improve the attendance of women. Introduction of economic incentives may also increase the participation of women. Unless women learners attend the centres more regularly, even a well planned Adult Education Programme may not succeed. An earlier study by Vasudeva Rao (1984) has highlighted the importance of the relationship between attendance and learners achievement (IJAE, May, 1984).

There is an urgent need for the establishment and development of Women's organisations at the grassroot level. Such organisations can play a significant role in the education of women. Attendance and learners achievement is positively and significantly related. The studies of Hebsur (1981), Laxminarayana (1982), Rao (1983) have also established the above fact.

## NPE Implementation

The implementation of the National Policy on Education 1986 on any substantive scale was delayed for lack of funds for the first two years. Several centrally sponsored schemes, however, were launched:

1. In Non-Formal Education assistance was given to exclusive girls NFE centres on 90:10 basis: to co-educational centres on 50:50 basis; to voluntary organisations and academic institutions on 100 per cent basis.
2. A total of one million school teachers and 264,000 NFE instructors were given orientation in a multi-tiered programme by the NCERT during 1987-98.
3. Data base on girls education has been strengthened and over 100 districts identified where the primary enrolment rate per cent of population in the age group 6-11 years was found to be less than 50 per cent for girls. Problems of SC and ST girls were studied specially to identify bottleneck in the advancement of NPE among them. Textbooks were screened for removal of sexist bias. Mobilisation of women and the community for NPE of girls was done in a few States on an experimental basis.
4. More than 250 District Institutes of Education and Training (DIET) have been set up to provide the professional academic and administrative support to the programme of UEE and Adult Education.

## Suggestion

Some of the suggestions offered by the learners for improving the functioning of the centres were *(i)* giving information about credit facilities by banks; and *(ii)* extension of the course could be for a period of ten months to two years. Proper follow-up after the course is over, so that they get jobs.

# 10

# Summary and Conclusions

This study is aimed at examining the impact of tribal educational programme on the socio-economic conditions of the tribal households in one of the tribal concentrated districts of Andhra Pradesh namely Visakhapatnam, the problems and constraints in the implementation of educational development programme in the selected district were also examined in the study. Studies of tribal development have assumed greater significance since the introduction of Intensive Tribal Development Planning from Fifth Five Year Plan onwards.

## 1. Scope and Objectives of the Study

India is one of the countries having largest concentration of tribal population in the world. The extreme backwardness and poverty conditions of the tribals in the country have stimulated the attention of governments both during British regime and the Indian Government after independence of the country. The post-independence era witnessed a large number of developmental measures, policies and programmes focused on the overall development of the tribal areas.

After the initiation of the planned development programmes in the country from the First Five Year Plan, till the present VIII Five Year Plan, many programmes were implemented for the socio-economic upliftment of the tribals both by state and Central Governments. There are a few studies particularly in Andhra

Pradesh evaluating the impact of these tribal development programmes which are mostly done by the governmental agencies. However these studies fail to bring out the hindrances, in implementation of the programme. Therefore, what is necessary is to evaluate thoroughly the tribal development programmes in the highest tribal concentrated zones in the State where heavy investments and developmental efforts were made. But due to lack of time and resources prohibit undertaking evaluation study of all the tribal concentrated areas in the state.

The specific objectives of the study are:

1. The assess the existing pattern of education and educational facilities available to the scheduled tribes.
2. Finding out the bottlenecks, problems and constraints coming in the way of successful implementation of educational development programmes such as absenteeism, wastage and stagnation.
3. Suggesting suitable corrective and remedial measures for effective implementation of the educational programmes in the study area for achieving the desired results.

## 2. The Methodology of the Study

This study was taken up in Visakhapatnam, being one of the tribal concentrated districts in the State. Because of its ideal location, the State Girijan Cooperative Corporation of the Government of Andhra Pradesh had its headquarters at Visakhapatnam to extend all necessary assistance. Therefore, it has been decided to take Visakhapatnam District for the study. Among the 11 tribal concentrated mandals in the district, it was decided to select one mandal based on the following criteria.

For selection of a mandal two criterias have been adopted which are as follows:

1. Proximity to the Integrated Tribal Development Project Office;
2. Availability of infrastructural facilities with specific reference to education.

**(a) *By adopting the above criterias, one mandal namely, Paderu has emerged as the ideal mandal for conducting the study.***

The I.T.D.A., headquarters is located at Paderu because of its central location in the tribal track of the district. Paderu because of its central location, and location of various sectoral departments including I.T.D.A. exclusively meant for development of tribal population, is socially and culturally well developed. Thus the mandal selected for the study is representing different situation in the tribal areas of the Visakhapatnam district.

*(b) Selection of Respondents*

It total, the sample constituted 50 households for the study.

*(c) Data Collection*

Data for this study were collected from the researcher worked three months in this mandal. The main activities during the field work were to collect data from I.T.D.A. Paderu for projects such as education.

During the stay at Paderu, this researcher faced many problems concerned with officials, transport and food. Many officials in tribal areas were not available in time because they were not living with their families, they frequently visited their families and also many posts are vacant. Regarding transport many villages are not connected with bus routes. Regarding food, the researcher had to take food in tribal houses during his visits to the villages.

*(d) Tools and methods of Data Collection*

The tools of data collection include a household schedule, observation and unstructured interviews. The technique of participant observation was employed to gather data on interactions with development functionaries and people's participation in the developmental activities and their behaviour and attitude etc. The experience reveals that friendly talk, outside trips, gossiping are some of the best means of collection of information. All the information thus collected was counter-checked with reliable persons and their available records in doubtful cases.

### (e) Data Analysis

The data thus collected were two types, qualitative and quantitative. First, the qualitative data that were collected through the household schedule were transferred to I.B.M. sheets after carefully editing the schedules. All the data were analysed and tables were prepared with the help of computer.

The qualitative data gathered through interviews and observation were recorded in field diaries. These data were thoroughly edited before incorporating in the thesis.

The frame of reference in the present study includes both internal and external systems of education. Types of school, level of schooling, medium of instruction, accommodation, equipment, communication and proximity of facility, a school timings, syllabus, enrolment and attendance, absenteeism, stagnation and wastage. Management of hostels and Ashram schools constitute the internal system.

The response of studies, parents and teachers towards the internal system and the conditions in which scheduled tribe students have to seek education, pattern of life and study habits, career and performance in studies, participation in extra curricular activities, their aspirational levels, nature of encouragement received from parents and teachers, the social life and outlook of students, exposure to mass-media and politicization has been studied under the external system.

The selection of educational institutions in 12 villages has been made to have a representation of all five agencies in the area under study. Invariably the sampled students and teachers have been chosen from these institutions. However, the parent respondents were chosen at random in different selected villages. The key informant study technique, non-participation observation method and interviewing method for primary data collection and referring the school records and collecting relevant data from the offices related to education for secondary source information have been used in the present study.

The pattern of enrolment obtained from the study has been skewed in almost all the schools of the different agencies, however the present rate of enrolment among school going age children (98.60 per cent) in mandal as a whole, appears to encouraging, but the enrolment of girls has been a low compared to boys. Especially in some of the selected schools under study there has been a wide disparity between the enrolment and the actual attendance. This gives an idea that there exists a high rate of absenteeism. Again the incidence of absenteeism has been on the higher side as the level of educational standard increases. In other words the higher the standard, the higher the rate of absenteeism. Secondly, it is more among girls than the boys. Similarly the present data indicate that there has been a high rate of wastage in the first 3 standards in the primary level of institutions. Here the level of educational standard increases correspondingly the rate or wastage has been on decreasing. Further analysis helps us to know that the wastage among girls seem to be on the higher side. So it is confirmed that there is a problem of discontinuation of study among girls before reaching the fifth standard. As far as stagnation is concerned, it is observed from the study that more than 50 per cent of the students admitted in the 1st standard have not reached the final year (V standard) of primary school. It suggests that the students have detained at any standard more than once in between 1st to Vth classes. Although the enrolment is less among girls, the incidence of wastage and absenteeism has been found high. It could be because of the socio-economic pressures from the parents to make the girl students either to be irregular or to discontinue their studies. It is observed that the girl students are more keen on studies, this idea supplements with the observation of less percentage of stagnation among girls.

The number of educational institutions in mandal is not adequate considering the total area and its population. However, major thrust has to be paid to the improvement of the existing educational institutions rather than mere introducing some more institutions. It does not mean that mandal does not require additional educational facilities. What is required now is that proper stress has to be paid on the qualitative improvement first and then for quantitative development. The major problem lies in the area is because of single teacher schools with an enormous strength of students. Drinking water has been a problem in many of the hostels and Ashram schools. (78.00 per cent) Hill streams are being used as a source of water for drinking and other purposes. To go and lift the water from the hill streams which are situated at a far off places is a major problem. A majority of the schools (80.00 per cent) are attached with gardens. A few among them (16.66 per cent) under tribal welfare and ITDA have gardens with good maintenance. The contingent staff including cook and waterman (kamati) are used to attend the gardening work. The involvement of students in gardening is not so encouraging. It is due to lack of sufficient water, and non-participation of students, the gardens have not been properly maintained. Some such thing shall be a part of the general curriculum of a class upto X class by that the students will come to know the importance of plantation and gardening.

By increasing the strength of the school, the new demand automatically will rise up with the new situation to meet the additional number of students, so the accommodation and the number of teaching staff, equipment and other infrastructural facilities have to be generated. This has not happened in many of the schools under study (*). Classes are being conducted in huts in many of the school (*). In some cases these huts are drab and in dilapidated condition. In regard to other schools though the pukka buildings are provided, the available accommodation is in adequate and its upkeep and maintenance is very poor (90.00 per cent). The present strength of Ashram schools attached to primary schools is 65 as minimum and 91 as maximum. In case of upper primary schools, 84 is the minimum and 126 as the maximum, and Ashram schools attached with high schools, the strength is 127 as the minimum and 140 as the maximum. With this, one can easily say that the existing hostels and Ashram schools have exceeded the normal capacity and these institutions are caught with the problem of inadequate accommodation. These hostels and Ashram schools are not properly equipped with the necessary cooking vessels, plates, tumblers.

Along with the studies sports and games play an important role to make the student physically fit and mentally alert towards studies. As far as schools under study almost all of them have their own play grounds except a few (25.00 per cent), which have well laid out play grounds with play material the rest of them have been provided with some space with no proper maintenance.

It is found that the schools located at interior villages have several disadvantages because of lack of proper communication facilities. The student belonging to these areas are less exposed to the outside world, and also the level of awareness and assimilation of new ideas through formal education is apparently low compared to the students who are at schools situated at the road side. Even for the maintenance of hostel and Ashram school in these places is bound to be a problem as the transportation of provisions and other commodities to interior places is not an easy task. The locational and communicational limitations have its own far reaching consequences. Because of these disadvantages, supervising authorities may have little interest to visit these places. The teacher working in these schools used to be irregular. And it is more likely that the wardens are likely to mismanage the things. This can be treated as a bottleneck in the spread of tribal education.

The students have an unquestionable faith in the existence of God, however they are non-believers in fatalism. Contrary to this concept of fatalism, they over emphasize the idea that man is the architect of his own fate. The perception of teacher toward religion is traditional and conservative as they have expressed strong belief in the existence of God as well as in fatalism.

Exposure to mass media has become a part of their life to the students. Students seek to enjoy in witnessing cinemas mostly during vacations. Radio and newspaper have also been playing an important role in educating and entertaining the tribal students. News, songs and politics are treated to be the most liking features in Radio. Reading of newspaper has been confined to the Xth and Intermediate classes. Periodically or reading again is correlated with the availability of the newspaper and the level of educational standard of the student. Mostly the students intend to look for advertisements and employment news and political aspects. Although the students are against the active participation aspects. Although the students are against the active participation in politics, but they have their own favourites in politics.

With respect of familial relations, the father and the parents still hold the decision making process on any issue in the tribal family system. There is a little change in the selection of life-partner for Adult sons and daughters. Now the educated students perceive that the consent of a boy or girl is equally important when an attempt is made for marriage. The authoritative approach of Father in this regard is not at all acceptable to them. The educated tribal student has come to a stage to prescribe some yardsticks for the selection of their life partner. The tribal educated boy aspires his wife to be with good character, education and adept in domestic chores. For the tribal educated girl, 'husband' needs to have good education, employment and free from all sorts of vices.

The making of friendship among the students belonging to different committees will throw light on the elements of integration and isolation. The situation obtaining from the study, purports that there exists friendly relations between tribal and non-tribal students. There has not been any rupture in the network of their relationship pattern. The majority of the students do not consider the identify of caste, kinship, area, and other parochial parameters in the selection of a friend. Mostly mutual intimacy and understanding of common interests facilitate one's friendship with somebody. And it has been noticed that observance of social distance among the students of different tribal committees belonging to primary schools seems to be a matter of reality even now.

For the students the locality and the people at those places where they are now are new. According to them, the level of empathy of the students with the new environment, has been found so encouraging. And they do not visualise any major hindrance to their studies to be at the new environment. Coming to the teaching staff those who almost all of them are non-tribals, the present place of stay is a punishment area. It is so pathetic to note that the teachers have not developed any liking and close attachment towards the area inspite of their long standing service. The teachers have mentioned some problems like higher education for their offspring, transport, accommodation and health facilities. Some of them have felt that the climate is not congenial because of severe cold throughout the year in the agency. It is due to lack of calcium content in water in this area; the place has become a health hazard. A majority of them evaluated the tribals as bad, drunkards, not trustworthy, uncivilized, illiterate and immobile. Among them, valmikis are the most intelligent and non-cooperative. The tribal elite and the urbanised tribals, with their formal positions as a member of panchayat and president of panchayat expect that the teachers should yield to their pressures. In case the teachers go against them, they make complaints to the higher authorities. And for those who have some special liking for the agency area and the tribals, the reasons for liking such as the life here for them is so simple, serene and their is lot of scope for one's educational development. Some teachers would attend the tribal festivals on invitation of the tribal elders, and the tribal elite would also come and participate in the functions of the schools. Students have not felt isolated from the main group though they are at the new environment, whereas the teaching community have looked at the area and people altogether in different perspective. Students have developed special liking towards their teachers as both of them keep maintaining smooth relations. Almost all students are familiar with the Telugu language. It indicates that the Telugu as medium of instruction is not a problem in the area. In regard to syllabus of all classes, it is found that it is heavy and overburdened according to the students and teachers. The teachers have suggested that the content of the curricula should be reoriented towards the practical problems of tribal situation. Instead of creating tension and fear towards studies among tribal students, and the studies should be able to generate thinking and interest in them; whatever the type of education they get it should be useful in their life. Then task becomes easier to create confidence in them. The teachers felt that some portions of Mathematics, General Science and even in Social Studies in high school sections need to be reduced. According to students, Mathematics and Science are as difficult. It is so interesting to note that some students could develop special interest in some subjects. Probably they must have had a better coaching at the primary level education which helped them to develop such interest. The same aptitude would remain with them even at the higher levels of their education. Devotion of time towards studies seems to be such less than the average requirement. It also reveals that there is no proper check and supervision of higher authorities as to the way of students are spending their time. Cooperation is most essential from the teaching staff even when a student wants to meet him after working hours for some clarification on any subject. Proper aptitude and initiative of a teacher and inquisitiveness of student and equally necessary to realise better results.

Both the teachers and students have expressed that inspections by supervising authorities are said to have a therapeutic treatment to the working of a school. Teachers, students and other staff will have an opportunity to expose their problems and seek solutions with them.

There is no persistent resistance from the parents in sending their children to schools. However, it is because of ecological constraints and policy limitation, some parents are unable to make use of the educational facilities to the extent possible. Incentives and presence of Ashram schools have made a dent on the mental make up of the tribal parents. It is very much revealed that the students are pursuing their studies in order to secure jobs of their interest. Due to educational tours, pilgrimage, and other trips to urban centres, both parents and tribal students have formed favourable opinion towards the urban mode of life. But they are hesitant to settle down at these centres as they have no means to survive in these areas.

The tribal students are dull and their comprehension level is low according to the teaching community. They are inferior to the plain students in this regard. The parents prefer the non-tribal is teacher. The teachers are said to have shown the discriminatory attitude towards tribal students.

The selection of educational institution is based on the presence of Hostel facilities, standard of education along with the proximity. Some times personal choice or liking would not matter at all. In case the students fail to get admission on one school, he goes on trying to secure a place in other places as a last resort.

Regarding working hours the day scholars and some of the teaching staff have felt that the present system needs some change. Rainy and winter seasons are not convenient to attend the school, these seasons are desired to be declared as holidays at the dispense of some days in summer vacations. The students could be helpful to their parents at the time of harvesting, if the harvesting season is converted as vacation. On the other a majority of the parents have felt that the hostel and Ashram schools should keep open during the vacations also, the interested students may have a chance to attend to studies. But the students intend to be at their homes during vacations to see their parents and relatives and enjoy their time by visiting movies. The students invariably abscond from the hostels with or without permission to attend to their festivals. To enlist the cooperation of the tribals and proper appreciation of tribal cultural values and to avoid the present stalemate, tribal festivals are to be declared as public holidays.

A considerable number of students have evinced interest in literacy debates. A few of them have participated in NCC, Scouts, and gardening. This is more true in the case of students belonging to X and II year Intermediate classes. As many as students have expressed to continue their studies at least upto degree level. It is confirmed from their views that the studies have developed a rational outlook in choosing the type of qualification to seek the type of employment. It implies that there is a sense of direction and uncompromising faith among the students in the attainment of education. A majority of them are ready to break their traditions if necessary to realise their goal of development. There is little dispute to comment with the present state of conditions, the students are change prone to raise their living condition. Already they have started advocating the validity of modern values in their social set up. And the change is quite visible in their dress, diet, habits, mannerisms. This is due to the impact of education.

Parents have a great appreciation about the attitude of educated tribal youth. They do not possess any inhibitions to send their children for higher education. Moreover they are fully confident that the educated children will work for the welfare of the fellow tribals. They will never become deviant from their social milieu. Further they have stated that the educated children will become a source of motivation to the other non-school going children.

With regard to the enrolment of tribal children the teachers divided themselves evenly. Presence of boarding, and lodging facilities have been found to be the factor of attraction for higher rate of enrolment in the schools. As to the parents, disinterest of students, financial condition of parents, ill health of a child, economic necessity, non-availability of a high order, educational facility in and around their villages and sudden demise of the parent are the different contributing factors for the drought and poor attendance.

A majority of teachers, parents and students, have approved the policy provisions made available to the tribal children for the development of tribals. They have approved its relevance. While the students and parents emphasizing the importance of Ashram school in the extension of tribal education in the area, the tribal parents and students have expressed their dissatisfaction about the style of management of Ashram schools and implementation of different incentives.

The teaching community is satisfied with the existing pay structure, and a few among them have expressed their resentment in regard to their probation, security and promotional prospects. For them transfer is a natural course, it is clear that the teachers do not spend enough time for the preparation of their subjects. Interaction between teacher and tribal parent is very much minimal. Once the child was admitted, then the parents will feel a sigh of relief and are in the spell of euphoria as if their is no further responsibility for them. Parents and teachers like to have to the students himself, in regard to the selection of job. Teaching community have further stressed that if a student is bright, he should be encouraged to go in for higher studies, and avail the policy of reservation to secure better employment. It has become easier for them new even to become BDO, Tahasildar, Doctor and Engineer.

Girls' education is not much liked by tribal parents due to some traditional inhibitions. Having seen the change around in the name of development, they are prepared to swim across the currents of modern values and give up their dichord customs. Liberalisation of government policy in regard to the admission into

Ashram schools, job guarantee schemes after studies, simplification of official procedures in obtaining certificates from schools and Government officers, introduction of some more primary schools are very much desired. Tribal parents and students emphasize that the administrative machinery is deemed to show their active involvement in discharging their duties.

It is felt that the environment in which the tribal children were brought up at times acts as a deterrent to the development of their education. The tribal children are reluctant by nature to go to schools. Sitting in the four walls of an institution is a punishment for them. There is little dispute about the inadequacy of transport, housing, higher education and health facilities in tribal areas which will no way encourage the teacher to be committed and dedicated. Educational infrastructure at schools such as teaching aids, laboratories and libraries are either inadequate or altogether absent in some schools (48.00 per cent). A majority of them expressed that the teaching on health and hygienic habits has to become a part of the curricula in the schools. There is a provision to keep the medicines at schools. There is a provision to keep the medicines at schools and hostels to treat the emergency cases and attend to small ailments. But the system of functioning has not been found so effective in this aspect. As to the high wastage and poor enrolment in the schools among tribal children the teaching community felt that the daily wage for a worker per day in coffee plantation is Rs. 8.00, it is so attractive for the parents to make their children as wage earners. In some cases, if the parents are old, the children do not incline to go to school regularly if they were admitted and they discontinue from their studies after sometime. The parents who have confidence in securing job for the child after studies have been showing proper care in sending their children to schools. And there is no special drive from the Government to accelerate the rate of enrolment and lessen the rate of drop out among the tribal children. Besides the proper atmosphere ought to be necessary where tribal student must not suffer from want of minimum requirements like accommodation, teaching aids, furniture and other infrastructural amenities in a school.

Education has a role to play in changing life styles of people in any society. This change need not a positive type always, it may have its mixed impact also. Other factors being equal, it has been established that formal education acts as a facilitator for change that is felt desirable.

The selection of a village is mostly dependent on the presence of educational institution. Sufficient care has also been taken to have a representation from the different levels of lower primary, upper primary and secondary schools.

Tribal parents, tribal students and teachers from the composition of the respondents in the present study. Technique like informal discussions, observations along with interviewing with structured schedule, have also been used for primary data collection. Secondary sources are utilised by referring the records, the other relevant literature pertaining to the educational institutions.

Thus, it is no iota of doubt that the education system in tribal areas is beset with some impediments. Enough ideas, views, suggestions and recommendations have been floated to set right the system. A few of them are quoted here which will help us to size the pulse of magnitude of educational situation. They are: A problems of adjustment and assimilation with formal education system and new environment and unknown and unheard to tribal students (Srivastava 1968), Problems of implementation of various incentives (Singhi 1979), inconvenient schools timings (Tippa 1979), ill equipped schools and unsuitable teachers (Ruth S.N. 1981), ignorance of Parents, Family environment, unhappy school atmosphere and medium of instruction through unknown language (Joshi N.D. 1982).

The study conducted by the research scholar in Andhra Pradesh with a view to identify the problems of education would also add to our understanding. Before dealing with actual problems, the background about the ecology, economy and society of tribals in each state are discussed at the outset as there is ample scope of its influence on the working pattern of educational institutions. Andhra Pradesh is under Vth Schedule of Indian Constitution. Economic development is preceded by education in Andhra

Pradesh. The tribals under study in Andhra Pradesh, is mostly dependent on agriculture both 'Podu' or 'Jhum' cultivation and settle type of cultivation. The tribals under study of Andhra Pradesh *viz.* Bhagathas, Valmikis and a few others have been undergoing a lot of change by accumulating the traits of non-tribal Hindu culture. While in Andhra Pradesh the tribals and Hinduised.

Perception of tribal parents in Andhra Pradesh is quite contradictory. They prefer non-tribals as teachers by evaluating the non-tribals as their reference group to the tribal students. Tribals are in minority, the non-tribals are dominating the tribals.

The tribals in Andhra Pradesh speak Telugu also alongwith their tribal dialect. As such tribal children studying in educational institutions do not find Telugu as medium of instruction as a constraint. If we analyse state-wise situation, the schools under Government are much better managed and equipped as compared to private management schools in Andhra Pradesh. The schools, hostels and Ashram schools are neither properly equipped nor maintained. Single teacher schools, differential attitude of parents towards girl's education and policy of admission into Ashram schools are found as bottlenecks.

The uniform approach to the problems of education is unrealistic as the tribal situation is so complex. Flexibility in our approach is highly desirable. Problems relating to education in tribal areas have to be viewed in different context and not in terms of the general average situation as obtaining in the country. Education should be suited to the needs of tribal people, otherwise, it will be deterimental to their well-being. If properly planned and invested, educational efforts for the scheduled tribes has to be somewhat different from general mass. In non-tribal areas, demand for education is already there. Establishment of an educational institution itself is sufficient to attract the children from the advanced communities, because the parents in these areas have already developed interest in education. This is not the case with scheduled tribes. The message of formal education has not yet reached the more backward areas where the people are not much aware about the practical utility of education.

Efforts in the development of education in isolation is not appropriate, it should be simultaneous along with economic development.

Apart from other measures to tackle the specifics, voluntary spirit is immensely needed to serve the tribal areas and implement the different programmes, as these areas have inbuilt inadequacies.

Time and again the attempts of identifying problems and suggesting remedial measures have become a routine affair. We have to go a step further and test them for its operational suitability. What is urgently need now is to instill an ounce of interest in them. If necessary periodic review of the present policy and modification should be ensured from time to time based on experiences and research findings.

Thus, education, no doubt, has the potential to change the life styles of people. But it can not be presumed that education alone can bring about changes and are necessary for the development. It is not a panacea to weed out the social evils automatically. Factors like location specific and culture specific will also have a role to play in the system of education in a direction that is desirable for realising the anticipated results.

**Figure—1: Pie Showing Distribution of Population Categorywise in Vizag Dist.**

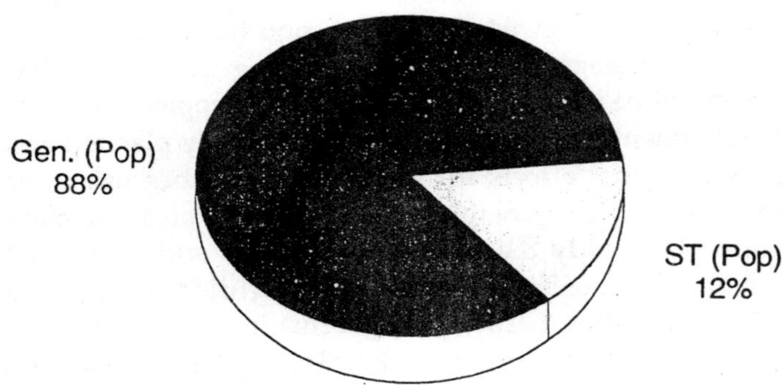


1991 Census Data

**Figure—2: Number of Schools Managementwise**

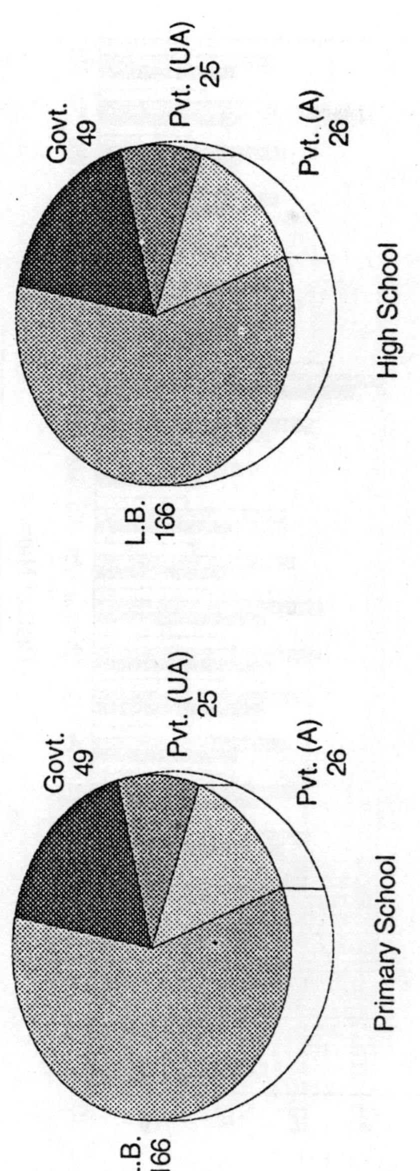

**Figure—3: Districtwise Literacy Rates (7 Years and Above)**

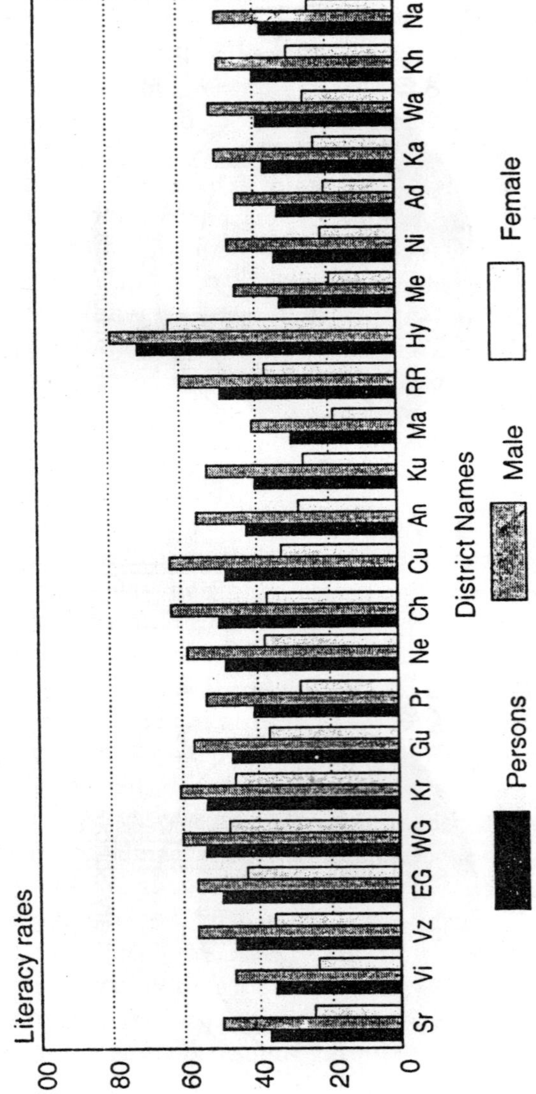


1991 Census data

**Figure—4: Comparison of Indicators**

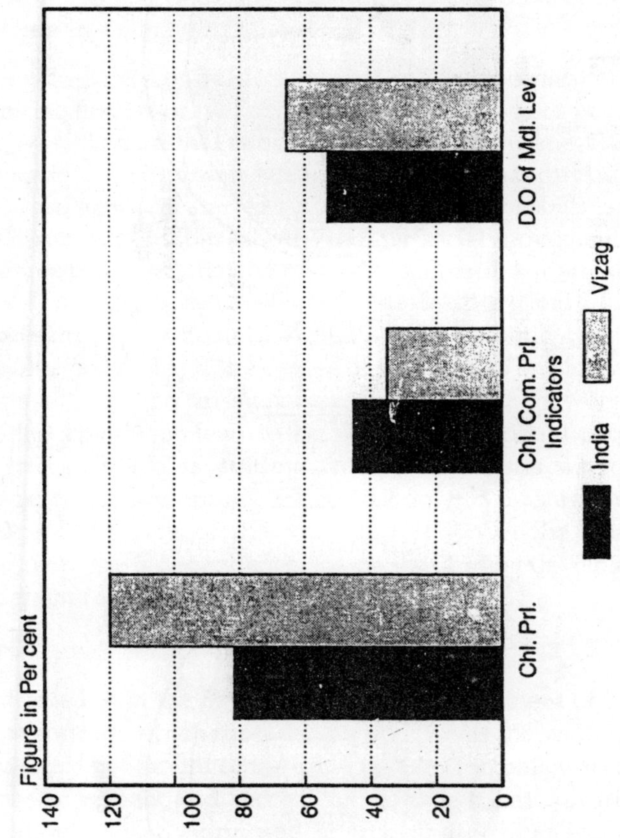


Source: DSE/SCERT Data 1988

**Figure—5: No. Schools Vs. No. of Teachers (Primary School) Vizag District**

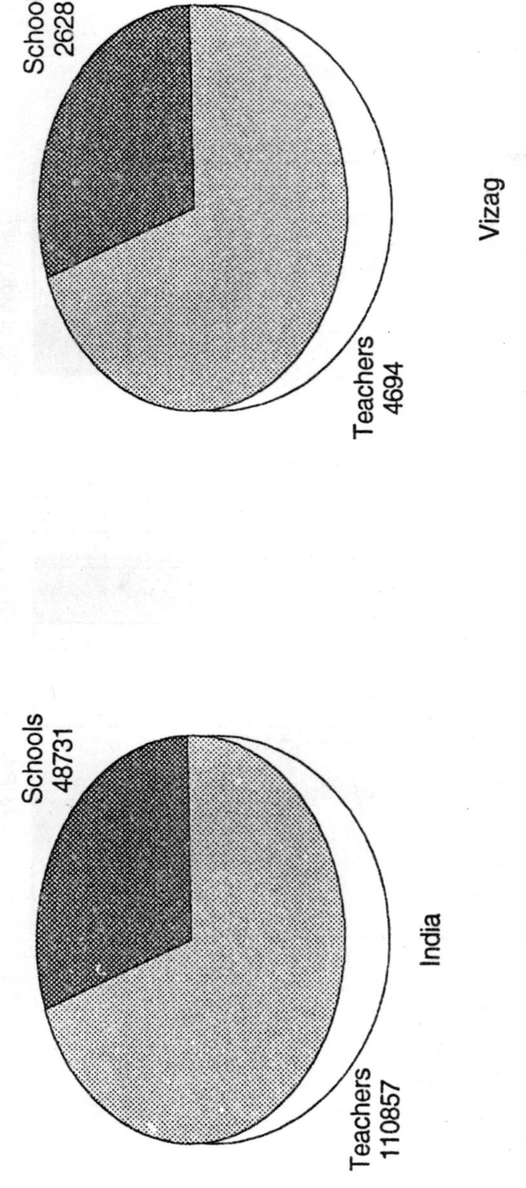


Source: DSE/SCERT Data 1988

**Figure—6: Rural Literacy Rates Comparison**

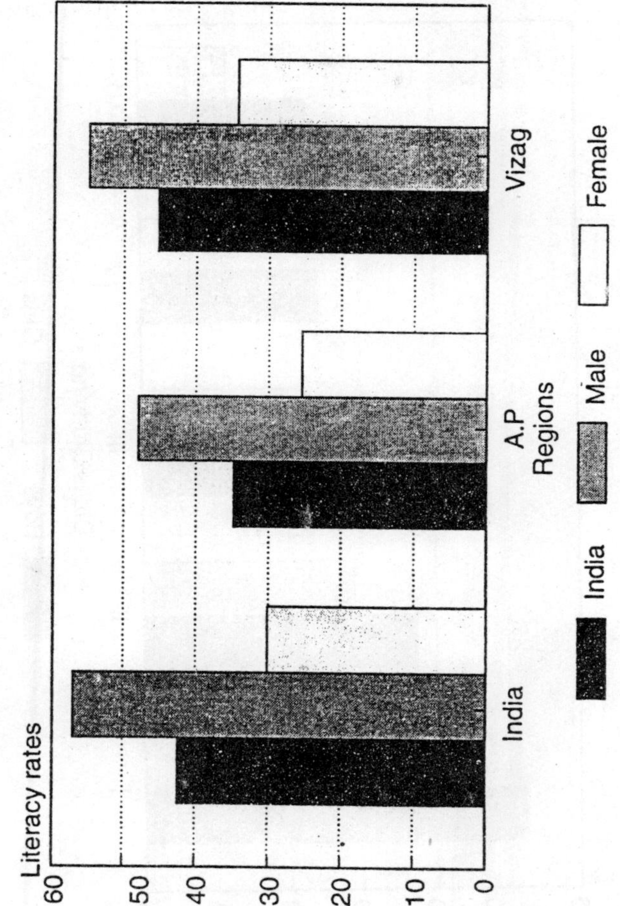


1991 Census Data

**Figure—7: Bar Depicting dropout of Children in Middle Level—Vizag District**

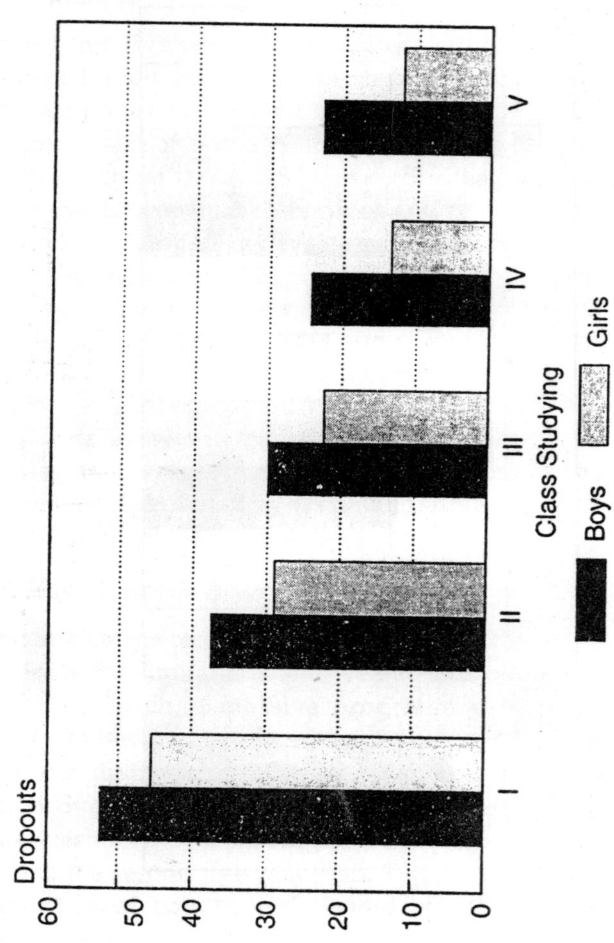


Source: 1994 Education Profile

# REFERENCES

Ambasht, N.K. (1970), A Critical Study of Tribal Education, New Delhi: S. Chand and Co.

Anon. "Literacy Statistics at a Clance", Yojana, 22 (n. 18, 1978), pp. 37-40.

Avalos, Beatrics (ed.) (1986), Teaching Children of the Poor-Ethnographic Study in Latin America, Ottawa: IDRC.

Balakrishna. 1984, Effect of Socio-Cultural Deprivation on Some Cognitive and Non-Cognitive Abilities of Tribal Adolescents, Ph.D. Psychology, Magadh Univ.

Bhattacharya, S.N. Community Development Programme, Adivasi, Delhi: Publication Division, Government of India, 1960, 144.

Bihari, Wastage and Stagnation in Primary Education among the Tribals; Srivastava, Utilisation of Financial Assistance by Tribal Students.

Bastia, Study of the National Adult Educational Programme in the Tribal Region of Orissa State; Joshi, Problems faced by Tribal Groups in Trivendrum District.

Bhowmick, P.K. The Lotless of West Bengal—A Socio-Economic Survey, Calcutta: Punthi Pustak, 1963, 27-28; Chitnis, Scheduled Caste and Scheduled Tribe College Students in Maharashtra; Singh, Pandey, Dubey and Yadav, Scheduled Caste and Scheduled Tribe Students of Secondary Schools in U.P. East and Singh, S.P. High School Examination, Aptitude, Teachers' Estimate as Predictors of Achievement in Science at the Intermediate Level, Ph.D. Education, Garwal University, 1975.

Binata, S. 1984. Education of the Santals-Identification of Educational Needs, Probabilities and Problems. Ph.D. Edu., Visva Bharathi, Univ.

Bihari, L.R. Wastage and Stagnation in Primary Education Among the Tribals, Ahmedabad: Tribal Research and Training Institute, Gujarat Vidyapith, 1969.

Cenkner, William, The Hindu Personality in Education: Tagore, Gandhi, Aurobindo (New Delhi; Manohar, 1976).

Chand, J. 1985. A Comparative Study of Various Naga Tribal Pupils in Relation to their Self Perception, Socio-Economic Status, Vocational and Educational Aspirations and Academic Achievement, Ph.D. Edu, NEH, Univ.

Chaudhari, B. (1982), Tribal Development in India-Problems and Prospects, New Delhi: Inter-India Publications.

P. Chowdari, "Report of an Investigation into the Problem of Wastage and Stagnation in Primary Schools in the District of 24 Paraganas", Directorate of Public Institute, Calcutta.

Chitnis, Scheduled Caste and Scheduled Tribes College Students in Maharashtra.

Chitnis, Scheduled Caste and Scheduled Tribe College Students in Maharashtra; Gangrade, Educational Problem of Scheduled Caste in Haryana; and Sachchidananda. Education Among Scheduled Castes and Tribes in Bihar.

Chowdhury, S.S. 1985. Education and Social Change Among the Scheduled Tribes of North Bengal, Ph.D. Soc. and Social Anthropology, NB Univ.

Das, A.K. Influence of City Life on Educated Tribals, Bulletin of the Cultural Research Institute, Calcutta, Government of West Bengal, 1962, Vol, 1. No. 2, 69-70; Shah and Patel, Who goes to College?; and Srivastava, Problems of Early, Schooling of Tribal Children.

Daniel Lerner, 1962. The Passing of Traditional Society, New York, The Free Press, 61.

Desai and Pandoor, Scheduled Caste and Scheduled Tribe High School Students in Gujarat.

Desai and Pandoor, Scheduled Caste and Scheduled Tribe High School Students in Gujarat; Lal, S.K. Educational Progress and Problems of Scheduled Caste and Scheduled Tribe College Students in Rajasthan, Department of Sociology, Jodhpur University, 1974; Salma, R., A Comparative Study of Values and Level of Aspiration of Harijan and Higher Caste Secondary Level Students, M.Ed. Dissertation, Kumaon University, 1980; Singh. Adjustment Problems of the Scheduled Caste and the Scheduled Tribe Students; Shah, B. A study of Co-Curricular Participation Amongst the

Graduate Level Students in Relation to their Caste and Educational Development, Journal of Higher Education, 1985-86 II (2), 182-186.

Desai and Pandoor, Scheduled Caste and Scheduled Tribe High School Students in Gujarat.

Desai, I.P. and Pandoor, G.A., The Scheduled Caste, and the Scheduled Tribe High School Students in Gujarat, Surat; Centre for Regional Development Studies, 1974; Rath and Misra, Scheduled Caste and Scheduled Tribe college Students in Orissa; Parvathamma, C. The Study of Scheduled Caste and Scheduled Tribe College Students in Karnataka. Department of P.G. Studies and Research in Sociology, Mysore University, 1974; and Sachchidananda, Education Among the Scheduled Castes and Tribes in Bihar (School Students), A.N.S. Institute of Social Studies, Patna, 1974; Solanki, S. A Study of the Problems of Tribal Students going for Higher Education, Tribal Research and Training Centres, Gujarat Vidyapith, Ahmedabad 1976; Jain, P.A. Study of the Educational Problems of Scheduled Tribe Students of Secondary Level of Chamoli District, M.Ed. Dissertation, Garhwal University, 1981; and Srivastava, Tribal Students of Mirzapur.

Desai and Patel, Ashram School of Gujarat.

Desai, Profile of Education Among the Scheduled Tribes and Gujarat; and Ramamani, V.S. Tribal Economy: Problems and Prospects, Allahabad: Chugh Publications, 1988.

Desai, A.R. "Social Change and Educational Policy", in M.S. Gore and others (eds.) Papers in the Sociology of Education in India (New Delhi, NCERT, 1967), pp. 91-126.

Desai and Patel, Ashram Schools of Gujarat.

Dubey, Scheduled Caste and Scheduled Tribe College Students in Assam; Singh, Pandey, Dubey and Yadav, Scheduled Caste and Scheduled Tribe Students of Secondary Schools in U.P. Est; Shah, Educational Problems, Educational Aspirations and Need for Academic Achievement.

Dubey, Scheduled Caste and Scheduled Tribe College Students in Assam; Shah, B. Study of Caste Distance Among Graduate Students of Kumaun University, Indian Journal of Social Work, 1983, XXI (1), 41-47; and Shah, Educational Problems, Educational Aspirations and Need for Academic Achievement.

Dubey, S.N. and R. Murdia, Administration of Policy and Programmes for Backward Classes in India (Bombay: Somaiya Publications Pvt. Ltd., 1976).

Dutt, M.L. 1983. Socio-phycological Study of the Tribal High School Male Students of Himachal Pradesh with High Achievement Motivation. Ph.D. Edu., MS Univ.

Elwin, (1954), A Philosophy for NEFA Shillong: North Eastern Frontier Agency, Shillong: Government of India.

Fernandes, Walter, Philip Viegas, Geeta Menon, and Philip Viegas, forests, Environment and Forest Dweller Economy in Orissa: A Report of a Study done Jointly by Orissa Action Groups and the Indian Social Institute, New Delhi (New Delhi: Indian Social Institute, 1984).

Fernandes, Walter, Philip Viegas, Geeta Menon, and K.T. Chandy, Forests, Environment and Forest Dweller Economy in Chattisgarh: A Report of a Study on Deorestation, Marginalisation and Search for Alternatives (New Delhi: Indian Social Institute, 1985).

Gopal Rao, N. 1987 (Jan) Primary Education Among the Scheduled Tribes of Andhra Pradesh, Problems and Perspectives, Vanyajati, 22-26.

Gupta, S.P. 1965, "A Study of Adivasi Students on Ranchi District", the Bihar Welfare Research Institute.

Haddad, Wadi D. (1971), "Theoretical and Methodological Problems in the Study of School", in Wax, M.L. and Others (ed.) Anthropological Perspective on Education, New York: Basic Books Inc.

Furer Haimendorf, (1982), Tribes of India, Delhi: Oxford University Press, pp. 57-66.

Von Furer-Haimendorf, C. 1985, Tribes of India, Delhi: The Struggle for Survival, Oxford University Press, Delhi.

Halsey, A.H. 1970, The Sociology of Education in Neli J. Smelser, Sociology—An Introduction New Delhi, Wiley Eastern, p. 414.

Jetley, Surinder, Modernising Indian Peasants: A Study of Six Villages in Eastern Uttar Pradesh (New Delhi: Asian Education Service, 1977).

Joshi, Problems Faced by Tribal Groups in Trivendrum District; Shah, Educational Problems, Educational Aspirations and Need for Academic Achievement.

Joshi, Educational Problems of Scheduled Castes and Scheduled Tribes of Baroda District: Lakshmanna, Scheduled Caste and Scheduled Tribe High School Students in Andhra Pradesh; Shah and Patel, Who goes to College?

Joshi, Educational Problems of Scheduled Castes and Scheduled Tribes of Baroda District.

Joshi, Vidyat, "A Century of Tribal Education in Gujarat", in V. Joshi, et al. (eds). Tribal Education in Gujarat (Delhi: Ajanta Publications, 1985), pp. 19-49.

Joshi, N.D. Problems Faced by Certain Tribal Groups in Trivendrum District in Relation to Provision and Use of School Facilities, Department of Education, Kerala University, 1981.

Joshi, S.D. Educational Problems of the Scheduled Castes and the Scheduled Tribes of Baroda District, Ph.D. Educational, M.S. University of Baroda, 1980.

Khan, M.A., Scheduled Castes and their Status in India, New Delhi; Uppal Publishing House, 1980; Singh, S.N. A Study of Pattern of Education and Occupation of Persons Living in Varanasi (Rural) with Special Reference to Scheduled Caste, Demographic Research Centre, Banaras Hindu University, 1971; and Dumont, L. Home Hierarchism: The Caste System and its Implication, Delhi: Vikas Publication, 1961.

Koul, L. 1983 Case Study of Scheduled Tribe Failure Students at Middle and Matriculation Level in Himachal Pradesh, Deptt. of Edu., Univ.

Kumar. 1978. Higher Education Among Scheduled Tribes: An Evaluation Study. Ph.D. Thesis (Education), Ranchi Univ.

Lachaiah, G. 1990, The Impact of Education in Socialising the Tribal Children, Hyderabad, Osmania University, Ph.D. Thesis.

Lakhera, Educational Problems of the Scheduled Tribe Pupils.

Lakshmanna, C. The Study of Scheduled Caste and Scheduled Tribe High School Students in Andhra Pradesh, Department of Sociology, Osmania University, 1975.

Majumdar, D.N. The Tribal Problem. In the Adivasis, New Delhi: Ministry of Information and Broadcasting, Government of India: 1960; Bhatia, S.C. Education and Socio-Cultural Disadvantage, Delhi: Xerox Publications, 1981; Srivastav, Problem of Early Schooling of Tribal Children; Kattakayam, Social Structure and Change Among the Tribals; Shayam Lal, Education Among Tribal.

Marla, Sarma, Bonded Labour in India: National Survey on the Incidence of Bonded Labour, Final Report (New Delhi: Biblia Impex, 1981).

Masavi, M. Wastage and Stagnation in Primary Education in Tribal Areas, Ahmedabad: Tribal Research and Training Institute, Gujarat Vidyapith, 1976.

Minz, Nirmal, "Higher Education in the Tribal Context", New Frontiers in Education, XII, (No. 1, Jan.—March, 1982) pp. 50-53.

Mohan Rao, (1989), "Strategy of Tribal Development in Andhra Pradesh", Conference Paper, March.

Nagaiah. 1986. The Effect of Home Environment and Parenting Style on Some Personality Variable: A Study of Disadvantaged Tribal Student Population of Madhya Pradesh. Ph.D. Thesis (Psychology), DHSGVV.

Naidu, N.Y. and Pradhan F.M. Elementary Education in Tribal Development Block, Hyderabad: National Institute of Rural Development, 1973.

Naik J.P., Education of the Scheduled Tribes (1965-66), (New Delhi: ICSSR, 1971).

Naik, J.P., Some Perspectives of Non-Formal Education (New Delhi: Allied Publishers Pvt. Ltd., 1971).

Nayer, Scheduled Caste and Tribe High School Students in Kerala; Pathak, Changes in Attitudinal Orientation Aspiration; and Shah and Patel, Who goes to College?

Nayer, Scheduled Caste and Tribe High School Students in Kerala; Shah, Educational Problems, Educational Aspirations and Need for Academic Achievement.

Nayer, Scheduled Caste and Tribe High School Students in Kerala; Rajgopalan, Educational Programme and Progress of Scheduled Caste and Scheduled Tribe Students in Karnataka; Rath and Misra, Scheduled Caste and Scheduled Tribe College Students in Orissa; Chitnis, Scheduled Caste and Scheduled Tribe College Students in Maharashtra.

Nayer, Scheduled Caste and Tribe High Schools Students in Kerala.

Nurullah, S. and J.P. Naik. A History of Education in India, 2nd Edition, (Bombay: Macmillan and Co. Ltd., 1951).

Pamecha, Renuka, Elite in a Tribal Society (Jaipur: Printwell Publishers, 1985).

Panda, B.N. 1989. Personality Adjustment, Mental Health and Acculturation Among Saora Tribals, Ph.D., Edu., Kur Univ.

Patel, Tara, Development of Education Among Tribal Women (Delhi: Mittal Publications, 1984).

Pattanayak, D.P., Multilingualism and Mother-Tongue Education (Delhi: Oxford University Press, 1981).

Parvathamma, Scheduled Caste and Scheduled Tribe College Students in Karnataka: Sachchidananda, Education Among the Scheduled Castes and Tribes in Bihar; Lakshmanna, Scheduled Caste and Scheduled Tribe High School Students in Andhra Pradesh; Desai, Profile of Education Among the Scheduled Tribes of Gujarat; and Solanki, Problem of Tribal Students going for Higher Education.

Parvathamma, Scheduled Caste and Scheduled Tribe College Students in Karnataka; Lakhera, Educational Problems of the Scheduled Tribe Pupils; and Shah, Educational Problems, Educational Aspirations and Need for Academic Achievement.

Patel et al. Tribal Education in Gujarat.

Pathak., K.D., Anusuchit Jati Awam Jana Jati Ke Vidyarthion Ki Ananksha Aur Abhivrittyatmak Unmukhata Main Parivartan (Changes in Attitudinal Orientation and Aspiration of Scheduled Caste and Scheduled Tribes Students), Ph.D. Sociology, Banaras Hindu University, 1981.

Pathak, Changes in Attitudinal Orientation and Aspiration.

Pathak, Changes in Attitudinal Orientation and Aspiration; Lakshmanna, Scheduled Caste and Scheduled Tribe High School Students in Andhra Pradesh.

Phadke, J.K. and Shukla, R.C. A Study of Drop-outs Among the Scheduled Tribe Students in Vyara, Arts and Commerce College, Vyara, 1980.

Prasad, N. Land and People of Tribal Bihar, Ranchi: Bihar Tribal Research Institute, 1961, 285-320.

Pratap et al. Ashram Schools of Andhra Pradesh.

Pratap, D.R. et al. Study of Ashram Schools in Tribal Areas of Andhra Pradesh, Hyderabad: Tribal Cultural Research and Training Institute, 1971.

Rajgopalan, Educational Progress and Problems of Scheduled Caste and Scheduled Tribe Students in Karnataka; Scheduled Caste and Scheduled Tribe Students in Karnataka; Sachchidananda, Education

Among the Scheduled Castes and Tribes in Bihar; Singhi, Educational Problems of Scheduled Caste and Scheduled Tribe School Students in Rajasthan.

Rajgopalan, Educational Progress and Problems of Scheduled Caste and Scheduled Tribe Students in Karnataka; Lakshmanna, Scheduled Caste and Scheduled Tribe High School Students in Andhra Pradesh; Schchidananda, Education Among the Scheduled Caste and Tribes in Bihar.

Rao VKRV, 1966 Education and Human Resource Development, New Delhi, Allied Publication, p. 60-61.

Rao, V.N., and R. Parthasarathy, 1993, "School Mental Health Problems: Relevance in Indian Context", The Educational Review, XXCIX 12): 207.

Rajgopalan, C. Educational Progress and Problems of Scheduled Caste and Scheduled Tribe Students in Karnataka (High School) Department of Sociology, Banaras Hindu University, 1974.

Rath and Misra, Scheduled Caste and Scheduled Tribe College Students in Orissa.

Rathnayya, Structural Constraints in Tribal Education.

Rathnayya, E.V. Structural Constraints in Tribal Education: A Regional Study, Ph.D., Sociology, Andhra University, 1974.

Ratnaiah, E.V. (1978), Structural Constraints of Tribal Education, New Delhi: Sterling Publication.

N. Subba Reddy, (1988), "Depriving Tribals of Land", Economic and Political Weekly, July 16.

G. Prakash Reddy, (1987), "Politics of Tribal Exploitation, New Delhi: Mittal Publications, p. 61.

Rist, R. (1970), Students Social Class and Teacher Expectations: The Self-Fulfilling Prophecy in Ghetto Education, Harvard Educational Review, 40 (3): 411-450.

Rout, P.C. 1985. A Multi-Dimensional Approach for Analysis of Trends, Perspectives and Education Programmes in Tribal Education and Formulation of Action Strategies. Ph.D., Edu., Utkal Univ.

Roy Burman, B.K., 1985, "Issues in Tribal Development", Mainstream, January 5 and 12, New Delhi.

Sachchidananda, 1992. "Modernization, Development and the Predicament of Tribal Communities", Science, Culture and Development (Prof. L.K. Mahapatra Felicitation Volume), Behura, N.K. and K.C. Tripathy (eds.), Paragon Publishers, Bhubaneswar.

Sachchidananda, The Changing Munda, New Delhi: Concept Publishing Company, 1979, 16; Shah, Educational Problems, Educational Aspirations and Need for Academic Achievement.

Sachchidananda, 1990, "Research in the Education of the Disadvantaged", in the Fourth Survey of Research in Education, M.B. Buch, NCERT, (II): 1414.

Sachchidananda, Education Among Scheduled Castes and Tribes in Bihar; George, E.T. Educational Problems of Scheduled Caste and Scheduled Tribe College Students in Kerala, Department of Psychology, Kerala University, 1975.

Sachchidananda, Education Among the Scheduled Castes and Tribes in Bihar.

Sachchidanda, (1967), 'Socio-Economic Aspects of Tribal Education', in Report of the National Seminar on Tribal Education in India, New Delhi: NCERT, pp. 78-99.

Shah, Educational Problems, Educational Aspirations and Need for Academic Achievement.

Shah, Educational Problems, Educational Aspirations and Need for Academic Achievement.

Shah and Patel, Social context of Tribal Education in Gujarat; Punalekar, S.P. Migration and Social Stratification: A Case Study of Dhedias of Surat City, Surat: Centre for Social Studies, 1980; and Shah, Educational Problems, Educational Aspirations and Need for Academic Achievement.

Shah, Educational Problems, Educational Aspirations and Need for 'Academic Achievement.

Shah, V.P. and Patel, T. Who goes to College?: A Study of Schedule Caste/Tribe Post-Matric Scholars in Gujarat, Department of Sociology, Gujarat University, 1977; and Shah, G. Socio-Economic Conditions of Chaudhries: A Restudy, Surat: Centre for Social Studies, 1981.

Shah, Educational Problems, Educational Aspirations and Need for Academic Achievement.

Shah, Educational Problems, Educational Aspirations and Need for Academic Achievement.

Shah, V.P. and T. Patel, Social Contexts of Tribal Education (New Delhi: Concept Publishing Company, 1985).

C.L. Sapra, (1966), "Wastage and Stagnation at the First Level of Education in India", (Report Presented at UNESCO Seminar held at Bangkok, September 5-12, 1966, Ministry of Education, Government of India, New Delhi.

C.L. Sapra, and G. Khurana, (980), "Wastage and Stagnation in Primary and Middle Schools in India", Research Monograph 2, NCEFT, New Delhi.

Sharma, B.D., 1986-87, Twenty eighth Report of the Commissioner for Scheduled Castes and Scheduled Tribes, Government of India, New Delhi.

B.D. Sharma, (1984), Planning of Tribal Development, New Delhi; Prachi Prakashan, pp. 80-81.

Sharma, B.D. (1978), Tribal Development—The Concept and the Frame, New Delhi: Prachi Prakashan.

Shyam Lal, Education Among Tribals.

Shyam Lal, Education Among Tribals.

Singh, R.R. Adjustment Problems of the Scheduled Caste and the Scheduled Tribe Students in Residential Schools of Rajasthan, Vidya Bhavan G.S. Teachers' College, Udaipur, 1981.

Singh, Pandey, Dubey and Yadav, Scheduled Caste and Scheduled Tribe Students of Secondary Schools in U.P. East; Shah, B.V. and Thakre, J.D. Educational Problems in Scheduled Caste, Scheduled Tribe college Students in Gujarat, Department of Sociology, S.P. University, 1974.

Singh, Predictors of Achievement in Science at the Intermediate Level.

Singh, Adjustment Problems of the Scheduled Caste and the Scheduled Tribe Students.

Singh, L.B. 1979. A Study in Personality of Tribal Students. Ph.D. (Psy.), Bhagalpur Univ.

Singh, Adjustment Problems of the Scheduled Caste and the Scheduled Tribe Students; Desai B. and Patel, A. Ashram Schools of Gujarat: An Evaluative Study, Ahmedabad: Tribal Research and Training Institute, Gujarat Vidyapith, 1981.

Singhi, N.K. Education and Social Change (Jaipur: Rawat Publications, 1979).

Solanki, S. Tribals in Primary and Secondary School Textbooks, Tribal Research and Training Centre, Gujarat Vidyapith, Ahmedabad, 1977.

Solanki, Problems of Tribal Students going for Higher Education; Parvathamma, Scheduled Caste and Scheduled Tribe College Students in Karnataka.

Srivastava, Pr̂oblem of Integration of the Tribal People; and Joshi, Problems Faced by Tribal Groups in Trivendrum District.

Srivastava. 1986. A Socio-Psychological Study of Stagnates Among Tribal and Non-Tribal of Class VII. Ph.D., Thesis (Education), Lucknow Univ.

Srivastava, L.R.N., Utilisation of Financial Assistance by Tribal Students, Tribal Education Unit, NCERT, New Delhi, 1970; Dubey, Scheduled Caste and Scheduled Tribe College Students in Assam; and Rath and Misra, Scheduled Caste and Scheduled Tribe College Students in Orissa.

Srivastava, A.K. An Investigation into the Factors Related to Educational Underachievement, Ph.D. Psychology, Patna University, 1967; Douglas, J.B., Ross, J.N. and Simpson, H.R. All Our Future—A Longitudinal Study of Secondary Education, London: Peter Davies, 1968; Gangrade, K.D. Educational Problems of Scheduled Caste in Haryana (College Students), Delhi School of Social Work, Delhi University, 1974; and Harnquist, K. The International Study of Educational Achievement, American Journal of Educational Research, 1974.

Srivastava, Utilisation of Financial Assistance by Tribal Students; Desai, Profile of Education Among the Scheduled Tribes of Gujarat; Nayar, Scheduled Caste and Tribe High School Students in Kerala; Rajgopalan, Educational Progress and Problems of Scheduled Caste and Scheduled Tribe Students in Karnataka; Rath and Mishra, Scheduled Caste and Scheduled Tribe college Students in Orissa; and Lakshmanna, Scheduled Caste and Scheduled Tribe High School Students in Andhra Pradesh.

Srivastava, S.S. Problems Aspirations, Values and Personality Patterns of Tribal Students of Mirzapur, Faculty of Education, Banaras Hindu University, 1981.

Srivastava, L.R.N. (1967), Some Basic Problems of Tribal Education in Report of National Seminar on Tribal Education in India, New Delhi: NCERT, pp. 68-77.

Sujatha, K. (1987), Education of forgotten Children of the Forests, New Delhi: Konark Publishers.

Venkata Reddy, M.V. 1990, Development of Scheduled Tribes in Andhra Pradesh with Special Reference to their Education, Hyderabad, Osmania University, Ph.D. Thesis.

Vyas, M.N. and Mann, R.S. Indian Tribes in Tradition, Jaipur: Rawat Publications, 1980.

Mandals in East Godavari are Divided into Three Categories on the Basis of Rural Literacy Rate and One Mandal is randomly Selected from each Category. For details of Methodology see S. Subrahmanyam, and V. Rama Raju, (1988), "Wastage in Primary Education: A Study of East Godavari", Hyderabad, Centre for Economic and Social Studies, (Mimeo).

See D.V. Chickermane, (1962) "A Study of Wastage in Primary Education", Education and Psychology Review, Volume II, January.

UNESCO, (1970), "The Statistical Measure of Educational Wastage", Paris.

When the Available Cross-Section Data are used, it is not Possible to Distinguish between the Two Components of Wastage *viz.* drop-out and Stagnation.

In many Cases, the Teachers Handling Grade I Also Handle some Other Classes. Hence the Average Roll and Attendance of these Teachers are Calculated by Considering All the Classes they are Handling. This Represents the Burden on the Teacher.

National Committee on Development on Backward Areas, Report on Development of Tribal Areas (New Delhi: Govt. of India, 1981).

Poverty Line is Fixed at Rs. 100/- per Capita Monthly Income and Rs. 75/- is the Norm for Identifying the Very Poor.

Tribal Sub Plan, 1989-90. Department of Tribal Welfare, Government of Andhra Pradesh.

Tribal Sub Plan, 1975, Tribal Welfare Department, Government of Andhra Pradesh.

Ibid.

Report of the Scheduled Areas the Scheduled Tribes Commission, Ministry of Home Affairs, 1961.

Report of the Working Group on Development of Scheduled Tribes during Seventh Five Year Plan, Ministry of Home Affairs, 1984, pp. 20-22.

Calculated from the Data Presented in the Tribal Sub Plan for the Fifth Plan Period, Tribal Welfare Department, Government of Andhra Pradesh 1975.

Seventh Five Year Plan, Tribal Sub Plan (Revised) 1985, p. 197.

Report of the Parliamentary Committee on Scheduled Castes and Scheduled Tribes, 1985-86, p. 14.

Working of the ITDAs, Report of the Parliamentary Committee, 1985-86, p. 103.

**Reports**

Ministry of Education, Challenge of Education—A Policy Perspective (New Delhi: Govt. of India, 1985).

W.H.O. 1973. Technical Report 613, Child Mental Health and Psycho-social Dev., Geneva.

Census of India. Primary Census Abstracts: Scheduled Castes, Series 1, Part II-B (vi), India, 1981a.

—Primary Census Abstract: Scheduled Tribes, Series 1, Part II-B (iii) India, 1981b.

—General Population and Population of Scheduled Castes and Scheduled Tribes, Series—1, Paper 2 of 1984.

Commissioner for SCs and STs. A Report (Calcutta: Govt. of India Press, 1951).

—,Sixth Report, Part I (Delhi: Govt. of India Press, 1955).

—, Twenty Seventh Report Part II, Appendices (New Delhi: Govt. of India, 1979-81).

Dept. of Social Welfare, Women in India: A Statistical Profile (New Delhi: Govt. of India Publication, 1978).

Govt of Bombay, A Review of Education in Bombay States—1855-1955 (Bombay: Govt. of Bombay, 1958).

Government of Andhra Pradesh (Department of Labour) and UNICER 1993 (March).

G.O.I. 1986. National Policy on Education. New Delhi: Ministry of Human Resources Development.

Career and Placement Study of Scheduled Caste and Scheduled Tribe Students in Selected Districts of Tamil Nadu (1974-76), Madras: SCERT, 1979.

UNICEF 1994, The State of the World's Children, New Delhi, Oxford Univ. Press, p. 45 and 64-66.

Education Among Tribals; and Shah, Educational Problems, Educational Aspirations and Need for Academic Achievement.

—(1990), Inter and Intra-Tribal Disparities in Education, Man and Life, 16 (1-2): 19-29.

Also see Sayeed, A.A. Investigation of Social, Economic, Cultural and Home Conditions Affecting the Education of Boys and Girls in Naliasopara Area (Taluka Bassein, District Thana), M.Ed. Dissertation, Bombay University, 1968; Chitra, M.N. The Social Background of Some Undergraduate Women Students in Mysore City, Ph.D. Sociology, Delhi University, 1969; and Shah, B. Study of Caste Effect upon the Achievement of Graduate Students, Social Change, 1984, 14 (1), 41044.

# Index